W9-BNE-889

The Money Chase

THE MONEY CHASE

Congressional Campaign Finance Reform

David B. Magleby
and Candice J. Nelson

The Brookings Institution
Washington, D.C.

Copyright © 1990 by
THE BROOKINGS INSTITUTION
1775 Massachusetts Avenue, N.W., Washington, D.C. 20036

Library of Congress Cataloging-in-Publication Data

Magleby, David B.
  The money chase : congressional campaign finance reform /
David B. Magleby and Candice J. Nelson.
    p.   cm.
  Includes index.
  ISBN 0-8157-5434-5   ISBN 0-8157-5433-7 (pbk.)
  1. Campaign funds—United States.   2. United States. Congress—
Elections—Finance.   I. Nelson, Candice J., 1949–   .   II. Title.
JK1991.M25   1990
324.7'8'0973—dc20   90-2092
                                                                          CIP

9   8   7   6   5   4   3   2   1

The paper used in this publication meets the minimum requirements
of the American National Standard for Information Sciences—Per-
manence of Paper for Printed Library Materials, ANSI Z39.48-1984.

℔ THE BROOKINGS INSTITUTION

The Brookings Institution is an independent organization devoted to nonpartisan research, education, and publication in economics, government, foreign policy, and the social sciences generally. Its principal purposes are to aid in the development of sound public policies and to promote public understanding of issues of national importance.

The Institution was founded on December 8, 1927, to merge the activities of the Institute for Government Research, founded in 1916, the Institute of Economics, founded in 1922, and the Robert Brookings Graduate School of Economics and Government, founded in 1924.

The Board of Trustees is responsible for the general administration of the Institution, while the immediate direction of the policies, program, and staff is vested in the President, assisted by an advisory committee of the officers and staff. The by-laws of the Institution state: "It is the function of the Trustees to make possible the conduct of scientific research, and publication, under the most favorable conditions, and to safeguard the independence of the research staff in the pursuit of their studies and in the publication of the results of such studies. It is not a part of their function to determine, control, or influence the conduct of particular investigations or the conclusions reached."

The President bears final responsibility for the decision to publish a manuscript as a Brookings book. In reaching his judgment on the competence, accuracy, and objectivity of each study, the President is advised by the director of the appropriate research program and weighs the views of a panel of expert outside readers who report to him in confidence on the quality of the work. Publication of a work signifies that it is deemed a competent treatment worthy of public consideration but does not imply endorsement of conclusions or recommendations.

The Institution maintains its position of neutrality on issues of public policy in order to safeguard the intellectual freedom of the staff. Hence interpretations or conclusions in Brookings publications should be understood to be solely those of the authors and should not be attributed to the Institution, to its trustees, officers, or other staff members, or to the organizations that support its research.

For
Joseph, Katie, Daniel, and Benjamin
and
David and Peter

Foreword

The role of money in elections is a recurring problem in American politics. Both the 100th and 101st Congresses struggled with campaign finance reform under the shadow of partisan disagreement and distrust. Meanwhile, the problems that led policymakers to consider reform continue: the obsession with raising campaign funds, the growing influence of special interests, and declining electoral competition in the House of Representatives.

Too often the debate over campaign finance reform has bogged down because the most interested parties—incumbent members of the House and Senate—cannot agree on the problems with the current system, much less on proposed solutions. The rhetoric becomes so intense that compromise becomes impossible.

This book attempts to get beyond the rhetoric, to examine the real problems with the present system, and to analyze the likely partisan and institutional consequences of proposed reforms. The authors point out that to be successful, reform must be bipartisan, must recognize the differences between House and Senate campaign finance practices, and must be approached comprehensively. They suggest an integrated package of reforms that would increase competition among congressional candidates, reduce dependence on special interests, decrease the time candidates spend in fundraising, strengthen the role of the parties, lead to full disclosure of contributions and expenditures, and improve administration of campaign finance laws.

David B. Magleby is professor of political science at Brigham Young University, and Candice J. Nelson is a former visiting fellow in the Brookings Governmental Studies program. The authors benefited from the comments of anonymous reviewers and of Dee Allsop, Calvin Andrus, Anne Bedlington, Byron W. Daynes, David Flanders, and Richard L. Jacobson, who read the manuscript in whole or in part. They also thank the following people who willingly shared their expertise: Gary C. Bryner, Joseph Cantor, Kent Cooper, Fred Eiland, Ellen S. Miller, Herb

K. Schulz, and Sharon Snyder. The authors also wish to thank the experts and participants in the current congressional campaign finance system who granted interviews.

Federal Election Commission data were provided by the Interuniversity Consortium for Political and Social Research and by the FEC. The Brigham Young University College of Family, Home, and Social Sciences Computer Center provided assistance in merging and managing data tapes. The authors wish to acknowledge the assistance of Robert Biersack, supervisory statistician at the FEC.

The authors gratefully acknowledge the research assistance provided at Brookings by Rebecca L. Noah, Mitchell Rabinowitz, and David A. Richter, and at BYU by Janna Brown, Thel W. Casper, Michelle Gardner Detweiller, Harold M. Gregory, Kelleen Lieshman, Daniel Neilson, David Passey, and Laure Rawson. Computing assistance at BYU was provided by Steven R. Britton, York M. Faulkner, Bradley B. McLaws, Martin C. Nichols, Robert B. Speakman, Jr., and Rodney J. Symes.

Financial support for the project was provided by the Dillon Fund and for Magleby by the College of Family, Home, and Social Sciences, the BYU Young Scholar Award, and the Department of Political Science. Both authors also gratefully acknowledge the support given them during their year as American Political Science Association congressional fellows in 1986–87 and the learning opportunities provided them in the offices of U.S. Senators Robert C. Byrd and Alan Cranston.

Administrative support was provided by Sandra Z. Riegler and Eloise C. Stinger, and secretarial assistance by Renuka D. Deonarain, Ellen P. Isan, Vida R. Megahed, and Teresita V. Vitug at Brookings and Suzanne Harding at BYU. James R. Schneider and Nancy D. Davidson edited the manuscript. Todd L. Quinn verified its factual content, Susan L. Woollen prepared it for typesetting, and Margaret Lynch prepared the index.

The views expressed in this book are those of the authors and should not be ascribed to the people or organizations whose assistance is acknowledged above or to the trustees, officers, or other staff members of the Brookings Institution.

BRUCE K. MACLAURY
President

June 1990
Washington, D.C.

Contents

Text Tables

Appendix Tables

Figures

1

Introduction

Money is a necessary means to achieve the democratic ends of American politics. Candidates, political parties, and interest groups all raise and spend money for political purposes, including such essential activities as communicating with voters, registering them, and mobilizing them on election day. These activities are universally seen as important and laudable. But the way candidates, groups, and parties raise and spend the money needed to finance such activities has been the subject of considerable controversy and ongoing debate. The issues of who should pay for elections, in what way, and with what expectations have again moved to center stage in American politics.

The first session of the 101st Congress was overwhelmed with problems of compensation and the ethical handling of money. Early in 1989 members fought a bruising battle over a congressional pay raise. Speaker Jim Wright was charged with evading House rules on accepting outside income, which led to his unprecedented resignation. Five members of the Senate were accused of being improperly influenced by Charles Keating, executive of the Lincoln Savings and Loan in California, which was in financial trouble. Although the House succeeded in adopting a proposal that raised salaries in return for the elimination of honoraria, concerns remain that money has a suffocating and corrupting influence on Congress.[1] And nowhere have these concerns been more evident than in debates on how to reform the financing of congressional election campaigns.

Because of rising campaign costs, politicians have been forced to follow a never-ending money chase. They spend countless hours and

---

1. The Senate enacted a more modest pay raise for itself and reduced the amount of money senators could accept in honoraria from 40 percent of their salaries to 27 percent. However, it is possible that the Senate will reconsider a ban on honoraria in the 101st Congress, or after the 1990 elections.

1

tremendous energy in fundraising, often to the detriment of their legislative duties. Incumbents in both parties and both houses have increasingly been drawn to political action committees and other big contributors to fill campaign war chests, raising questions of whether these special interests are unduly shaping decisions on public policy. Meanwhile, potential challengers have had an even more difficult job of raising enough money to run competitive campaigns. The result is that in the past few elections House incumbents have been reelected about 98 percent of the time, a situation that threatens to create an entrenched and less responsive legislature.

Nevertheless, the forces inhibiting a major overhaul of the campaign finance system are formidable. Self-interest separates incumbents and challengers, Democrats and Republicans, House and Senate. Reform has also been stymied because of deep philosophical differences over the proper role of government in financing and regulating campaigns. Finally, distrust and perceptions of unfair treatment by leaders and members on both sides of the partisan divide have made this a difficult issue at the interpersonal level. And these divisions have been made worse because students of campaign finance cannot agree why these problems have arisen and how they can best be solved.

This book examines the congressional campaign finance system and its weaknesses, evaluates alternative ideas for reform, and proposes specific reforms to slow the money chase, reduce the influence of special interests, and increase competition in congressional elections. It gives special attention to the political feasibility of various reforms as well as to possible unintended consequences.

Overview of the Issues

The American congressional campaign finance system is burdened with rising costs and marked by decreasing competition. Both too much and too little is spent in congressional elections. Hundreds of House challengers are seriously underfinanced and largely invisible. Instead of contests in 435 congressional districts, competitive elections often take place in fewer than 50. In 1988 just 11 percent of House incumbents were elected with less than 60 percent of the vote; on average 24 percent were elected with less than 60 percent of the vote since 1970.[2]

---

2. Calculated from Norman J. Ornstein, Thomas E. Mann, and Michael J. Malbin, *Vital Statistics on Congress, 1989–1990* (Washington: Congressional Quarterly, 1990), p. 59.

Incumbents can and do spend increasing amounts of money on decreasingly competitive seats. As incumbents become safer in their seats, a permanent majority in the House becomes more and more a reality.[3]

The dynamic in Senate elections has been much different. Twice during the 1980s control of the chamber changed hands, with Republicans picking up several close victories in 1980 and then losing several of those same seats in 1986. Incumbent senators now expect to have competitive challengers, and thus campaign spending per voter has increased dramatically. Rising costs and competitive elections also mean longer campaigns and a much greater commitment of time from challengers, who now routinely start fundraising two years before the election. Because this is a full-time job, they must have an independent means of support early in the period, which means wealthy candidates have a tremendous advantage.

Given such expensive campaigns, where does the money come from? For most House incumbents, the largest source is political action committees, or PACs; for Senate incumbents PACs are not yet so important, but the share of campaign funds that come from them has been growing. Most challengers for seats in either house receive little from such special interests; PACs do not generally want to offend the politicians in power. Candidates also turn to individual donors who can contribute $500 to $1,000. Such relatively wealthy people share with PACs a policy focus and contribute with the expectation that a legislator they have helped win will respond to their concerns. Given congressional incumbents' preoccupation with reelection, campaign contributions are greatly valued, and those who provide the funds are given special treatment.

The consequences of the money chase are also serious for Congress as an institution. Because limits on what individuals and PACs can give do not take account of inflation, members must constantly expand their donor base. This takes more and more time and effort. Although Congress once prohibited fundraising in congressional offices on Capitol Hill, now one or more staff members in each office may be designated to receive campaign contributions. Fundraising also affects the legislative process itself. Leaders of both parties have commented on the difficulty of scheduling floor business in the evenings because of the competition

3. The reelection rate in the House will probably decline somewhat following the redistricting that will occur after the 1990 census. Even if districts are drawn to protect incumbents, members in states that are losing seats fear being put in a district with another incumbent.

from Washington fundraising events and the need to accommodate members traveling around the country to raise money. In short, fundraising has become a larger part of the job description of House and Senate members and more important to both houses and both parties than it ought to be.

The Approach and Plan of the Book

Not everyone agrees on the specific problems attendant to the current system of campaign finance; indeed, there are very different perceptions of what the problems are. However, observers generally agree that the system needs to be changed. Many of the strongest advocates of reform are confident that their favored solutions would have only positive consequences.[4] But an irony of the current system is that the importance of PACs, often listed as one of the major problems, is itself a product of post-Watergate reform legislation. Others conclude that reform is so complicated and so rife with potential problems that change is likely to do more harm than good.[5] Neither position is tenable. Some reforms in and of themselves would only make existing problems worse. For example, enacting spending limits without providing public financing, or more ready access to money, would make it even more difficult for challengers to run competitive campaigns. But some reforms—reducing the costs of communicating with potential voters, for example—would almost certainly improve the current system.

Congressional campaign finance reform has been a seemingly intractable area of public policy, and the rhetoric of the debate has often been inflamed and prone to overgeneralizations. Advocates of limiting PAC influence have charged that "Washington is corrupt to the core."[6] Defenders of the status quo often divert attention from the issues of rising costs, the increased role of PACs, and declining competition by shifting the terms of argument to "the real corruption," namely honoraria, free trips home for legislators, and the conversion of unused campaign funds to personal use when a member retires from the House.[7] One of the objectives of this book is to move beyond such rhetoric.

4. Philip Stern, *The Best Congress Money Can Buy* (Pantheon Books, 1988).

5. Frank Sorauf, *Money in American Elections* (Scott, Foresman, 1988).

6. Amitai Etzioni, *Capital Corruption: The New Attack on American Democracy* (New Brunswick, N.J.: Transaction Books, 1988), p. xi.

7. Larry Sabato, "Campaign Finance Reform Ideas: The Good, the Bad & the Ugly," Project for Comprehensive Campaign Reform, April 1989.

Congressional campaign finance has been frequently written about in the press. It is a subject tailor-made for editorial writers because of its apparent simplicity and its easily espoused solutions that are seemingly without costs. But editorial writers and news reporters are not alone in these tendencies; academics are also prone to overgeneralization, mere description, or an extremely narrow definition of the research question. This is perhaps best illustrated in the literature on PACs. Although careful authors and scholars have written about this problem and have made significant contributions to understanding it, they have focused on the current system rather than on possible reforms and their likely consequences. In short, there is a need for a book that has reform as its primary concern.

The purpose of this book is to evaluate possible reforms of congressional campaign finance in light of experience, the judgment of key participants in the current system, and political realities. Most research on campaign finance has either scrutinized the current sources of funds— parties, PACs, or individuals—or examined the relationships between the amount of money spent and electoral success.[8] Books that have examined possible reforms have typically done so only in a concluding chapter; reform has not been their main purpose.[9]

Assessing possible changes in the congressional campaign finance system requires anticipating the behavior of individual contributors, PACs, parties, and candidates, although it is true that no one knows for sure how these participants will behave. Changes have and will continue to occur in the way congressional campaigns are financed, whether or not Congress adopts any of the reforms we discuss. Some of the changes that have occurred since the passage of the last set of reforms include dramatic growth in campaign costs, increases in the number of PACs

8. See, for example, Paul S. Herrnson, *Party Campaigning in the 1980s* (Harvard University Press, 1988); Theodore J. Eismeier and Philip H. Pollock III, *Business, Money and the Rise of Corporate PACs in American Elections* (Quorum Books, 1988); Richard P. Conlon, "The Declining Role of Individual Contributions in Financing Congressional Elections," *Journal of Law and Politics,* vol. 3 (Winter 1987), pp. 467–507; Gary C. Jacobson, "The Effects of Campaign Spending in Congressional Elections," *American Political Science Review,* vol. 72 (June 1978), pp. 469–91; and Donald Green and Jonathan Krasno, "Salvation for the Spendthrift Incumbent: Reestimating the Effects of Campaign Spending in House Elections," *American Journal of Political Science,* vol. 32 (November 1988), pp. 884–907.

9. See Larry Sabato, *PAC Power: Inside the World of Political Action Committees* (Norton, 1984); Brooks Jackson, *Honest Graft: Big Money and the American Political Process* (Knopf, 1988); Stern, *The Best Congress Money Can Buy;* Herrnson, *Party Campaigning in the 1980s;* Eismeier and Pollock, *Business, Money and the Rise of Corporate PACs;* and Sorauf, *Money in American Elections.*

and in their importance to candidates' overall campaign funds, a diminished role for contributors of modest means, and longer campaigns. In sum, recent changes in the system have had important consequences in their own right and need to be evaluated.

Our approach to the study of campaign finance is unusual. There already exists a substantial literature on the present system and past reform proposals as well as the consequences of the present system for competition, political parties, and interest groups.[10] But this literature does not examine information in light of the debate on reform. Our focus is to examine reform ideas in light of experience and our understanding of political behavior.

One other reason why much of what has been written about the current system is of limited usefulness is that reform would significantly change the campaign finance system itself. For instance, if all candidates in general elections were given public funds sufficient to enable them to achieve significant voter recognition, candidate recruitment would undoubtedly be made easier and at least some election outcomes less one-sided. We know that the presidential nominating rules have affected the pool of candidates and their strategies.[11] There is every reason to believe that this would be true in congressional elections as well. It is less certain what parts of current behavior will carry over into the new world of reformed campaign finance. This is a topic to which we will return, but for now it is important to note that although studies of current practices may help predict behavior under reform, it is also likely that in some important respects they will not.

Some issues in the debate on campaign finance reform are empirically resolvable, but many of the most important are not. Take, for instance, the question of whether too little or too much is spent on campaigns. The answer will finally be a judgment based on spending patterns, the implications of spending for competition—or, as we will define it,

10. For past reform proposals, see Herbert E. Alexander, *Financing Politics: Money, Elections and Political Reform* (Washington: Congressional Quarterly Press, 1976); Robert E. Mutch, *Campaigns, Congress and Courts: The Making of Federal Campaign Finance Law* (Praeger, 1988); and Larry J. Sabato, *Paying for Elections: The Campaign Finance Thicket* (New York: Priority Press, 1989). For effects of the current system on competition, see Jacobson, "The Effects of Campaign Spending in Congressional Elections"; and Green and Krasno, "Salvation for the Spendthrift Incumbent." Consequences for political parties are discussed in Herrnson, *Party Campaigning in the 1980s*; and Sorauf, *Money in American Elections*. Eismeier and Pollock, *Business, Money and the Rise of Corporate PACs in American Elections*; and Sabato, *PAC Power*, treat interest groups.

11. Byron Shafer, *Quiet Revolution: The Struggle for the Democratic Party and the Shaping of Post-Reform Politics* (New York: Russell Sage Foundation, 1983).

visibility—and how the costs of campaigns affect the pool of candidates. As we will show, too much is spent in some campaigns and not nearly enough in others. But our assessment is premised on a belief in the importance of real electoral competition, something readers may or may not agree with as a basic assumption.

A similar problem arises as to whether special interests are unduly influential. These interests will always have the influence that results from a politically active membership, the ability to provide relevant information, and the like.[12] But what effect do PACs have on Congress? One school of thought defines influence narrowly, using only the results of floor roll call votes. These votes, however, are only one step in the legislative process.[13] Focusing only on them overlooks the involvement of PACs and their affiliated organizations in lobbying for committee assignments for favored members, setting the legislative agenda of subcommittees and committees, helping organize hearings, drafting legislation and amendments to legislation, preparing committee reports, and stopping or redirecting the activities of members and committees in their legislative or policy oversight responsibilities. This more inclusive definition raises two questions: how involved are PACs in these activities, and to what extent is their influence the result of their large and growing role in financing congressional campaigns? Unfortunately, very little attention has been paid to PAC activities in parts of the legislative process that occur away from floor votes.

The problem is not that political science cannot determine the answer to these questions, but rather that to do so requires a very different approach from those already taken.[14] It is also not true that one must adopt an all-or-nothing approach to PACs, as the organizations' defenders often assume. If one believes campaign contributions or honoraria payments give special interests influence over senators and representatives, that does not mean interest groups per se should have no influence. The question is what additional leverage special interests obtain as a result of their ability to give money directly to members of Congress, to play a large and growing role in financing their campaigns through PACs, and to retire their campaign debts. It also begs the question to

---

12. Raymond Bauer, Ithiel de Sola Pool, and Lewis Anthony Dexter, *American Business and Public Policy: The Politics of Foreign Trade* (Atherton Press, 1963).

13. John Kingdon, *Congressmen's Voting Decisions* (Harper and Row, 1973).

14. In some ways this is analogous to the debate over community power in American cities. See Nelson Polsby, *Community Power and Political Theory* (Yale University Press, 1963); and Robert Dahl, *Who Governs?: Democracy and Power in an American City* (Yale University Press, 1961).

argue that PACs are little different from individual donors who make large contributions. If giving campaign money changes the relationship between individuals, groups, and members of Congress, as common sense suggests it must, then this leads to a definition of undue influence for both individuals and groups who contribute to campaigns.

Given our focus on what we see as problems with the present system of congressional campaign finance and our desire to assess the consequences, intended and unintended, of possible reforms, we cannot avoid discussing values. Much of what we will present in this book is open to different interpretations. In fact, in our description of the various partisan positions on these issues, that will be one of our central points.

The proper role for government in financing and regulating campaigns, the effects of the present system or possible alternatives on candidate recruitment and electoral competition, and the extent to which campaigns should be financed by organized interests with legislative agendas all are examples of topics on which there is substantial disagreement. We do not presume to resolve these disagreements. What we seek to do is identify the issues, evaluate the extent to which their importance is supported by experience, and assess their political consequences.

One of our most important objectives is to assess alternative reform proposals as well as the status quo. What are the administrative limitations of the Federal Election Commission? What would be the implications of public financing for candidate recruitment? Do spending limits by their nature help incumbents? If new restrictions or limitations are placed on campaign money, where is it likely to surface next? Will money spent in these new ways have detrimental effects on the political system? What can be learned from the experience of the states or other nations in the financing of elections? This is a partial list, but it illustrates the important questions that reform raises. To what extent will the empirical regularities summarized in this book and elsewhere hold under the new rules? The answer is that no one knows for sure, but this very calculus is precisely the one that ought to be made as reform proposals are evaluated.

Another justification for a book on campaign finance reform is that the politics of reform itself needs additional analysis. A record eight cloture votes attempting to override a partisan filibuster were taken on a reform bill in the 100th Congress. Support for reform surfaced in the 1988 vice presidential debate and was frequently discussed in the ethics and congressional salary disputes of 1989. President Bush's proposed changes in campaign laws were the first from an administration on the subject in more than a decade. Both houses of Congress revisited congressional campaign finance in the 101st Congress. A bipartisan task force worked for several months in the House and seemed to be making progress before breaking down along the predictable partisan lines. The Senate created a panel of outside experts to "stimulate discussion and perhaps even break the legislative logjam in Congress."[15] While Congress was deliberating, the Supreme Court handed down another in a series of campaign finance reform decisions, this time concerning independent expenditures.[16] The actions by all three branches of government in 1989–90 are evidence that congressional campaign finance and related ethics issues are now part of the agenda of American politics.

Although there is no agreement on the types of reforms that should be made, the public feels that something needs to be done. Democrats and Republicans, House and Senate candidates, incumbents and nonincumbents all perceive problems with the current system of campaign finance. We hope our discussion will provide the relevant data, inform those who may not have considered all sides of the issue, and facilitate the debate to come.

Part I of this book examines the problems with the current system that have led to discussions of the need for campaign finance reform. Chapter 2 provides the legal and political context for reform. Chapter 3 compares election costs for Senate and House races, competitive and noncompetitive races, and spending by incumbents, challengers, and candidates for open seats. Chapter 4 examines how campaign money is raised and spent and how the mix of funding sources varies by party and by type of candidate. Chapters 5, 6, and 7 analyze PACs, political parties, and the Federal Election Commission, all of which have come under attack from proponents of reform for being too influential or not influential enough. Part II of the book builds on this discussion to analyze the attitudes these participants in the electoral process will have toward specific reform proposals. Particularly, these chapters examine the influence of various proposals on six core values that reform should promote: increased competition, reduced dependency on money from special interests, slowing the money chase, a stronger role for political parties, full disclosure of contributions and expenditures, and ease of administering campaign laws. Chapter 8 examines changes in contribution limits for individual donors, PACs, and political parties. Chapter 9

15. Campaign Finance Reform Panel, "Campaign Finance Reform: A Report to the Majority Leader and Minority Leader, United States Senate," March 6, 1990, p. 1.

16. *Austin v. Michigan State Chamber of Commerce,* 110 S. Ct. 21 (1990).

investigates public financing and limits on candidates' spending. Chapter 10 evaluates proposals aimed at changing the way money is raised and spent in congressional campaigns. Finally, chapter 11 offers a comprehensive reform proposal and tries to anticipate the consequences of reform for congressional campaigns and for Congress as an institution.

Part I
The Context of Reform

2

Rules, Practices, and Partisan Expectations

To understand much of the debate over campaign finance reform requires an understanding of the background of the issue, the successes and failures of prior reforms, the rules and practices currently used, and the partisan and institutional perceptions. The charge that money can corrupt democracy is not new. It has been a recurrent concern in American politics. Past laws written to deal with this concern serve to set the stage for much of the current debate. Reform brings with it both intended and unintended consequences, a lesson that is important to remember when evaluating possible future changes. An insight into likely behavior under new or changed rules can be gained from a careful assessment of current behavior. Because the House and Senate operate with different election timetables, constituencies, and fundraising opportunities, they often have different perspectives on the topic of reform. Equally important are the different partisan positions on the issue. For all of these reasons it is important to consider the context of reform.

The Federal Election Campaign Act

In January 1972, amid reports that President Nixon's reelection campaign had raised millions of dollars from wealthy backers and had received millions more in illegal corporate contributions, Congress passed the Federal Election Campaign Act of 1971. The FECA replaced the Corrupt Practices Act of 1925, which, although it required disclosure of receipts and expenditures by political candidates and committees, was written in such a way that virtually all of them were exempt from its provisions.[1] The 1972 act established uniform disclosure requirements for political committees and candidates for federal office and restricted candidates' use of their own money in campaigns. It also limited advertising expenses to ten cents per eligible voter in a candidate's state or district, or $50,000, whichever was greater. Sixty percent of this limit could be spent for broadcast advertising.[2] A companion measure, the Revenue Act of 1971, established public funding of presidential campaigns as of 1976, to be paid for through an optional checkoff of $1 on federal tax returns, and allowed tax credits for political contributions.

The FECA statutes also legitimized political action committees, or PACs. These committees had existed since the 1940s, and labor PACs had become widespread after the creation of the AFL-CIO's Committee on Political Education in 1944, but their legal status had never been affirmed. Fearing that a pending case would lead the Supreme Court to decide that the committees were nonvoluntary and thus illegal, Congress added provisions to the FECA to allow corporations and unions to use funds from their treasuries for the "establishment, administration, and solicitation of voluntary contributions to a separate, segregated fund to be utilized for political purposes."[3]

These provisions were made even more far-reaching by amendments passed in 1974 in the wake of the Watergate investigation's disclosures that an estimated $5 million in large individual and corporate contributions had been received by President Nixon's reelection campaign.[4] The amendments set limits on candidate spending and established new limits on how much individual donors, political parties, and political action committees could contribute to presidential and congressional campaigns. They also limited independent expenditures, those made on behalf of (or in opposition to) candidates, with or without the candidates' approval. Finally, the amendments placed ceilings on how much of their own money candidates could spend on their campaigns, provided for

1. For a discussion of pre-1971 campaign finance reforms, see Robert E. Mutch, *Campaigns, Congress and Courts: The Making of Federal Campaign Finance Law* (Praeger, 1988), pp. 24–26.

2. Herbert E. Alexander, *Financing Politics: Money, Elections and Political Reform* (Washington: Congressional Quarterly Press, 1976), p. 270.

3. Ratified as 18 U.S.C. 610 (1972). The Tillman Act, passed in 1907, prohibited corporations from contributing corporate funds to candidates for federal office. The Taft-Hartley Act, passed in 1947, prohibited labor unions from using members' dues to make campaign contributions to candidates for federal office.

4. Herbert E. Alexander, *Financing Politics: Money, Elections and Political Reform,* 2d ed. (Washington: Congressional Quarterly Press, 1980), pp. 51–52, 73–81.

partial public funding for presidential primary contests, and created the Federal Election Commission to administer the laws.

In January 1975, however, a few days after the new statutes went into effect, they were challenged in court. An unusual combination of liberals and conservatives, led by New York Senator James Buckley, former Democratic senator and presidential candidate Eugene McCarthy, and Stewart Mott, heir to the General Motors fortune and a major contributor to Democratic candidates, challenged the contribution and spending limits on the grounds that they violated the free speech provisions of the First Amendment.

The Supreme Court's decision in *Buckley* v. *Valeo* on January 30, 1976, is crucial to understanding the congressional campaign finance system that has since evolved. The Court ruled that money was a form of speech, and thus spending it to attain political office was protected by the First Amendment. Consequently, the limitations in the 1974 amendments on campaign expenditures were unconstitutional because they restricted free speech. However, the Court ruled that limitations were constitutional when they were tied to public financing; if candidates voluntarily accepted public funds, they also had to accept spending limitations. Because the FECA provided public funds only for presidential campaigns, the *Buckley* decision in effect allowed candidates to spend as much money as they could raise in congressional campaigns. The decision also disallowed limitations on independent expenditures and candidates' expenditures of their own money. However, the Court upheld provisions in the 1974 amendments that restricted campaign donations, arguing that the laws were justified to "limit the actuality and appearance of corruption resulting from large . . . financial contributions."[5]

In addition to striking down spending limits, the *Buckley* decision also addressed the composition of the Federal Election Commission. The 1974 amendments had called for two members of the commission to be appointed by the president, two by the president pro tempore of the Senate, and two by the Speaker of the House, all subject to confirmation by both houses of Congress. This provision, the Court decided, was unconstitutional because it violated the separation of powers established by the Constitution and the clause in Article 2 that gives the president sole authority to make such appointments. In 1976 Congress amended the act once again to require that all six members of the commission be appointed by the president and confirmed by the Senate.

5. *Buckley* v. *Valeo,* 424 U.S. 1 (1976).

The most recent amendments, in 1979, although seemingly mere technical changes, have also had serious consequences for campaign financing. One change allowed state and local parties to spend unlimited amounts of money on voter registration, get-out-the-vote drives, and other "party-building activities." This amendment opened the way for individual contributors, political action committees, and political parties to spend potentially unlimited and often undisclosed amounts, commonly referred to as soft money, in presidential and congressional campaigns.

Current Congressional Campaign Finance Laws

The results of the actions of Congress and the Supreme Court in the 1970s are the congressional campaign finance disclosure and contribution laws now in force. Individual donors may contribute up to $2,000 per candidate in each election cycle ($1,000 in the primary and $1,000 in the general), up to $5,000 to a political action committee each year, and up to $20,000 to a national party committee each year, but an individual donor's total campaign contributions in any one calendar year may not exceed $25,000 (table 2-1). PACs may contribute no more than $10,000 per candidate in each election cycle ($5,000 in the primary and $5,000 in the general), no more than $15,000 to a national party committee each calendar year, and no more than $5,000 to any other committee, but there is no limit on the total contributions they may make.[6]

Political parties are limited both in the amount of direct contributions they may make to candidates and in the amount that can be spent in coordinated expenditures—those made on behalf of candidates for polling, mailings, and media production, and in some cases purchases of air time on television and radio. The national party committees, the congressional campaign committees (both House and Senate), and the state and local party committees may each contribute $10,000 per election cycle directly to House candidates. Senate candidates may receive a total of $17,500 from the national party committees and the senatorial campaign committees; the House, state, and local party

6. If a runoff election is necessary, individual donors may contribute another $1,000 to a candidate and PACs may contribute another $5,000.

TABLE 2-1. *Limits on Contributions to Congressional Campaigns,*
January 1990
Dollars

| | | Receiver | | |
Contributor	Candidate (each election)ª	National party committees (calendar year)	Any other committee (calendar year)	Total limit (calendar year)
Individuals	1,000	20,000	5,000	25,000
PACs	5,000	15,000	5,000	None
Party committeesᵇ	5,000	None	5,000	None
All other groups	1,000	20,000	5,000	None

a. Includes contributions to a candidate's campaign committee.
b. See text for details of party committee contribution limits.

committees can contribute another $10,000 each.[7] In addition, both the national and state party committees may spend $10,000 in 1974 dollars, adjusted for inflation, on behalf of House candidates. On behalf of Senate candidates and House candidates in at-large districts, the national and state party committees may spend two cents times the voting age population of the state, or $20,000, whichever is larger, adjusted for inflation. In 1988 national and state party committees each were permitted to make such coordinated expenditures of $23,050 in each House race and between $46,100 and $938,688 in Senate races and at-large House races, depending on the size of the state.[8] State and local party committees may cede their spending authority for these expenditures to the national party committees, effectively doubling the amount of money the national party committees may spend on behalf of their candidates.

Although limitations on spending in presidential campaigns are indexed to inflation, only coordinated expenditures are indexed in congres-

---

7. In a few cases in 1986 and 1988, but more often in special elections since 1986, the national senatorial campaign committees made contributions to House candidates and the House campaign committees to Senate candidates. The campaign finance laws do not explicitly prohibit these contributions, and in 1989 the Federal Election Commission decided not to challenge them. Both the Republican and Democratic Senate campaign committees made contributions to House candidates running in special elections in 1989, and it seems likely that such contributions will continue in close, competitive elections.

8. Federal Election Commission, "F.E.C. Announces Party Spending Limits For 1988 General Elections," press release, February 8, 1988.

sional elections. Spending in congressional elections rose dramatically between 1974 and 1988, partly because of inflation, but contribution limits for individual donors and PACs remain the same as they were in 1974.

Consequences of the FECA

By upholding limits on contributions but striking down those on candidates' spending unless linked to public financing, the Supreme Court set the stage for a dramatic change in the funding of congressional campaigns. Before 1974 there was little difference in the opportunities for individual donors and organized interests to influence congressional campaigns; both could contribute as much as they wished. But now, because PACs have much higher limits on contributions to individual candidates and have no aggregate limit, organized special interests are far more important.

Before passage of the Federal Election Campaign Act most of the few PACs that did exist represented labor unions. But because the act restricted the opportunities for the concerns of business to be voiced through individual contributions, corporations and trade associations followed labor's lead and created their own committees.[9] The total number of PACs grew from 1,146 in 1976 to 4,828 in 1988. The number of corporate PACs increased from 433 to 2,008; labor PACs increased from 224 to 401.[10] The combination of PACs' higher contribution limits and their proliferation has meant that candidates increasingly turn to them to finance campaigns. The committees are more than willing to go along: they spent $12.5 million in 1974 and $151 million in 1988.[11] Candidates' increasing dependence on PAC financing has led to higher campaign spending and more and more vocal concerns that special interests may be unduly influencing congressional policymaking.

A second consequence of the act, more particularly of the Supreme

9. Edwin M. Epstein, "Business and Labor under the Federal Election Campaign Act of 1971," in Michael J. Malbin, ed., *Parties, Interest Groups and Campaign Finance Laws* (Washington: American Enterprise Institute for Public Policy Research, 1980), p. 114.

10. Federal Election Commission, "PAC Growth—from 1974," press release, July 18, 1988; and Federal Election Commission, "FEC Finds Slower Growth of PAC Activity during 1988 Election Cycle," press release, April 9, 1989.

11. Michael J. Malbin, ed., *Money and Politics in the United States: Financing Elections in the 1980s* (Washington: American Enterprise Institute for Public Policy Research, 1984), p. 298; and Federal Election Commission, "FEC Finds Slower Growth of PAC Activity during 1988 Election Cycle."

Court's interpretation of it, has been the growth in independent expenditures by PACs. Although they have not increased as rapidly as direct contributions to candidates and the amounts involved are far smaller, they totaled $21.1 million in 1988.[12] Given the current constitutional protection of independent expenditures, increases in this form of spending would be a likely consequence of any reform that further restricted direct PAC campaign contributions.

The growth of so-called soft money in both presidential and congressional elections has been another unintended consequence. By allowing state and local parties to spend unlimited amounts of money on voter registration efforts, get-out-the-vote drives, and party mailings, the laws have in effect enabled individual donors, political action committees, and in some cases corporations and labor unions to contribute unlimited, and in some states undisclosed, amounts for these activities. Although such money is supposed to benefit only state and local parties, it is difficult to argue that it does not also affect federal elections. Soft money seems to be undermining the contribution limits of the FECA. In 1988 at least 375 people contributed $100,000 in soft money to the Democratic and Republican parties.[13] These large contributions were aggressively sought by the parties and brought large contributors back into the game of presidential campaign finance.

The FECA as it now stands has also magnified the importance of personal wealth as a qualification for congressional office. Because of the rising costs of running for office and PACs' preference for supporting incumbents, seed money for the campaigns of challengers and candidates for open seats must often come from candidates' own pockets. Those who are wealthy or who can borrow sizable amounts are increasingly becoming the only ones who can mount serious campaigns. Party congressional committees also consider potential candidates' ability to provide personal funds to their campaigns as a sign of serious commitment.

Campaign finance reform has also inadvertently encouraged use of so-called bundling by both individual donors and PACs to circumvent contribution limits. When contributions from a number of people are presented as a package to a candidate, individual contributors are able

12. Federal Election Commission, "Independent Expenditures of $21 Million Reported in '88, FEC Study Shows," press release, May 19, 1989.
13. David Ignatius, "Return of the Fat Cats," *Washington Post,* November 20, 1988, p. D5; and Charles R. Babcock, "$100,000 Donations Plentiful Despite Post-Watergate Restrictions," *Washington Post,* September 22, 1988, p. A27.

to enhance their influence. In 1986 ALIGNPAC collected contributions of more than $250,000 from individual insurance agents and presented them in a bundle to Senator Robert Packwood, who was chairman of the Senate Finance Committee.[14]

Finally, campaign finance reform has proved a boon to direct mail operations. The various limitations on contributions have meant that candidates and parties can no longer rely on a small number of very wealthy contributors to bankroll campaigns. Direct mail fundraising has helped both candidates and parties develop large donor lists.

The Politics of Reform

In 1980 the Republicans experienced a political resurgence that boosted their morale and held out the possibility that they might become the dominant party in Congress. In Ronald Reagan they had a leader who broadened the appeal of the party and could, by lending his name, help in fundraising and other activities. But more important for the politics of campaign finance reform were the seats Republicans picked up in the Senate. Several of these races had been close, and observers would later debate how much effect weakened incumbents, Reagan's landslide, or the activities of the National Conservative Political Action Committee (NCPAC) had on the outcome. Whatever the causes, the Republicans were a majority in the Senate for the first time since 1953–54. The advantages of being in the majority were soon realized—control of all Senate committee chairmanships, an infusion of Republican staffers to occupy committee positions, and the ability to control the legislative agenda, both in committees and on the floor.

Republicans also picked up thirty-four House seats in the 1980 election. They were still far short of the number needed to take control, but they had unseated some powerful Democrats, including Al Ullman, chairman of the Ways and Means Committee; John Brademas, the majority whip; Harold "Bizz" Johnson, chairman of the Public Works Committee; and James Corman, chairman of the Democratic Congressional Campaign Committee. And it became clear as 1981 unfolded that Republicans could, with the help of conservative Southern Democrats, muster a working majority on issues important to the president. The most notable

14. Brooks Jackson, *Honest Graft: Big Money and the American Political Process* (Knopf, 1988), p. 131.

results of this coalition were the passage of the 1981 tax cuts and the institution of the Gramm-Latta-Hollings budget reconciliation process.

Republicans held real hope that they would be able to build on their success in the Senate and their legislative accomplishments to become the majority party in the House as well. An especially strong group of challengers was recruited to run in 1982, and the party pulled out all the stops to raise money for them. But although it did better than most presidential parties in a midterm election, it still lost twenty-six seats. Fatalistic and embittered, many Republicans are now convinced they constitute a permanent minority party in the House.

Democrats were also changed by the events of 1980 and 1982. Many had never served in a House not controlled by their own party and had taken such control for granted. Moreover, they had been the beneficiaries of Americans' tendency to dislike Congress but like their own congressman.[15] In short, they had been buoyed by the postwar tendency to reelect incumbents. The Reagan victory meant divided government, a reality Democrats had lived with in the Eisenhower, Nixon, and Ford years. But the idea of working in a divided Congress was new for all but a few members. In the aftermath of the 1980 election and the 1981 Republican legislative victories, Democrats professionalized their party committees and became more aggressive in soliciting contributions from PACs. Candidates raised far more money for their 1982 campaigns than they had in some time. After the 1982 election the party was ready to be tougher with its own membership and with the Republicans.

The more marked partisan lines were reinforced by a dispute in 1984 over who had won the House election in Indiana's Eighth Congressional District. Two days after the election, one-term Democratic incumbent Frank McCloskey officially had a seventy-two-vote lead over his Republican challenger, Richard McIntyre. Indiana Secretary of State Edwin J. Simcox, a Republican, refused to certify McCloskey the winner, saying he would wait for a recount in Gibson County. The recount gave McIntyre a thirty-four-vote lead and Simcox certified him the winner. When Congress convened in January, the House voted 238–177 along party lines to declare the seat vacant and refer the contested election to the House Administration Committee. A month later the committee appointed a recount task force, made up of two Democrats and one Republican. In the meantime, Simcox had completed his own recount

---

15. Richard Fenno, *Home Style: House Members in their Districts* (Little, Brown, 1978), pp. 245–46.

and found McIntyre the winner by 418 votes. In February, March, and early April, the Republicans offered resolutions to seat McIntyre, which barely failed to pass.

The task force found McCloskey the winner by four votes. The Republican on the task force, William M. Thomas of California, demanded a special election. When the committee rejected Thomas's motion, its Republican members walked out. The committee's Democrats then voted 12–0 to recommend that the House seat McCloskey. Partisan tempers ran high. Bill Frenzel, the ranking committee Republican, had told the committee, "Democrats decided their pal needed another chance. If you vote for the report, you are guilty of a crime I can't even describe." Republican Pat Roberts, in a statement that would describe the feelings of his party for years to come, added, "You're going to win here, but you're losing by tearing at the fabric of this place. If you worry folks like me, we're in serious, serious trouble."[16]

This partisan rift persisted into the 1986 elections. The only House race in which Ronald Reagan personally campaigned was in Indiana's Eighth District, where a rematch between McCloskey and McIntyre resulted in McCloskey's victory by 13,000 votes. The battle has had implications well beyond a single house seat. House Republican campaign professionals blamed former Speaker Jim Wright and former Majority Whip Tony Coelho for the events that led to McCloskey's seating. As long as the two were in the Democratic leadership, Republican attitudes were that it made no sense to deal with them or with other Democratic leaders on electoral reform issues because they had been neither fair nor reasonable. While Speaker Thomas Foley has done much to restore partisan goodwill to the House, Republicans remain suspicious. They agree that Republican challengers are at a disadvantage under the present campaign finance system but do not trust a legislative process controlled by Democrats to reform it. They know that the system perpetuates a Democratic House majority, but they reject any alternative supported by Democrats because they assume that the changes will only further entrench the Democratic majority.

During the first six months of the 101st Congress, matters of ethics dominated deliberations: the proposed elimination of honoraria in return for increased salary, the propriety of former Senator John Tower's consulting fees charged to defense contractors, the charges and coun-

16. Andy Plattner, "Republicans Seethe over Indiana 8th Decision," *Congressional Quarterly Weekly Report,* April 27, 1985, p. 775.

tercharges involving the misconduct of the Speaker of the House and the whips of both House parties. Perhaps the most dramatic event was the resignation of a sitting Speaker of the House. Republican distrust of Wright had burst into the open in 1988. An ethics investigation initiated by Republican Newt Gingrich ultimately led the House Committee on Standards of Official Conduct to bring charges against Wright. He was accused of having exceeded the limits on outside earned income through the sale of his book, *Reflections of a Public Man*. He was also charged with being the recipient of undisclosed gifts from a friend and business associate, George Malick, and accepting gifts from a person with an interest in legislation, again Malick. Just as the Wright matter was coming to its conclusion, Democratic Whip Tony Coelho admitted to having entered into a deal to purchase junk bonds that was financed by an officer of a California savings and loan. He had not listed the transaction on his financial disclosure forms. While the charges against him appeared on their face to be less extensive than those against Wright, he resigned soon after the first news report. A few days later Wright also resigned.

Meanwhile Gingrich himself was charged with ethics violations involving the financing of his book, *Window of Opportunity,* and income received by his wife in conjunction with its promotion. The evidence of wrongdoing was insufficient for the outside counsel to recommend action by the House Ethics Committee.[17] Additional charges against Gingrich were filed by Democrat Bill Alexander. The Democratic hostility stemmed from Gingrich's leadership in the battle against Wright and from his assertion that the list of ethics violators included more than Wright and Coelho, perhaps as many as ten House Democrats.[18]

Democratic distrust was further fueled by the release of a Republican National Committee memorandum that referred to Tom Foley, Democratic majority leader and soon-to-be-elected Speaker, in derogatory terms. When the memorandum became public, the RNC official who had written it resigned and received a stern reprimand from President Bush and his chief of staff John Sununu.

In July 1989 President Bush offered his own program of campaign finance reforms. He proposed banning PACs affiliated with corporations, unions, and trade associations and reducing from $5,000 to $2,500 per election the amount of money nonconnected PACs (those not connected

---

17. Don Phillips, "Gingrich Book Probe Falters," *Washington Post,* October 21, 1989, p. A1.

18. Tom Kenworthy, "Coelho Exit Seen as Good to Wright," *Washington Post,* May 29, 1989, p. A4.

with corporations, unions, or trade associations) could contribute to candidates. He also proposed raising the party contribution limits, reducing the number of congressional mailings permitted under the frank, forcing the disclosure of soft money, and eliminating the carryover of campaign funds from one election to the next. But although the president and his aides argued that the proposal would "free our electoral system from the grip of special interests" and "level the playing field," Democrats in Congress were quick to label the package as partisan politics. Senate Majority Leader George Mitchell said that the plan was "obviously crafted with one objective—to help Republicans."[19]

It is in this context that the 101st Congress confronted the matter of money in congressional campaigns and congressional life. Whether it will feel added pressure to enact reform remains to be seen.

Partisan and Ideological Differences

Party opposition to various proposals for campaign finance reform stems from both self-interest and philosophy. Republican party committees have been able to raise much more money than the Democratic party committees, but this advantage has not translated into success at the polls. Democratic candidates raise sufficient money to be competitive, and Republicans cannot take full advantage of their fundraising edge because of limits on party spending. The Democrats have been especially successful in cultivating PAC contributions, reinforcing their hold on power in the House, and making the job of Republican challengers particularly difficult. But the realities have not dissuaded Republicans from resisting giving up their fundraising advantage for spending limits, with or without public financing. The Republicans also believe that they need to spend more than their opponents to compensate for fewer party supporters, weaker organization in most states, the help Democrats receive from organized labor, and the fact that Democrats more often have opportunities to build name recognition through election to local or state office.

Republican philosophical objections to reform stem from distaste for government regulation, aversion to a larger role for government generally, and alarm at the potential cost of any campaign finance reform legislation that includes public financing. Democrats, on the other hand, are willing to enlarge the role of government in campaign finance reform and

19. Ann Devroy and Helen Dewar, "Bush Unveils Campaign Regulation Package," *Washington Post,* June 30, 1989, p. A11.

generally are less concerned about costs. They believe that the present system discourages people from seeking office and elevates the interests of those who can afford to make political contributions. Ironically, however, it is the Democrats who, by most assessments, have mastered the present system of campaign finance, at least in the House, and stand to lose the most by changing it. Why then, ask many Democrats, should they support fundamental changes in the way congressional campaigns are financed?

The answer depends more on philosophy than self-interest. To the extent that people disapprove of the present system, they see the Democrats as the leaders of efforts to reduce the influence of PACs. Until the late 1980s, Republicans were the most vocal defenders of the present campaign finance system, and particularly of PAC contributions, even though House Republicans receive less money from PACs than Democrats do. But as the 1980s came to a close, Republican congressional leaders roundly criticized PACs, and President Bush called for banning most of them. This change of attitude reflected the frustration of Republicans with heavy corporate PAC giving to incumbent Democrats and a desire to gain the high ground in the debate on campaign finance reform.

House Republicans find themselves in a distressing circumstance. On one hand, they are at a strategic disadvantage, with Democratic incumbents seemingly invulnerable to challenge. On the other, they read partisan intent into Democratic reform proposals and think it safer not to take a chance on reform. Their aversion to public financing and their distaste for a larger government role in elections are secondary to their anger at their seemingly permanent status of minority party.

House-Senate Differences

Since 1979 the expectation has generally been that the Senate must act first on campaign finance reform, but that House action would quickly follow. This expectation stemmed in part from the experience of the 1970s, when the House passed campaign finance reform legislation only to see it die in the Senate.[20] Because the politics of reform are so volatile

20. The Obey-Railsback bill, as the legislation was called, passed the House in October 1979. An amendment to the Federal Election Commission authorization bill, it would have prohibited House candidates from accepting more than $70,000 from PACs in any two-year cycle and would have lowered the limit on PAC contributions to individuals from $10,000 to $6,000 per election cycle. Senators Mark Hatfield and Hubert Humphrey threatened a filibuster on the bill and thus there was no Senate action on it. "PAC Contribution Limits," *Congressional Quarterly Almanac, 1979*, vol. 35 (1980), p. 556.

and the costs of assembling a coalition so high even within one party, the House put the Senate on notice that it must act first on the next campaign finance reform legislation.

This informal political understanding made the Senate the initial battleground in 1977 and again in 1987–88 and permitted the Republicans to use Senate rules to delay or defeat any reform measure. In both instances they successfully mounted a filibuster and maintained sufficient party unity to fend off cloture.[21] In 1987 and 1988 opposition to the reform bills came from both Senate and House Republicans. There was close communication between them, and it was understood that if campaign finance reform legislation passed the Senate, there was little House Republicans could do to stop it from passing in the House as well.

Another dynamic of congressional campaign finance reform is the understanding that each chamber will write its own bill. Thus S.2, the 1987–88 reform package, primarily addressed campaign finance for Senate elections. Had it passed, the House would have developed a bill acceptable to the House. There is thus no guarantee that the two houses will develop similar solutions to the campaign finance problem. The Senate could enact a system of spending limits and partial public financing with aggregate PAC limits, while the House might choose to provide public financing at modest levels but not cap spending or PAC receipts— the so-called floor with no ceiling. Whether one chamber would object to the other's solution is not known. What we do know is that the different perspectives and circumstances make a single approach difficult to achieve.

---

21. In 1977 there were three attempts to invoke cloture. In 1987–88 there were a record eight cloture votes. Mutch, *Campaigns, Congress and Courts,* p. 132; and *Congressional Record,* daily ed., February 26, 1988.

3

Campaign Costs

The price of admission to Congress has risen dramatically in the past two decades. Taken as a whole, spending on campaigns has increased far faster than the rate of inflation and well beyond what would appear to have been necessary, given the lack of competition in most House races and many Senate races. Although it is of course necessary to spend money to establish a campaign organization, mobilize voters, and communicate ideas, the ceaseless search for campaign money causes major problems. Higher costs mean a longer and longer fundraising cycle and force candidates to spend more time seeking funds. To raise what they consider adequate campaign funds, candidates turn ever more frequently to PACs and wealthy individual contributors who have their own particular interests to advance. Moreover, some candidates raise money to discourage opposition, and others to foster careers in Congress or to prepare for campaigns for other offices.

Much of the increase in spending has been caused by the high cost of modern communications. As Roger Craver, one of the most successful direct mail fundraisers, has said, there is "a direct correlation between the rise of television costs and campaign spending."[1] Fundraising to meet these costs falls squarely on the candidate, especially since campaigns focus on candidates rather than on parties. Because current law permits candidates to spend as much as they can raise, and current campaign conditions encourage them to raise as much as they can if they want to compete seriously, candidates are caught in a money chase. "Everybody," commented Susan Manes, former staff director of the Senate Democratic Policy Committee and now with Common Cause, "raises and therefore spends more and more money in order to stay one step ahead of what [they think their] opponent might do."[2]

1. Interview with Roger Craver, March 22, 1988.
2. Interview with Susan Manes, March 22, 1988.

But how much spending are we talking about? And in what configurations? Are spending patterns the same for House and Senate, Democrats and Republicans, incumbents and challengers, sharply contested races and those in which one candidate is clearly dominant? And are candidates really spending too much? Perhaps more spending would lead to higher voter turnout or a better-informed electorate. Answering these questions is crucial if the effects of fundraising on candidates, legislators, the electorate, and the institution of Congress itself are to be sorted out and problems resolved.

How Much Have Costs Risen?

Since the Federal Election Campaign Act became law in 1972, total expenditures in general elections by candidates for House and Senate seats have risen from $66 million to $407 million (figure 3-1). Expenditures by Senate candidates have increased more than 600 percent; those of candidates for the House, 456 percent. The increases were sharpest between 1976 and 1978 and between 1980 and 1982. The surge in spending by candidates for the House in 1982 is explained by the Republican successes in the 1980 presidential and Senate elections and by the defeat of some prominent House Democrats, which motivated House Republicans and Democrats alike to go all out.

Spending by House general election candidates as a group has consistently been higher than for Senate candidates, but the gap has been narrowing: House candidates' share of all spending dropped from 61.5 percent in 1976 to 55.1 percent in 1988.[3] Since 1972, House candidates have normally accounted for about three-fifths of all House and Senate general election campaign expenditures, although House candidates outnumber Senate candidates by more than twelve to one.

Part of the variation shown in figure 3-1 results from the spending surge in midterm election years. In the three midterm elections since the Federal Election Commission began keeping records in 1976, spending by House candidates was an average of 38 percent higher than in the preceding election year, while in the presidential election years it was 18 percent higher. Senate candidates follow the same pattern: the average increase for midterm years is 52 percent and for presidential

---

3. When all candidates (that is, including those in primary races) are considered, the pattern is similar. House candidates' share of total spending declined from 62 percent in 1976 to 53 percent in 1986.

FIGURE 3-1. *Total Campaign Expenditures by House and Senate General Election Candidates, 1972–88*[a]

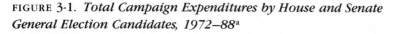

Millions of dollars

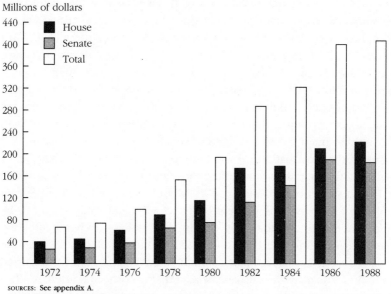

SOURCES: See appendix A.
a. Includes primary and general election expenditures by major-party general election candidates only (net expenditures, where possible).

FIGURE 3-2. *Total Campaign Expenditures by House and Senate General Election Candidates in 1988 Constant Dollars, 1972–88*[a]

Millions of dollars

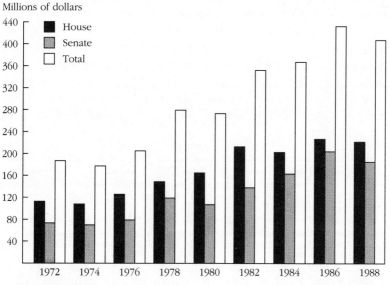

SOURCES: See appendix A.
a. Includes primary and general election expenditures by major-party general election candidates only (net expenditures, where possible).

election years 18 percent.[4] Competition for funds by presidential candidates and the attention focused on the presidential election are some of the causes.

Figure 3-1 shows only expenditures by general election candidates. Challengers who lost in the primaries since 1980 account for an additional $25 million in both the House and the Senate. Including these candidates increases overall expenditures since 1972 by $150 million for House races and $138 million for Senate races. The pattern of higher expenditures in midterm races persists. Because the pool of candidates varies more dramatically from year to year when primary election losers are included, in subsequent discussions, unless otherwise noted, we will refer only to major-party candidates' spending in general elections.

Part of the explanation for the increase in campaign expenditures is inflation. But even after controlling for that, expenditures of candidates for House seats doubled between 1972 and 1988, and those of Senate candidates rose by 148 percent.[5] Figure 3-2 plots total spending by House and Senate candidates by year in 1988 dollars. (When comparing spending over time, we have converted nominal dollars into inflation-adjusted real or constant dollars.) Much of the increase has been caused by the dramatic growth in broadcast advertising costs. In constant dollars the largest jump in expenditures by House candidates came in 1982, when spending rose 29 percent. In the Senate the largest increase was in 1978, when expenditures rose 50 percent. Again, expenditures tended to rise more in midterm years than in presidential election years and somewhat more in the Senate than in the House. This same pattern exists when all candidates, not just those who ran in the general election, are included. For House candidates, expenditures in constant dollars increased an average of 24 percent in midterm election years; in presidential election years they increased only 1 percent. For all Senate candidates, expenditures increased an average of 34 percent in midterm election years and 2 percent in presidential election years. Although the predictable elections to watch for increased spending are those in

4. The midterm spending surge is also evident for all candidates, including losers in primaries. In nominal dollars, spending by candidates for House seats in midterm elections since 1976 rose an average of 40 percent; in presidential election years, 16 percent. Spending by Senate candidates rose an average of 51 percent in midterm elections but only 14 percent in presidential election years.

5. It is important to remember that only one-third of the Senate is up for election at any one time and that the sample of states having current Senate races may skew the data. For instance, when California and New York both have Senate races, average spending could be substantially higher.

midterm years, spending will probably also increase in 1992, a presidential election year, because redistricting will result in more open-seat and competitive races, and because in the Senate the "expensive" class of 1986—California, New York, and a group of competitive small states—will be up for reelection.

In constant dollars, spending has not always increased; it declined in the Senate between 1978 and 1980, in the House between 1982 and 1984, and in both between 1986 and 1988. Moreover, spending growth, in constant dollars, is slowing. The increase for House candidates was 26 percent in 1978, 29 percent in 1982, and 12 percent in 1986. Presidential election years show the same declining rate of increase: 17 percent in 1976, 4 percent in 1980, − 5 percent in 1984, and − 2 percent in 1988. Senate candidate spending in midterm elections rose by 50 percent in 1978, 29 percent in 1982, and 25 percent in 1986, while in presidential elections it rose by 14 percent in 1976, 10 percent in 1980, 18 percent in 1984, and − 9 percent in 1988. Senate candidate spending deviated from the pattern of declining rates of increase in 1986, just as House candidate spending deviated from the pattern in 1982. The campaign environment in these two years may be part of the explanation.

Because comparing Senate election spending every two years is difficult—the subset of states in any given election is different from the preceding cycle—interpreting the drop in spending in real dollars in Senate elections between 1986 and 1988 is also difficult. In fact, spending per voter rose between 1986 and 1988, and spending also rose dramatically between 1982 and 1988, when the same sample of states held elections.

Because not all states have Senate elections in each election cycle, it is important when discussing changing costs to compare the same set of states over time. Table 3-1 compares the mean costs per voter in constant 1988 dollars for Senate elections since 1978. The table also reports the mean expenditure per voter for the ten most expensive and ten least expensive states in each cycle. In each six-year cycle since 1978, spending in Senate elections rose faster than the rate of inflation, 45 percent to 41 percent. There is, however, a wide range within each cycle. For instance, in 1986 the ten most expensive states had a mean expenditure of $6.45 per voter while the ten least expensive states had a mean of $0.80. While this is the widest discrepancy, the pattern was the same in the other five elections. The most dramatic increase occurred between 1980 and 1986 among the ten least expensive states, where

TABLE 3-1. *Average Spending per Voter in Senate Election Cycles,*
1978–88
Constant 1988 dollars

States	Year and amount	Year and amount
	1978	*1984*
All states	1.64	2.34
Ten most expensive	2.81	4.65
Ten least expensive	0.63	0.62
	1980	*1986*
All states	1.94	2.81
Ten most expensive	4.69	6.45
Ten least expensive	0.35	0.80
	1982	*1988*
All states	2.06	2.91
Ten most expensive	4.30	6.10
Ten least expensive	0.52	0.82

SOURCES: FEC data tapes; see appendix A.

expenditures per voter rose by 129 percent after controlling for inflation, a growth rate well beyond that of the ten most expensive states. Spending in Senate elections is typically increasing 40 percent in constant dollars over a six-year cycle.

One way to get a sense of this growth is to compare it with the growth in costs of presidential elections (figure 3-3). Expenditures in presidential elections have declined, leveled off, and begun to grow again since 1972, the last presidential election year before spending limits took effect. Before 1972 the long-term trend had been toward increased spending, with fairly dramatic jumps in expenditures reported for 1964 and 1968.[6] In the absence of spending limits, presidential election expenditures would probably resemble those of congressional elections.[7]

Congressional elections show a very different pattern. In 1972 congressional election expenditures were $138 million less than presidential election expenditures. In 1984 they exceeded presidential spending by $208 million. Adjusted for inflation, expenditures in congres-

6. Herbert Alexander and Brian A. Haggerty, *Financing the 1984 Election* (Lexington, Mass.: D.C. Heath, 1987), p. 84.
7. Because the expenditure data before 1976 are reported differently and may be less accurate, it would be a mistake to overdraw these comparisons. But given the consistency of the long-term patterns, we include them here.

FIGURE 3-3. *Campaign Expenditures of President and Congress,*
1972–88[a]

Millions of constant 1988 dollars

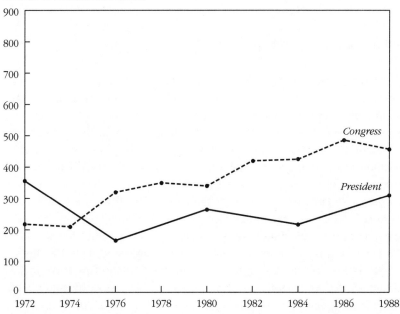

SOURCES: FEC data tapes; see appendix A.
a. Includes primary and general election expenditures by major-party general election candidates only (net expenditures, where possible).

sional elections more than doubled between 1972 and 1988, although the rate of increase has been slowing. Expenditures in presidential elections have remained much flatter since the spending limits took effect, ranging from $167 million to $266 million, except for the increase to $311 million in 1988.[8] Expenditures in presidential primaries and general elections by major-party presidential candidates have not grown as dramatically as expenditures by congressional candidates, and they dropped substantially as limits took effect in 1976, rose with the election of 1980, but then dropped again in 1984. The jump in spending by presidential candidates in 1988 was at least partly caused by the large number of candidates seeking the nomination in both major parties.

8. We do not include spending on the party conventions, "miscellaneous spending," or soft money, as do Alexander and Haggerty, *Financing the 1984 Election,* pp. 84–85. Were we to do so, our estimates would be much higher.

Despite these now substantial differences in spending between congressional and presidential elections, raising the limits on spending in
presidential elections has not been proposed.[9]

Who Does the Spending?

Although campaign spending has generally been increasing for House
and Senate candidates, is it because of more spending by all candidates
or by only a few? To explore this question, we divided all House general
election candidates into deciles according to their expenditures in
constant dollars and compared the mean for each decile over time. The
striking fact is that average spending rose most dramatically for the top
50 percent of House candidates since 1980; for the other 50 percent of
House candidates, the lower the decile, the less the change. The difference
between deciles is evident in figure 3-4. For the top 50 percent of House
candidates the typical increase in average spending by decile was nearly
50 percent in real dollars. The increase in mean spending in the highest
decile is 29 percent, rising from just under $700,000 in 1980 to just
under $900,000 in 1990 in 1988 constant dollars. Most of the increase
in average spending is occurring in only half of the House campaigns.
At the other end of the distribution, candidates may be spending too
little to attain sufficient visibility to be competitive. Fifty percent of all
House candidates have spent less than $200,000 in constant 1988 dollars
since 1980. In the Senate, mean spending by decile has increased more
uniformly. Excluding the highest and lowest deciles, which include the
extremes, spending increased by an average of 60 percent between 1980
and 1988.

In which contests are these increases occurring? Table 3-2 shows
average costs for all House and Senate general election candidates and
for winning candidates. The average House candidate in 1988 spent
about $274,000, and the average winning candidate spent over $100,000
more.[10] This gap has been widening in both houses. In 1976 the average
Senate general election candidate spent $1,238,000 in 1988 dollars, and
the winners roughly $250,000 more. By 1988 average Senate candidates

9. One reason is the availability of soft money to presidential candidates. See Elizabeth
Drew, *Politics and Money: The New Road to Corruption* (Macmillan, 1983); and Alexander
and Haggerty, *Financing the 1984 Election.*
10. Here and elsewhere in the book we have rounded dollar figures to the nearest
$100.

FIGURE 3-4. *Mean Spending for House Candidates, by Decile, 1980–88*

Thousands of 1988 dollars

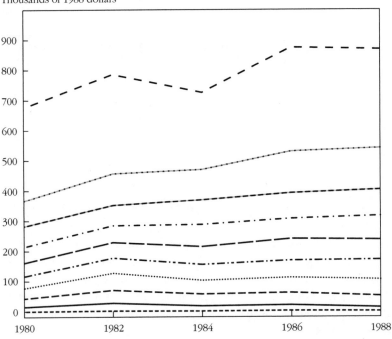

SOURCES: FEC data tapes; see appendix A.

spent $2,802,000 and winners $3,745,500. Senate candidates and Senate winners spent ten times more than House candidates and winners.

Since 1976, spending in constant dollars by winning House candidates has more than doubled, as it has for winning Senate candidates. House spending increased most between 1980 and 1982; spending for winning Senate candidates also rose substantially in these years. Holding constant the sample of states with Senate elections, spending in constant dollars rose from $1,693,500 for winners in 1980 to $3,311,400 in 1986. Thus it is in the competitive races that the greatest increase in expenditures occurs.

The most important distinction between congressional races is contests in which incumbents are running and those in which they are not. Since 1960, 10 percent of House and 20 percent of Senate contests have been for open seats.[11] For both parties, candidates for open seats are the

11. Data on the number of incumbents running are from Harold W. Stanley and Richard

TABLE 3-2. *Average Campaign Expenditures of House and Senate Candidates, 1974–88*[a]

Thousands of constant 1988 dollars

	House		Senate	
Year	All candidates	Winning candidates	All candidates	Winning candidates
1974	128	n.a.	1,050	n.a.
1976	152	181	1,238	1,461
1978	196	230	1,685	2,193
1980	201	255	1,516	1,693
1982	259	323	2,097	2,534
1984	249	332	2,404	3,367
1986	282	383	2,844	3,311
1988	274	388	2,802	3,745

SOURCES: See appendix A.

n.a. Not available.

a. Includes primary and general election expenditures by major-party general election candidates only (net expenditures, where possible). Numbers have been rounded.

ones who most successfully raise and spend money. In races with an incumbent, campaign spending by incumbent candidates in the House and Senate nearly tripled in constant dollars between 1974 and 1988 (table 3-3). Spending by challengers for Senate seats also rose substantially, but spending by House challengers has decreased in each successive cycle since 1982.

There are clear differences between Republican and Democratic challengers in their ability to raise and spend money. In 1988 House Republican challengers spent less than half as much in constant dollars as they spent in 1984, dropping from an average of $217,600 to $99,400 (table 3-4). House Democratic challengers are also underfinanced, but their ability to spend money has not declined, nor has average spending by Senate challengers declined as precipitously as spending by House Republican challengers. Republican incumbents consistently outspent both Democratic incumbents and Democratic challengers. But the sharpest contrast in spending is between House Democratic incumbents and House Republican challengers: House Democratic incumbents spent three and one-half times more than their Republican challengers in 1988.

Because challengers for House seats clearly have not been able to

G. Niemi, *Vital Statistics on American Politics* (Washington: Congressional Quarterly Press, 1988), pp. 91–92. Data on the number of Senate seats up in any given election are from *Congressional Quarterly Almanac*, annual editions, 1960–88. Data on the number of open House and Senate seats in 1988 are from *Congressional Quarterly Weekly Report*, November 12, 1988, pp. 3249, 3266.

TABLE 3-3. *Average Campaign Expenditures of House and Senate Candidates, by Candidate Status, 1974–88*[a]
Thousands of constant 1988 dollars

Year	Incumbent	Challenger	Open seat
House			
1974	135.7	96.0	217.0
1976	165.1	105.6	258.9
1978	201.8	136.1	361.9
1980	235.9	143.5	298.9
1982	321.4	158.6	358.7
1984	318.0	144.7	401.8
1986	364.0	135.8	454.4
1988	378.3	118.9	480.7
Senate			
1974	1,333.8	798.2	963.6
1976	1,351.1	900.8	1,573.8
1978	2,434.6	1,279.8	1,436.4
1980	1,887.6	1,213.3	1,606.8
1982	2,161.5	1,435.8	5,078.9
1984	2,831.3	1,185.6	5,088.6
1986	3,570.3	1,920.0	3,383.5
1988	3,750.7	1,816.1	2,886.4

SOURCES: See appendix A.
a. Includes primary and general election expenditures by major-party general election candidates only (net expenditures, where possible). Numbers have been rounded.

compete with incumbents in fundraising, their competitive position has worsened in the past decade. Moreover, incumbents seem to spend money to preempt serious challengers as well as to react to them.[12] "One thing an incumbent can do which has almost no direct effect on the *quality* of the challenger he or she will face," according to Jonathan Krasno and Donald Green, "is to raise and spend campaign money early in the election cycle." These findings, limited to 1977–78, run counter to the widely held view that the more incumbents spend the worse they do. Spending is not the only factor; as Krasno and Green argue, preempting challengers is best accomplished by soundly defeating the challenger in the previous election.[13] The consequence for challengers is that they need to raise and spend large sums to be competitive.

12. Edie N. Goldenberg, Michael W. Traugott, and Frank R. Baumgartner, "Preemptive and Reactive Spending in U.S. House Races," paper prepared for the 1983 annual meeting of the Midwest Political Science Association.
13. Jonathan S. Krasno and Donald Philip Green, "Preempting Quality Challengers in House Elections," *Journal of Politics,* vol. 50 (November 1988), pp. 932–33.

TABLE 3-4. *Average Campaign Expenditures of House Candidates, by Party and Candidate Status, 1974–88*[a]
Thousands of constant 1988 dollars

Party	Incumbent	Challenger	Open seat
Republican			
1974	192.8	49.5	193.8
1976	190.2	110.9	211.7
1978	228.6	139.7	343.3
1980	254.7	199.8	321.9
1982	352.6	199.1	385.7
1984	317.7	217.6	424.6
1986	395.6	118.8	527.1
1988	408.7	99.4	500.6
Democrat			
1974	93.0	142.2	239.4
1976	152.4	96.3	302.5
1978	187.8	128.7	384.4
1980	227.0	134.0	259.0
1982	303.6	173.4	313.9
1984	318.2	141.9	399.7
1986	337.1	154.3	452.3
1988	358.2	143.5	461.6

SOURCES: Norman J. Ornstein, Thomas E. Mann, and Michael J. Malbin, *Vital Statistics on Congress, 1989–90* (Washington: Congressional Quarterly, 1990), pp. 71–72.
a. Numbers have been rounded.

The reelection rate for House members is very high: in the 1988 election, 98 percent of those seeking reelection won. While this was an all-time record, an average of 91 percent of incumbents in post–World War II elections have been successful. Incumbency has not been as great an advantage in Senate elections. During the 1960s the proportion of incumbent senators who won was nearly as great as for House members. In the 1970s the proportion decreased, reaching a low in 1980 when thirteen of the twenty-nine incumbents running were defeated in primary or general elections, allowing the Republicans to take control of the Senate for the first time since 1953.[14] In 1982 and 1984, however, more than 90 percent of the senators seeking reelection won, and in 1986, another turnover year, 75 percent won.

14. The 1980 election defeats of Senate Democrats have been blamed on many factors—the Reagan victory, a desire for change in the Senate, and the independent and negative campaign waged by the National Conservative Political Action Committee (NCPAC). See Thomas E. Mann and Norman J. Ornstein, "The Republican Surge in Congress," in Austin Ranney, ed., *The American Elections of 1980* (Washington: American Enterprise Institute for Public Policy Research, 1981), pp. 270–73.

Incumbents have an incentive to raise large sums of money early in campaigns as a way of showing strength. But, according to Gary Jacobson, "Spending the money does them comparatively little good. What matters much more is the amount spent by the challenger (and related to it how qualified and skillful he or she is). This means that *the incumbent's most effective electoral strategy is to discourage serious opposition.* The most effective way to do this is to avoid showing signs of electoral vulnerability."[15]

Another important determinant of spending is whether the race is for an open seat. Candidates for open House seats consistently spend more on average than incumbents or their challengers, and the increase has been greater than it has been for incumbents. Spending by candidates for open Senate seats has shown the most dramatic rise, climbing from an average of just under $1 million in 1974 to more than $5 million in 1982 and 1984.[16] That average expenditures in constant dollars dropped to less than $3 million in 1988 is explained in part by the particular group of states with open seats that year.

Average campaign expenditures of the two parties' general election candidates show surprising parity: for the period 1976–88, only about $4,500 separates them in the House and about $80,000 in the Senate. There is, however, significant variation between the parties in some election cycles. In the Senate the difference has been somewhat larger, with the greatest disparity in 1986 when Republicans spent about 40 percent more, in part because of the large number of incumbent Republicans (eighteen) seeking reelection. But are these findings true where money is likely to matter most—competitive races (in which the winner receives 55 percent or less of the vote)? Table 3-5 compares average expenditures in competitive races, in constant dollars, for the two parties in both houses. Republicans have been more successful than Democrats in funneling money to competitive races in the House. Except for 1984 and 1988, House Republicans' average expenditure in these races has been about $100,000 larger, in 1988 constant dollars, than that of the Democrats. Looking at Senate elections in constant dollars per voter, in competitive Senate races Republican incumbents have spent

15. Gary C. Jacobson, *The Politics of Congressional Elections*, 2d ed. (Little, Brown, 1987), p. 53 (emphasis added).

16. There is some variation in the number of open seats in a given year. Between 1978 and 1988 the average in the House was forty and in the Senate nine. There does not appear to be a correlation between the number of open Senate seats and the average expenditure in contests for them.

TABLE 3-5. *Average Campaign Expenditures of House and Senate Candidates in Competitive Races, by Party, 1980–88*[a]
Thousands of constant 1988 dollars

Year	House		Senate	
	Democrat	Republican	Democrat	Republican
1980	351.4	453.5	1,903.5	1,671.4
1982	354.0	486.7	2,896.9	2,878.6
1984	508.3	503.4	5,371.1	5,138.6
1986	500.2	597.6	3,804.2	4,818.0
1988	613.2	600.2	3,661.6	4,159.9
Average	465.4	528.3	3,527.5	3,733.3

SOURCES: See appendix A.

a. Includes primary and general election expenditures by major-party general election candidates only (net expenditures, where possible). Numbers have been rounded.

an average of $2.07 since 1980; Democratic incumbents have spent $1.26. Democratic and Republican challengers both have spent $1.28. Democratic candidates for open seats have averaged $1.67 and Republicans $1.05.

Too Much or Not Enough?

Congressional campaign costs will likely continue to increase because of the lack of restraints on them, the abundant supply of money from contributors, and candidates' uncertainty about winning. Assuming the current rate of increase, the average winning candidate for the House in 1990 will spend more than $500,000 in 1988 dollars, and the average Senate winner $4.8 million. Costs for winners of competitive races and winners of open-seat contests will be even higher. This increase is one of the most frequently mentioned reasons for reforming the present system of congressional campaign finance. Still, not everyone agrees that spending is too high. In a 1987 Senate floor debate, Robert Packwood said that the United States does not spend "anywhere near what other democratic countries do in their elections. We do not come near spending what we do in this country on toothpaste or lipstick or beer or pet food or even advertising for pet food. So, in terms of priorities and importance, let us not get things out of scale. I would like to think that the value of an election for Congress or the Senate is worth as much as a can of cat food or dog food."[17] And some years ago Herbert Alexander

17. *Congressional Record,* daily ed., June 3, 1987, p. S7548.

FIGURE 3-5. *Voter Turnout and Aggregate Campaign Spending in Congressional Races, 1972–88*

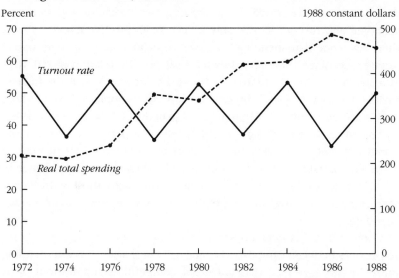

Percent   1988 constant dollars

SOURCES: Turnout data are from the *Statistical Abstract of the United States, 1988*, p. 250; and "Where They Voted ... and Where They Didn't: 1988 Presidential-Election Turnout as Percentage of Voting-Age Population," *Congressional Quarterly Weekly Report*, January 21, 1989, p. 136. Spending data sources are in appendix A.

drew a similar comparison: "Procter and Gamble, with the largest advertising budget of any American corporation, spent $270,000,000 for advertising in 1968, only slightly less than the amount spent for all political campaigning that year."[18] There is, of course, such an obvious difference between promoting products and spending for congressional elections that the comparison is misplaced. Nonetheless, the large amounts spent on product advertising and the increasing number of advertising opportunities reinforce the candidates' perceived need to spend more and more money to compete for voters' attention.

An additional aspect of the argument that the United States does not spend enough on election campaigns is the idea that spending more is better. Senator Robert Dole has expressed the view of many Republicans that the reforms considered in 1987–88, which included limiting spending, would decrease political participation.[19] This assumption can be tested directly. Campaign spending in congressional elections has

18. Herbert E. Alexander, *Political Financing* (Minneapolis: Burgess Publishing, 1972), p. 39.

19. *Congressional Record*, daily ed., September 9, 1987, p. S11872.

more than doubled in constant dollars since 1972. What has happened to voter turnout? As figure 3-5 shows, the aggregate turnout rate has declined somewhat since 1972. Testing for a relationship between spending and turnout shows only a very small positive effect.[20] But is there evidence that spending increases voter turnout in specific states? Senate races since 1980 have shown a weak positive relationship (0.0164 at a significance level of 0.0001). However, the states with the highest variation in spending show no relationship. For example, in South Dakota expenditures in constant 1986 dollars equaled $12.50 per voter in 1980, $12.31 in 1984, and $13.49 in 1986, but 65.8 percent of the eligible population voted in 1980, 62.6 percent in 1984, and 58.9 percent in 1986. Other states with similar changes in spending saw little change in turnout. The results are the same in all Senate races, those with higher than average spending, and competitive races with higher than average spending.

Competition, however, *does* lead to higher turnout, while expenditure imbalances between candidates reduce it.[21] Once again, it is not spending more in the aggregate that enhances competition and turnout. It is getting more money into the hands of challengers.[22] While it is difficult to disentangle these independent variables—competitive races have higher spending—it appears that of the two, competition is more strongly related to turnout.

Are there other presumed salutary effects of increased spending? Will voters be more informed because more thirty- or sixty-second commercials are broadcast? Those who oppose legislating limits on campaign spending argue that when candidates spend more, the voting public is better informed. To test this contention, the Center for Political Studies at the University of Michigan in its biennial American National Election Study measured the extent to which voters could correctly recall the names of their district's candidates for the House—a minimal level of

20. We adjusted for the predictably smaller turnouts in midterm elections by adding 5 percent to them, a weight very close to the mean turnout differential for the two types of elections in this period.

21. Paul A. Dawson and James F. Zinser, "Political Finance and Participation in Congressional Elections," *Annals of The American Academy of Political and Social Science,* vol. 425 (May 1976), p. 64.

22. Our findings agree with those of Gregory A. Caldeira, Samuel C. Patterson, and Gregory A. Markko, "The Mobilization of Voters in Congressional Elections," *Journal of Politics,* vol. 47 (May 1985), p. 504. See also Dawson and Zinser, "Political Finance and Participation in Congressional Elections," p. 200, who find that campaign advertising stimulates interest in elections and influences voter participation.

awareness and knowledge.[23] Between 1978 and 1986, as expenditures in congressional elections grew dramatically, the proportion of voters who could name the candidate and his or her party declined from 25 percent to 22 percent. Although it is impossible to tell if increased spending prevented a sharper deterioration in recall, increased spending clearly has not improved it.[24] In short, there is no evidence that, in the aggregate, higher spending significantly improves voter knowledge or participation.

The final element of the debate over whether too much or too little is spent on congressional campaigns is comparisons of costs in the United States with those in other countries. Campaign finance is very different in the United States from that in countries with parliaments. The American model is a candidate-centered electoral system in which political parties play a subordinate and perhaps diminishing role. American campaign finance is also marked by a direct relationship between political action committees and candidates. The parliamentary model, however, is a "party-oriented political system in which interest groups often are the basis of the parties, and candidates are subordinated to the interests of the parties."[25] Given these differences, in some ways costs cannot be compared. Comparing spending in the aggregate can be misleading. Spending in the United States, for instance, is very unequally distributed between incumbents and challengers, a discrepancy not as likely to occur in more party-centered electoral systems. This caveat aside, it is worth noting that in terms of costs per voter, spending in the United States is lower than in Venezuela, West Germany, Israel, and Ireland. Other countries, such as Canada, spend more when the value of free radio and television time is included.[26]

Consequences for Congress

The cost of running for office, the time it takes to raise funds, the necessity of asking more and more people for money, the growing

23. Thomas E. Mann and Raymond E. Wolfinger, "Candidates and Parties in Congressional Elections," *American Political Science Review,* vol. 74 (September 1980), pp. 617–32.

24. If a less restrictive standard of recognition is applied—correct identification of the candidate's party but inability to recall the candidate's name—the same pattern persists: 31 percent were able to name the candidate or his party in 1978, and 29 percent in 1986.

25. Herbert E. Alexander, "Campaign Financing in International Perspective," in Michael J. Malbin, ed., *Parties, Interest Groups, and Campaign Finance Laws* (Washington: American Enterprise Institute for Public Policy Research, 1980), p. 338.

26. Howard R. Penniman, "U.S. Elections: Really a Bargain?" *Public Opinion,* vol. 7 (June–July 1984), pp. 51–53.

dependence on PAC contributions, and the advantages enjoyed by wealthy candidates affect decisions of whether to run and thus have had important institutional consequences for the House and the Senate. Potential challengers or candidates for open seats realize that unless they can raise a lot of money, they have little chance of winning. In a study of who decides to run for Congress, Linda Fowler and Robert McClure concluded that "races often become so one-sided because many unseen candidates want no part in a bruising battle with an incumbent rich in resources."[27] Staff members of party committees that we interviewed concurred: it is increasingly hard to convince people to run, given the low probability of success and the high investment of time and money necessary to even hope to be competitive.

What kinds of potential candidates tend to be excluded because of the cost? This is difficult to answer because those who choose not to run rarely announce their reasons. Nevertheless, for some potential candidates the need to raise large sums of money is a deterrent. Winning candidates spent, in constant 1988 dollars, an average of $525,000 in competitive House races and $3.5 million in competitive Senate races in the 1980s. Winning candidates have averaged $517,000 for open seats in the House and $4.8 million in the Senate. If House winners had maintained a steady pace over their two-year terms, they would have needed to raise more than $5,000 a week every week between elections. Senate winners would have needed to raise $11,200 a week every week over their six-year term of office. If they waited until the last two years of the election cycle, they would have had to raise $33,700 a week.

The demands of fundraising have serious institutional consequences for the House and Senate. In a survey of House and Senate members and their staffs, the Center for Responsive Politics found that 52 percent of the senators surveyed thought the demands of fundraising cut significantly into the time available for legislative work. Another 12 percent believed fundraising had some deleterious effect. Of Senate staff, 87 percent believed fundraising took time away from legislative activity and 73 percent saw it as having a significant impact. House members and staff were more evenly divided.[28]

Given these figures, the frequent observation that for House candidates the campaign never stops is understandable. It is not uncommon for

27. Linda L. Fowler and Robert D. McClure, *Political Ambition: Who Decides to Run for Congress* (Yale University Press, 1989), p. 5.

28. Center for Responsive Politics, *Congressional Operations: Congress Speaks—A Survey of the 100th Congress* (Washington, 1988).

fundraising to begin in earnest shortly after election or reelection. And although it was once assumed that winning Senate candidates could take a break from fundraising in their first three or four years in office, that is no longer the case. Senate candidates often raise money in their first year to retire their campaign debts and then immediately continue to build resources for their next election. By the middle of 1988, more than two and one-half years before they would run for reelection, Bill Bradley had raised $2.8 million and Phil Gramm $2.7 million. At the same time, Alfonse D'Amato had raised $2.3 million some four and one-half years before his reelection bid. Raising large sums early has the additional benefit of sending a message to potential opponents that a challenge will be expensive and time-consuming, and that they are already far behind.

Rising campaign costs, combined with static limits on amounts individuals and PACs can donate, give an advantage to candidates with personal wealth. Although incumbents rarely contribute to their own campaigns, for many challengers self-financing is an important source of money.[29] Party campaign committee staff members we interviewed said access to personal funds was a greater concern in Senate races, but that it was not uncommon for challengers in House races to spend $25,000 of their own money. Senate challengers often loan themselves much more than this. Mark Braden, former counsel to the Republican National Committee, commented, "The most attractive candidates are often those who can finance their own campaign, because no one else can raise sufficient money to reach the credibility level; besides, it is easier on everybody. It is easier on the local party to have a candidate that can finance his own campaign."[30] Martin Franks, former executive director of the Democratic Congressional Campaign Committee, concurred: "If two otherwise equally plausible political candidates are standing before you, you would rather have the one who could put $50,000 or $100,000 of his or her own money into the race than one who can't."[31]

The expectation that candidates, especially challengers, will commit substantial amounts of their own resources to their campaigns is not a new phenomenon. More than a decade ago David Adamany and George Agree observed, "The steady rise in campaign costs and the increasing difficulty of raising funds give men of means an increasing advantage in

29. Frank Sorauf, *Money in American Elections,* (Scott, Foresman, 1988), pp. 65–67.
30. Interview with Mark Braden, November 16, 1987.
31. Interview with Martin Franks, November 17, 1987.

politics. Party workers, interest group leaders, and others are likely to recognize a wealthy candidate as a serious aspirant and therefore give him weighty consideration in their own strategic planning."[32]

Conclusions

Spending in congressional elections has risen sharply during the 1970s and 1980s and at a rate usually well exceeding the rate of inflation. Spending has risen fastest in midterm election cycles, when there appears to be less competition for contributions. The rate of increase is therefore not constant, and it has in recent years risen less sharply. The increase in costs has occurred in campaigns for both House and Senate seats. Spending has not increased for all campaigns. For example, most of the increase in spending has occurred in the top 50 percent of House races. Spending in the other half of House races has averaged under $200,000 in real dollars since 1980. In the Senate, spending has increased more uniformly.

Even more important than the overall increase is the disproportionate growth in spending by House and Senate incumbents. Incumbents significantly outspend challengers, and House Republican challengers spent on average less than half as much in 1988 as they did in 1984. With expenditures by House Republican challengers averaging less than $100,000 in 1988, it is not hard to see why so few were successful. To be competitive requires raising and spending several times that amount.

Is too much or too little spent on congressional campaigns? The answer is both. Too much is spent by many incumbents. For these candidates there is the following logic: if they can raise the money, they do so because they might need it. If they have raised the money, they spend more than they think they will need to defeat their opponents. If they can raise more than they will need, they do so to scare away future opposition. But while incumbents often spend more than necessary, challengers typically raise and spend too little to become well known to voters. In this sense too little is spent in many congressional elections.

Although previous research suggests that spending more on challengers will improve voter turnout, the equation is not straightforward. Spending in the aggregate improves turnout very little. But competitive races have a stronger effect on participation, and those races are typically

---

32. David W. Adamany and George E. Agree, *Political Money: A Strategy for Campaign Financing in America* (Johns Hopkins University Press, 1975), p. 33.

more expensive. Similarly, additional spending by most incumbents will not appreciably improve voters' knowledge of issues, but greater balance in spending probably would.

The implications of all this are important. All candidates must now assume that contests for the House or Senate will be expensive. Incumbents are able to raise increasingly large sums of money, whether or not they are seriously challenged. Challengers, too, are aware of costs, but there seem to be fewer and fewer resources available to them. Some potential challengers will assume they are different, and a few are; but many look at the incumbent's war chest and the inability of previous challengers to raise enough money to be competitive, and they decide against running.

The frequently cited reasons to spend more on congressional elections—that it increases turnout, voter interest, and knowledge—are true only if the spending is done by challengers and heightens competition. In short, the problem is not only how much is spent on congressional elections but also the distribution of that spending between challengers and incumbents, especially in the House.

4

Raising and Spending Money

For some time, candidates for Congress, especially winning candidates, have received less campaign funding from small individual contributions and more from large contributions by political action committees and wealthy individuals. These large contributions tend to reflect specific legislative interests—of automobile dealers, realtors, labor unions, doctors and dentists, supporters of Israel, tobacco companies, and so forth. Constituents and small individual contributors are thus being replaced by more "interested" money, often from outside a candidate's state or district.

Regardless of whether the present system is good or bad, the costs of campaigns would probably not have risen so dramatically without the ability of candidates, especially incumbents, to raise increasingly larger amounts of money. Not that raising money is easy; it is, Gary Jacobson has concluded, "by consensus, the most unpleasant part of a campaign. Most find it demeaning to ask people for money and are uncomfortable with the implications of accepting it."[1] New candidates are told to "learn how to beg and to do it in a way that leaves [them] some dignity."[2]

This chapter discusses where the money comes from, who is most successful at raising funds and why, how money is spent, and to what effect. It covers partisan differences and differences in candidate status—incumbent, challenger, candidate for an open seat—that can affect the way money is spent. It considers when money is spent and whether such timing affects the competitive balance between candidates and

1. Gary Jacobson, *The Politics of Congressional Elections,* 2d ed. (Little, Brown, 1987), pp. 61–62.
2. Diane Granat, "Parties' Schools for Politicians Grooming Troops for Election," *Congressional Quarterly Weekly Report,* May 5, 1984, p. 1036.

parties. Finally, it analyzes the relationship between spending and electoral success.

Sources

Before the passage of the Federal Election Campaign Act and its amendments, candidates could raise and spend money without serious restrictions. Comparatively little is known about their efforts then because disclosure laws did not apply to most candidates and it was in the interests of neither the candidates nor those who gave money to reveal their activities. Candidates could finance campaigns through gifts from wealthy contributors far more easily than they can today.[3] Campaigns cost comparatively less, and the need to raise large war chests was not as acute.

The passage of the FECA, with its disclosure provisions, has allowed the study of both the sources and disbursements of funds in a way not possible before. Since 1976, when the Federal Election Commission began keeping records, most of the money used to finance congressional campaigns has come from individual contributors. People may give directly to candidates in response to mail solicitation or other personal appeals, or indirectly through intermediary organizations such as political parties. They also frequently contribute to campaigns by buying tickets to dinners, receptions, and other events; these tickets may cost $5 to $1,000 a person. Blocks of tickets are often sold to interest groups, law firms, and lobbyists. A successful in-state dinner for an incumbent U.S. Senate candidate in 1986 typically raised between $200,000 and $500,000, with about 75 percent of that money as net proceeds.[4] But funds now increasingly come from groups—corporate, labor, trade association, and ideological—that form PACs to handle political contributions. According to Herbert Alexander, the "greatest change effected by the new campaign laws in the area of fund raising [is] the elimination of the prominent role previously played by the wealthy donor."[5]

As figure 4-1 shows, about three-fifths of the money used to finance

3. One person contributed $2 million to Richard Nixon in the 1972 presidential campaign. See Herbert E. Alexander, *Financing Politics: Money, Elections and Political Reform*, 3d ed. (Washington: Congressional Quarterly Press, 1984), p. 61.

4. Interview with H. E. Bud Scruggs, campaign manager for Senator Jake Garn (1986) and Senator Orrin Hatch (1988), July 7, 1988.

5. Herbert E. Alexander, *Financing the 1976 Election* (Washington: Congressional Quarterly Press, 1979), p. 511.

FIGURE 4-1. *Share of House and Senate General Election Campaign Receipts, by Source, 1980–88*

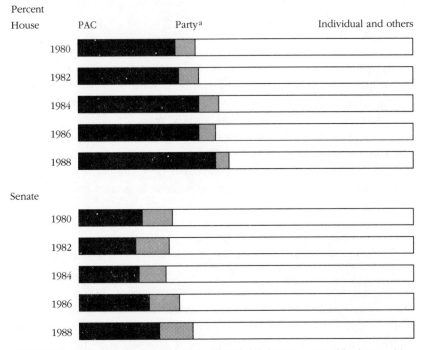

SOURCES: FEC data tapes; see appendix A. FEC data for 1980 and 1982 do not separate candidate loans, candidate spending, and other non-PAC, nonparty spending from individual contributions; thus in this figure the categories are PACs, parties, and others.
a. Includes party coordinated expenditures.

House general election candidates since 1980 and nearly three-quarters of that for Senate candidates has come from individual contributors and sources other than parties and PACs. Individual contributions make up the largest share of this category, but it also includes candidates' personal loans or contributions and interest earned on past campaign contributions.[6] For both the House and Senate, the proportion of receipts from PACs rose in 1988, while money from individuals and other nonparty sources declined. In 1984 individual contributions accounted for 53 percent of all receipts for House candidates and 67 percent for Senate candidates. The numbers for 1986 were very similar. PACs provided 41 percent of the receipts of House candidates and 24 percent of the

6. FEC reporting categories have changed over time. The only way to have comparable categories is to combine individual contributions with candidates' personal loans to their campaigns and interest earned on campaign funds.

receipts of Senate candidates in 1988, but Senate candidates receive, on average, about five times more money from PACs than House candidates in actual dollars. Parties play a much less significant role, contributing only 4 percent of House candidate receipts and 10 percent of Senate candidate receipts in 1988. Candidate self-financing is important in both houses. House candidates gave or loaned themselves 8 percent of total receipts in 1986 and 6 percent in 1988, and Senate candidates 4 percent in 1986 and 5 percent in 1988. Most self-financing occurs among challengers, who gave or loaned themselves 16 percent of their total receipts in 1986 and 10 percent in 1988.

Individuals

Individual contributors are the most important source of congressional candidates' campaign funds, but surprisingly little is known about them. Although Americans are more likely to make campaign contributions than to attend political meetings or rallies, wear a campaign button, or do campaign work, fewer than one in ten make political contributions to candidates for any office. In 1988 the proportion was 6 percent. From an analysis of the 1986 and 1988 American National Election Study, we found that a person's education, income, political interest, race, and age are the factors that most affect making campaign contributions. The higher the income and the more education, the greater the propensity to contribute. Only 2 percent of those with an eighth grade education or less gave money in 1986, while 28 percent of those with education beyond a bachelor's degree did so.[7] A similar distribution exists for income. Racial differences also are a factor. In 1986 whites were more likely than blacks or Hispanics to contribute. In 1988, however, blacks roughly equaled whites in the proportions giving money, perhaps a consequence of the presidential campaign of Jesse Jackson. Strong Republicans were the partisans most likely to make contributions, in proportions roughly double those of any other category of partisanship. Gender, union membership, and religious affiliation—with the exception of Jews—made no significant difference.

What motivates contributors or whether the motivations are different for large and small donors is unclear. Fundraisers indicate that motivations may include feelings of civic duty, a desire to belong to a cause or party, and a wish to influence the course of American government. Rodney

7. The same relationship between education and the propensity to contribute was found in the 1980 American National Election Study data.

TABLE 4-1. *Share of General Election Campaign Receipts from Individual Contributions of $100 or Less, by Candidate Party and Status, 1976, 1984*[a]

Candidate party and status	House		Senate	
	1976	1984	1976	1984
Republican incumbents	47	18	40	22
Democratic incumbents	38	14	23	12
Republican nonincumbents	31	14	30	17
Democratic nonincumbents	29	14	29	17

SOURCE: Richard P. Conlon, "The Declining Rate of Individual Contributions in Financing Congressional Campaigns," *Journal of Law and Politics*, vol. 3 (Winter 1987), p. 469.

a. Figures are determined by subtracting the sum of $100 contributors from the total individual contributors for 1976 and 1984.

Smith, formerly a fundraiser with the National Republican Senatorial Committee, sees the desire to belong to a special or select group as an explanation: supporters are motivated by ego and the need for security.[8] People also give out of self-interest: they expect to secure better access and political favors. And indeed, members of Congress often take extra steps to see that casework for contributors is handled more expeditiously than for others. Many contributors know this, especially those who have continuing contact with the federal government. Thus what motivates individuals is little different than what motivates most PACs.

While they account for the largest percentage, individual contributions represent a declining share of the totals. Richard P. Conlon, the late staff director of the Democratic Study Group, found that individual contributions fell from 75 percent of all receipts for Senate and House candidates in 1976 to only 61 percent and 47 percent, respectively, in 1984, although the amounts contributed rose from $54.8 million to $191.8 million.[9] The most precipitous drop occurred among those who give $100 or less. All categories of candidates have been affected, but House incumbents of both parties and Senate Republican incumbents have experienced the largest declines (table 4-1). Constituents and other small contributors now are less important in campaign funding and have been replaced, according to Conlon, by "money from special interests outside the congressman's district or state."[10]

8. Interview with Rodney Smith, December 2, 1987.

9. Democratic Study Group, "Troubling Trends in Election Financing ... Grassroots Money Shrinks as PAC Money Grows," Washington, October 22, 1985.

10. Richard P. Conlon, "The Declining Role of Individual Contributions in Financing Congressional Campaigns," *Journal of Law and Politics*, vol. 3 (Winter 1987), pp. 468–69.

Small individual contributions are increasingly raised in ways that exploit mass marketing techniques. Direct mail solicitations have become carefully targeted appeals popular with parties, individual candidates, and scores of issue and interest groups. Commonly sent in official-looking envelopes, the appeals appear important. The text of the letter "puts a premium on simpleminded presentation of issues, on scaremongering, and on creating boogeymen," according to Gregg Easterbrook. "In direct-mail copy writing there are no liberals or conservatives, only ultraliberals and ultraconservatives."[11]

The long-term potential of direct mail fundraising remains uncertain, however, because donors tend to wear out. The costs are very high: few people respond to initial mailings, referred to by practitioners as "prospecting." Because of the cost, much of the money raised must be put back into further appeals, leaving comparatively little to be spent on other campaign activities. Jesse Helms's Congressional Club spent 98 percent of its receipts ($93.3 million) in 1982 on internal expenses. Bob Dole's Campaign America collected $2.4 million in 1987 to help Republican Senate candidates other than Dole, but actually contributed only 2 percent of the funds raised.[12]

Groups and Political Action Committees

In 1988 PACs accounted for 37 percent of all contributions to House candidates and 23 percent of those to Senate candidates, a total of $148 million, up from an inflation-adjusted $62 million in 1978. PAC contributions constitute a much smaller proportion for most candidates than do contributions from individuals, but 211 of 408 House incumbents received more money from PACs than from individuals in 1984, and 255 received more in 1988. PAC money is very attractive to candidates because it can be raised more readily, in larger sums, and at a lower cost than money from individuals. Individual contributors are limited to giving $2,000 per election cycle to any one candidate; PACs are limited to $10,000. Thus the growth in PAC contributions is driven in part by the desire of candidates to raise money in larger sums more efficiently.

Do PACs prefer incumbents more than other types of contributors do? Larry Sabato asserts that "except for the ideological committees, they do display a clear and overwhelming preference for those already

---

11. Gregg Easterbrook, "Junk-Mail Politics," *New Republic,* April 25, 1988, pp. 17–21.
12. R. Kenneth Goodwin, *One Billion Dollars of Influence: The Direct Marketing of Politics* (Chatham House, 1988) p. 21.

FIGURE 4-2. *Share of General Election Campaign Contributions from Individuals, PACs, and Parties, by Candidate Status, 1986, 1988*

Percent

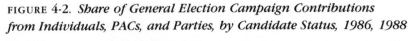

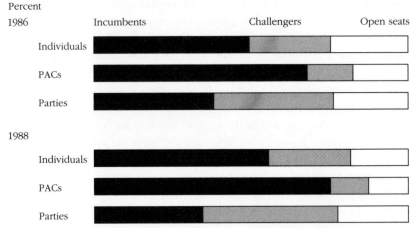

SOURCES: FEC, "FEC Releases Final Report on 1986 Congressional Candidates," press release, May 5, 1988; and calculated from FEC, *Final Reports on Financial Activity 1985–86: U.S. Senate and House Campaigns,* and *Final Reports on Financial Activity 1987–88: U.S. Senate and House Campaigns.*

in office. But the same bias is apparent in contributions from individuals, who ask the same reasonable, perhaps decisive, economic question: Why waste money on contenders if incumbents almost always win?"[13] But Sabato's assertion is incorrect. Individuals are less likely than PACs to give to incumbents; in fact, in both 1986 and 1988 they gave far less to incumbents than did PACs (figure 4-2). PACs gave more than two-thirds of their contributions to incumbents in 1986 and three-fourths in 1988. Parties gave more than 60 percent of their contributions to challengers or candidates for open seats in 1986 and 1988. If candidates for open seats are not considered, PACs gave less than $1 to a challenger for every $4 they gave to an incumbent in 1986; individuals gave $1 to a challenger for every $2 they gave to an incumbent. Excluding open seats, in 1988 PACs gave 85 percent of their money to incumbents. The heavy tilt of the campaign finance system toward incumbents is much more attributable to PACs than to other sources.[14]

13. Larry J. Sabato, *Paying for Elections: The Campaign Finance Thicket* (New York: Priority Press, 1989), p. 11.

14. The same pattern holds for individual, PAC, and party contributions if only general election candidates are considered. In 1986 PACs gave 69 percent of their contributions to incumbents, while individuals gave 55 percent. In 1988, in part because of fewer open seats, individuals gave 61 percent of their money to incumbents while PACs gave 77 percent.

PAC money has generated attention because it supports incumbents, often with more than an electoral objective in mind. For instance, in 1986 Florida Representative Sam Gibbons ran unopposed in both the primary and general elections, but took in nearly $900,000 in campaign contributions, $550,000 of it from PACs.[15] Gibbons was not alone. Of the 215 House and Senate members who collected more than half their campaign money from PACs in 1986, only 13 were in close races. And in 1988, of the 255 House incumbents who received more money from PACs than individuals, only 19 were in races where the winner got 55 percent or less of the vote.

That PAC money is interested money is reinforced by the fact that PACs often switch sides and contribute to the winning candidate after an election even though they may have contributed to the opponent during it. At least 150 PACs switched their backing to the winner after the 1986 Senate elections.[16] The willingness to switch has been a boon for new officeholders, providing a rich source of money for retiring campaign debts. The thirteen freshman senators elected in 1986 raised more than half their postelection funds in the first six months they were in office, and at least half of that was contributed by PACs. Senator Richard Shelby, for instance, had a $150,000 debt in January 1987 and by the end of June had raised nearly $387,000, of which $146,000 had been contributed by PACs.[17] Retiring campaign debts is a fairly new activity for most PACs. As recently as 1983 the National Realtors PAC had not earmarked any money for debt retirement; after the 1987 election it provided money to seven candidates, whom it had not supported before the election, to help retire campaign debts.[18]

Political Parties

Parties are important to congressional candidates' fundraising because they contribute money both directly and through coordinated expenditures—spending by political parties on behalf of congressional candidates. They provide important services such as polling, training, research

15. "Get Ahead of the PAC," *Record* (Hackensack, N.J.), April 15, 1987, p. A20.

16. "If at First You Don't Succeed, Give, Give Again," *Common Cause News,* March 20, 1987.

17. Jeremy Gaunt and Andra H. Armstrong, "Senate Freshmen Rewarded by Post-Election PAC Giving," *Congressional Quarterly Weekly Report,* September 5, 1987, pp. 2134–35.

18. Maxwell Glen, "Going For Broke," *National Journal,* January 8, 1983, p. 62; and Gaunt and Armstrong, "Senate Freshmen Rewarded by Post-Election PAC Giving," p. 2136.

on the opposition, and media advice; and they serve as liaison to PACs and wealthy people outside a candidate's state.

With the exception of the National Republican Senatorial Committee (NRSC), party committees have consistently contributed far less to candidates than the limits allow. For example, in 1988 the House Democratic Congressional Campaign Committee (DCCC) could have contributed $12.8 million directly to House Democratic candidates and could have spent another $19.7 million in coordinated expenditures, yet it made only $1.2 million in direct contributions and $2.6 million in coordinated expenditures. While the differences between actual and allowed expenditures for the House National Republican Congressional Committee (NRCC) and the Democratic Senatorial Campaign Committee (DSCC) are not as dramatic as for the DCCC, they still spent far less than permitted. The NRSC, in contrast, contributed $688,400 directly to Republican Senate candidates in 1988 out of an allowed limit of $907,500. Similarly, it came closer than the others to reaching the limit in coordinated expenditures. The operable criterion for allocating funds at the NRSC appears to have been competitive races. Any race considered competitive received the maximum contribution and coordinated expenditure.

There is a significant disparity in the campaign funds available to the Democratic and Republican campaign committees. Between 1980 and 1988 the Democratic Senatorial Campaign Committee increased the money available for coordinated expenditures from about 18 percent of the allowed limit to more than 50 percent. The National Republican Senatorial Committee contributed 69 percent of its allowable limit in 1980, 95 percent in 1982, 87 percent in 1986, and 80 percent in 1988.[19] The pattern for the House campaign committees is the same; the Republicans routinely outspend the Democrats.

The Senate campaign committees have consistently contributed more for coordinated expenditures than the House committees. In 1980 and, for the DCCC, again in 1982, the House committees gave more in direct contributions than in coordinated expenditures. However, by 1984 they had followed the lead of the Senate committees.

The two parties differed significantly in the number of times they spent the limit in direct contributions between 1978 and 1988. The

19. The DSCC gave 64 percent of its limit for direct contributions in 1982 while the NRSC gave 66 percent, figures a lot closer than total party spending would suggest. This implies that the DSCC may give more of its scarcer funds directly to candidates rather than provide support through coordinated expenditures.

Democratic committees did so in only eleven instances and the Republicans in seventy-eight. Both parties are more likely to contribute the maximum in coordinated expenditures than in direct contributions, but again the Republicans do so much more often than the Democrats. More than 90 percent of instances of spending to the limit were for coordinated expenditures.

The proportion of candidates receiving the maximum contribution or coordinated expenditure increased rapidly between 1978 and 1984. Only 64 House and Senate candidates received the limit in contributions or coordinated expenditures in 1978, and of these, 61 were Republicans. By 1984 the number was 244, of whom 198 were Republicans. In 1984 alone, 154 House Republicans received the maximum coordinated expenditure. By 1988, however, only 85 House Republicans received the maximum coordinated expenditure from their party, still roughly double the 45 House Democrats who did so. The same candidates are not constant recipients: over 70 percent of those who received a maximum direct contribution or coordinated expenditure did so only once in 1980–88. Finally, while there is some clustering at predictable levels—$250, $500, $10,000—amounts of direct contributions and coordinated expenditures vary widely.

Parties are not equal in their ability to help candidates. The Republican committees have been more important because of their remarkable ability to raise money.[20] But providing direct contributions and coordinated expenditures is only part of what can be done. In recent elections both parties have become adept at circumventing the limits on contributions. National parties have contributed beyond the limits to state parties for building purposes; this money inevitably has spillover effects on federal elections. Parties have also received checks from individuals made out to them, then passed the checks along to candidates who deposited them as if they were made out to the candidate directly. This practice, called earmarking, which is discussed more fully in chapter 6, enables a party to exceed its maximum contribution to a candidate by asserting that the money it has raised was really an individual contribution to the candidate. The Republicans used this technique in at least five Senate races in 1986.

20. Gary Jacobson, "Party Organization and Distribution of Campaign Resources: Republicans and Democrats in 1982," *Political Science Quarterly,* vol. 100 (Winter 1985–86), pp. 603–25.

Candidate Self-Financing

Although individuals, PACs, and parties are strictly limited in the total amounts they can give a House candidate in a two-year election cycle or a Senate candidate in a six-year cycle, candidates themselves are not limited in what they can give or loan to their own campaigns. Senate candidates are especially well known for providing large contributions to their campaigns: John Heinz loaned his 1976 Senate campaign $2.5 million, and Jay Rockefeller loaned his 1984 Senate campaign $10.3 million.[21] Not all who spend large amounts of personal funds are successful. Mark Dayton, the Democratic challenger to Minnesota Senator David Durenberger in 1982, contributed $5.7 million to his losing effort and made or guaranteed loans for another $1.3 million. New York Senate candidate John S. Dyson contributed nearly $86,000 and loaned $6 million to his unsuccessful primary run in 1986. Of the five Senate candidates since 1978 who spent more than $1 million of their own funds, only three have won. Of House candidates since 1978 who spent more than $100,000 of their own funds, a little more than one-third have won.

Party committees welcome, and sometimes expect, challengers and candidates for open seats in the House to be willing to spend $25,000 or more in personal funds.[22] Senate candidates are expected to give or loan their campaigns even more. It is presumed that a commitment of personal resources early in a campaign or at other strategic times will serve as seed money or provide a needed one-time boost to help raise other funds. Research has found that challengers in competitive districts and candidates for open seats are generally the ones most willing to spend their own money and that Senate challengers and candidates for open seats are more likely than others to use personal wealth.[23]

Candidates often loan their campaigns money rather than make contributions because if they win the election they can repay the loans

21. Data on candidates' self-financing reported here and elsewhere are to be found in FEC tapes and reports on financial activity. See appendix A.

22. Interviews with Mark Braden, Republican National Committee, November 16, 1987; and Martin Franks, DCCC, November 17, 1987.

23. Gary Jacobson, *Money in Congressional Elections* (Yale University Press, 1980), p. 97; and Edie N. Goldenberg and Michael W. Traugott, *Campaigning for Congress* (Washington: Congressional Quarterly Press, 1984), p. 64. Jacobson finds that candidate contributions are related only weakly to the competitiveness of the race, concluding that "hopeless candidates rely disproportionately on their own resources because they find others so much less accessible."

with further fundraising. In 1986 the average personal loan or contribution for all Senate general election candidates was about $59,000; for the twenty who made or guaranteed loans but not contributions, the average was $191,000. Such loans come almost exclusively from challengers or candidates for open seats. Only one incumbent, Alan Cranston, loaned his campaign money in 1986, while two loaned themselves $100,000 or more in 1988.

Most challengers and candidates for open seats are also expected to commit twelve months or more to campaigning and fundraising—and serious challengers, two years. Incumbents, of course, are paid while they campaign; many challengers are not, which probably very much limits the pool of potential candidates.

As Representative David Price, one of only six challengers to defeat an incumbent in 1986, has said, "I will also never forget how difficult it was to raise the first dollars. I understand quite well why many potentially strong challengers and potentially able representatives simply cannot or will not do what it takes to establish financial 'viability' and why so many who do reach that point do so only on the basis of personal wealth."[24]

In recent congressional debates over campaign finance reform, one idea that has enjoyed broad bipartisan support is to reduce or limit the use of personal wealth in campaigns. In 1987 Senator Pete Domenici introduced legislation designed to close this "millionaires' loophole" by requiring all candidates to declare at the outset of their campaigns how much personal money they would contribute. If the amount were more than $250,000, their opponents would be allowed higher contributions from individuals and PACs. "We ought," he said, "to seriously consider making this institution, as far as its campaigns, a fairer playing ground for the extremely wealthy versus those who have to go out and raise campaign money."[25]

24. David E. Price, "The House of Representatives: A Report from the Field," in Lawrence C. Dodd and Bruce I. Oppenheimer, eds., *Congress Reconsidered,* 4th ed. (Washington: Congressional Quarterly, 1989), p. 417.

25. *Senate Campaign Finance Proposals of 1987,* Hearings before the Senate Committee on Rules and Administration, 100 Cong. 1 sess. (Government Printing Office, 1987), p. 81. Senator Domenici's legislation (S. 625) proposed that a candidate who plans to spend or borrow $250,000 or more of his own money to be spent in either the primary or the general election campaign must declare that outright within fifteen days of becoming an official candidate. If he does not, he cannot spend it. If a candidate declares he will be spending his own money, the opposition can raise $10,000 per constituent instead of $1,000, raise $10,000 per PAC instead of $5,000, and receive an additional $25,000 above the current $25,000 limit for an individual American contributor. A candidate must announce all of the money he plans to spend from his own pocket within sixty days before

TABLE 4-2. *Share of House and Senate General Election Campaign Funds Received, by Source and Candidate Status, 1988*

Percent

Candidate status	Source				
	Individuals	PACs	Parties	Self	Other[a]
	House				
Democrats					
Incumbents	39	52	6	2	1
Challengers	47	32	6	14	0
Open seats	40	38	7	15	1
Republicans					
Incumbents	52	40	7	1	0
Challengers	57	10	14	19	0
Open seats	56	21	10	12	0
	Senate				
Democrats					
Incumbents	64	30	5	1	0
Challengers	68	16	11	3	2
Open seats	39	17	8	37	0
Republicans					
Incumbents	65	27	8	0	0
Challengers	64	12	18	6	0
Open seats	57	28	13	2	0

SOURCES: FEC data tapes; see appendix A. Figures are rounded.

a. Includes loans received, offsets to campaign operating expenses, interest on deposits, transfers from House campaign accounts to Senate campaign accounts, proceeds from joint fundraisers, and contributions from members of Congress or other candidates.

Differences in Access to Funds

Not all candidates have equal access to the financial resources of wealthy individuals, PACs, and parties. House incumbent Democrats differ from all other candidates in that they received more from PACs than from individuals in 1988—over $13 million more. House Democratic challengers and candidates for open seats also did comparatively well among PACs in 1988, averaging nearly $67,000. House incumbent Republicans are also dependent on PACs—much more than Senate incumbents of either party. House candidates in 1988 raised between 39 and 57 percent of their funds from individuals (table 4-2). Senate incumbents and challengers received between 64 and 68 percent. House incumbents of both parties neither gave nor loaned their campaigns very

the election. If the candidate borrows money under his own name, PAC money cannot be raised after the election to pay off personal loans (pp. 79–85).

much—generally 1 percent of total receipts, an average of about $5,000. For other 1988 House candidates, $1 in every $7 came from their own funds. Republican challengers' own resources amounted to about one-fifth of all receipts, double the amount they raised from PACs. Senate incumbents of both parties were even less likely to give or loan personal funds to their campaigns.

Where Money Is Spent

Although much has been written about the dramatic growth of campaign expenditures in congressional elections, there has been very little analysis of the causes of the increase. If, for instance, one cause has been rising costs of television and radio advertising, reforms may have to address these costs. If, however, spending has increased because candidates are doing more advertising, reforms may have to assume a different configuration. Where has the money gone?

The challenge in trying to determine where campaign money is spent is that the Federal Election Commission allows candidates to report expenditures in varying degrees of detail. Some give extensive break-downs; others only report large expenditures to professional campaign management firms. The firms conduct polls, purchase advertising, and provide printing, direct mail, and other services, but these expenditures need not be enumerated. Furthermore, although the FEC has maintained records of candidate expenditures since 1978, it has neither tabulated nor reported spending by category—media, consultants, staff, mail, and so forth. Such a tabulation was, however, made for the 1986 election cycle and released in July 1987 by the National Association of Broadcasters.[26] It shows that candidates spent more than $97 million on broadcasting in 1985–86. Senate candidates spent an average of $960,800 on broadcast advertising, 34 percent of their total; House candidates spent an average of 15.8 percent. The report also shows that candidates for open House seats averaged $127,000 for broadcast advertising, while incumbents and other challengers averaged about $36,000 and $25,000, respectively. Senate incumbents spent an average of $1.15 million on broadcast advertising; candidates for open Senate seats averaged $1.08 million and challengers $652,000.

26. National Association of Broadcasters, "1986 Candidates Spend Less Than 25 Percent on Broadcast Time; NAB Calls Focus of Campaign-Cost Debate on Radio, TV Unwarranted," press release and report on NAB/Aristotle Industries Study, July 13, 1987.

These are very conservative estimates because of the nature of FEC reports.[27] Previous studies have shown that advertising costs can range from 15 to 70 percent of a candidate's budget: one media consultant routinely recommends that challengers spend at least 70 percent.[28] Our interviews with media consultants indicated that at least half, and more likely two-thirds, of the budget must go to media advertising. Franklin Greer said, "If you look at the contested races, then that portion . . . is 75 percent of the budget."[29]

In a random sample of congressional districts in a study of the 1978 campaign, Edie Goldenberg and Michael Traugott questioned candidates and managers or other campaign officers and found that advertising and media expenses consumed sixty cents of every dollar. The costs of running an office and paying staff were a distant second. The percentages of the budget allocated for these categories differed little among incumbents, challengers, and candidates for open seats. But in dollar amounts, candidates for open seats and incumbents spent significantly more than challengers, both in total and on advertising. The study found less frequent use of television in House races than had previously been assumed. As the authors observed, "The modern fascination with political advertising on television, especially in presidential and statewide races, and the visibility given to several well-financed but atypical congressional races each term can create the impression that television is the communication vehicle of choice in all congressional races."[30]

Candidates or their campaign managers most frequently cited personal contact as the best means of getting information to voters. Still, one in four thought television most effective. The dichotomy in preference is largely a result of the lack of congruity between media markets and congressional districts. Candidates in urban areas must buy air time not only in their districts, but in as many as ten or twenty others (thirty-

27. Kenneth Thomas has found that candidates in competitive races in 1986 spent considerably more on media—an average 30.7 percent of their campaign funds for House candidates, or roughly double the NAB estimate, and 42.7 percent for Senate candidates. "Broadcast Media and Congressional Campaigns: An Explanatory Model," M.A. thesis, Brigham Young University, December 1987.

28. See Larry J. Sabato, *The Rise of Political Consultants* (Basic Books, 1981), p. 180. Sabato in turn cites as sources George H. White, *A Study of Access to Television for Political Candidates* (John F. Kennedy School of Government, Harvard University, May 1978), pp. 2–3; and National Republican Campaign Committee, "Campaign Manager's Study: 1978 Post-Election Research" (1979), pp. 2–6.

29. Interviews with Vince Breglio, January 26, 1988; Don Sipple, January 25, 1988; and Franklin Greer, January 27, 1988.

30. Goldenberg and Traugott, *Campaigning for Congress*, p. 117.

three in New York City).[31] In the six largest media markets in 1986, only 22 percent of House candidates spent $10,000 or more on television, compared with 58 percent of candidates in smaller media markets. House candidates are more likely to employ personal contact, campaign literature, buttons, direct mail, and radio; in the six largest media markets they spent 53 percent of their funds on direct mail.[32] Senate candidates generally spend more on television because they have more to spend and because there is a better match between media markets and state boundaries. It is commonly estimated that 60 percent of the overall budget in Senate races goes to broadcast advertising, while in contested House races the percentage is between 50 and 60 percent.[33]

The relationship between rising advertising costs and rising campaign costs was frequently cited in interviews with campaign professionals. Costs for television spots rose 169 percent between 1976 and 1990, a rate of inflation surpassing the consumer price index by more than 40 percent.[34] In 1987 Franklin Greer, an advertising media consultant to Democratic candidates, compared the costs of advertising in 1982 and 1988 in seventeen states with likely contested Senate races in 1988. He found that it would cost about twice as much in 1988 to buy the same amount of airtime in the news or on prime-time television as it cost in 1982.[35] In some media markets the increase has been even greater. Phoenix experienced a threefold increase in the cost per rating point for spots during its evening news programs. Costs of radio advertising, postage, and paper have also increased dramatically. Postage, for example, has more than doubled in the past six years.

Candidates not only pay more for advertising, but they also advertise more. Vince Breglio, a Republican campaign consultant, noted that "some campaigns [use television] to the exclusion of another medium that they

31. There are 215 media markets in the United States, and they have audiences ranging from several million in New York or Los Angeles to several thousand in Boise, Idaho, or Sioux Falls, South Dakota. *Broadcasting Yearbook, 1987* (Washington: Broadcasting Publishing, 1987), pp. C222–C224. See also Center for Responsive Politics, *Beyond the 30-Second Spot: Enhancing the Media's Role in Congressional Campaigns* (Washington, 1988), pp. 50–51.

32. Center for Responsive Politics, *Beyond the 30-Second Spot,* pp. 16, 103.

33. Statement of Franklin Greer, *Campaign Finance,* Hearings before the Subcommittee on Elections of the Committee on House Administration, 100 Cong. 1 sess. (Government Printing Office, 1987), p. 2.

34. Robert J. Coen, "Ad Spending Outlook Brightens," *Advertising Age,* May 15, 1989, p. 24; and Coen, "Tough Times for Ad Spending," *Advertising Age,* May 14, 1990, pp. 12, 59.

35. Statement of Franklin Greer, in *Campaign Finance,* Hearings, p. 3.

might choose to get their message through."[36] Finally, as Greer points out, television advertising adds more to campaign costs because "the presidential campaigns are longer. The Senate campaigns are longer."[37]

The availability of advanced technologies has further increased spending. Computerized voter lists are used in computerized direct mail. Tracking polls are used to ask constituents about their voting intentions and their reactions to the campaign, the opponent, and the advertisements. Using these data, candidates make new commercials and may target a mailing to particular types of voters—Catholics, weak partisans, residents of one county or city. Techniques such as these involve consultants for polling, canvassing, direct mail, media production, and campaign organization.[38]

When campaign consultants talk about the share of a budget spent on media, they are typically referring to net receipts—the funds that are available after the costs of fundraising have been paid. But as noted earlier, candidates also spend a substantial percentage of their budgets on fundraising itself. Depending on the nature of the effort—direct mail, campaign dinner, benefit concert, cocktail party—the rate of return can vary dramatically. A conservative estimate is that 15 to 20 percent of total receipts will cover the costs of fundraising in a campaign that does not do a lot of direct mail prospecting. For those campaigns that do use direct mail the costs rise substantially.

Some campaign funds must be spent to satisfy the requirements that election reform itself has imposed. Robert Huckshorn has reported that "most consultants are now advising clients to reserve from 5 to 10 percent of their total campaign budget for accounting, computer time, and the legal costs associated with increased campaign finance disclosure requirements."[39] One 1987 Senate proposal to limit spending (S. 2) would have permitted candidates to raise an additional 10 percent of the limit to pay the costs of compliance. Other important elements of candidates' budgets include professional staff, research consultants, office costs, and travel.

Although all candidates spend funds in the same budget categories, there are important differences among parties and types of candidates in where the resources are spent. Goldenberg and Traugott observed

36. Interview with Vince Breglio, January 26, 1988.
37. Interview with Franklin Greer, January 27, 1988.
38. Robert J. Huckshorn, *Political Parties in America*, 2d ed. (Brooks-Cole, 1984), p. 164.
39. Huckshorn, *Political Parties*, p. 165.

that "as members of the minority party, Republicans rarely can afford to appeal only to their own partisan supporters. To assemble winning coalitions, they need to broaden their appeal to independents and members of the opposite party as well."[40] This suggests that candidates in the two parties have different patterns in their campaign spending and explains why the desire to raise and spend more money than their opponents is so important to Republican strategies.

Incumbents, challengers, and candidates for open seats also vary in their spending strategies. Incumbents spend a smaller percentage of their budgets on television advertising than challengers do, yet they spend more in actual dollars because they have more to spend. Goldenberg and Traugott differentiate the spending strategy of incumbents by the nature of their districts—hostile or friendly: "incumbents from districts historically hostile to their party are likely to spend more money, regardless of their challenger, than those from districts with more support for their party."[41]

Another reason for incumbents to spend, irrespective of the nature of their district or the strength of the challenger, is a desire for higher party or political office. A candidate's prospects may be enhanced by a reputation as a successful fundraiser or as the person who can win big in his district. Henry Waxman, considered by *Congressional Quarterly* to be one of the House "leaders without portfolio," won his chairmanship of the Energy and Commerce Subcommittee on the basis of his contributions to the reelection campaigns of other committee members. He was able to contribute because of his fundraising abilities in Hollywood and because of his Twenty-fourth District California PAC. Tony Coelho won the office of majority whip in part because of his reputation for looking out for new members but perhaps more because of his fundraising abilities as head of the Democratic Congressional Campaign Committee.[42]

Candidates have different motives for spending. Incumbents' level of spending depends, in part, on their perceived electoral vulnerability but also includes broader political and personal motives. In contrast, challengers and candidates for open seats spend to establish name recognition and give voters a reason to vote for them. Yet, despite the very different levels of need among these House candidates, there is a remarkable

40. Goldenberg and Traugott, *Campaigning for Congress,* p. 29.
41. Goldenberg and Traugott, *Campaigning for Congress,* p. 100.
42. "Profiles in Power: Leaders without Portfolio," *Congressional Quarterly Weekly Report,* January 3, 1987, p. 18; and "Coelho Harvests the Fruits of His Labors," *Congressional Quarterly Weekly Report,* December 13, 1986, p. 3068.

similarity in the allocation of campaign resources, both in the proportion spent on advertising and the medium used. Goldenberg and Traugott found very little difference among incumbents, challengers, and candidates for open seats in the share of the campaign budget spent on advertising, except for sure winners who spent a large share on staff and financial matters—auditors, compliance costs, and so forth. Roughly 60 percent of the 1978 House candidates' budgets went to advertising.

When Money Is Spent

The timing of candidates' expenditures is perhaps as important as where the money is spent for winning congressional elections. Early money is generally considered especially important, not only because it helps pay for necessary polling and research, staff, organizing and planning, and developing a media strategy, but because it works to establish credibility, which in turn helps to secure funding for the later stages of the campaign.

About 40 percent of the expenditures of the average major-party House candidate occur before the general election period.[43] This ability to raise and spend money early in the campaign is an advantage enjoyed by incumbents far more than by challengers or candidates for open seats. Incumbents can combine surpluses from previous years with early fundraising to scare away opposition or to prepare for it. Peggy Connally, former communications director of the DCCC, has stated that the committee tries "to educate the incumbents that they do have the ability to raise money—particularly early money—much easier than the challengers."[44] Senator Jesse Helms's 1984 campaign against Governor James Hunt provided a striking example. Helms began airing television spots eighteen months before the balloting. In all, he spent more than $17 million on his campaign—an amount few challengers could hope to match.[45]

To spend money early, of course, candidates must raise it early. Table 4-3 shows the proportion of candidate receipts coming from different sources during the first eighteen months of election campaign cycles. In 1977–78, PACs as a group gave only 31 percent of their total contributions

43. Goldenberg and Traugott, *Campaigning for Congress,* p. 82.
44. Interview with Peggy Connally, March 21, 1988.
45. Alan Ehrenhalt, "A New Breed of Consultant Joins the Fray," *Congressional Quarterly Weekly Report,* December 7, 1985, p. 2563.

TABLE 4-3. *Share of Campaign Contributions during First Eighteen Months of Election Cycle, by Source, 1977–88*
Percent

Source	1977–78	1979–80	1981–82	1983–84	1985–86	1987–88
Political action committee						
Corporate	26	39	46	53	59	66
Labor	36	40	40	46	50	60
Nonconnected organization	22	24	27	42	43	58
Trade, membership, health	31	38	45	47	55	61
Cooperatives	54	40	41	45	60	65
Corporations without stock	33	36	45	59	52	72
Total PAC	31	38	42	47	54	62
Other	50	54	52	56	58	58

SOURCES: See appendix A; and Norman J. Ornstein, Thomas E. Mann, and Michael J. Malbin, *Vital Statistics on Congress, 1987–1988* (Washington: Congressional Quarterly, 1987), pp. 115–19.

in the first eighteen months. Aside from cooperative PACs, which gave a larger share early in the cycle, there was little variation in the timing of their allocations. Other contributors, however, tended to give half their contributions early. By 1988, however, PACs made 62 percent of their contributions in the first eighteen months, while other contributors gave 58 percent. The strategic importance of early money and the tendency of PACs to contribute heavily to incumbents amplify these committees' effects on elections.

Spending and Electoral Success

After all this consideration of who has given how much to whom and in what proportions, and of what the candidates spend money on and when they spend it, a fundamental question remains. Is money the key to winning elections? Intuitively, people seem to assume it is. Otherwise, contributors would not give as much as they do, candidates would not be motivated to spend more and more time chasing contributors, and editorial attitudes and public opinion would be far less interested in campaign funding reform. But is the relationship of money and success borne out by the facts?

Methodologically, it is difficult to untangle cause and effect in the relationship. Do incumbents win because they raise and spend more money or because they have a history of good service to constituents or a popular voting record?[46] Do they win because of the money they spend as incumbents or because of some other advantages of incumbency? Some scholars have suggested the importance of favorable treatment from the media or opposition by weak challengers or the declining importance of party identification as explanations for incumbents' success.[47] A related problem is how to explain why Senate challengers do better than House challengers.[48] And what about the nature of the district? There is substantial variation across districts in the extent to which they follow national trends. Voters' evaluations of local candidates seem to be more important in determining their choices than evaluations of the president, the national parties, or the state of the economy.[49] Presumably voter preference is influenced by the campaign and therefore by campaign spending.

But just how important is spending? David Magleby has found that heavy spending by statewide candidates, such as those running for governor, and spending on statewide ballot initiatives by either party or side of an issue are highly correlated with victory. Those who spend 56 percent or more of all the money spent in a campaign win more than 70 percent of the time. In candidate contests in which spending is higher than twenty-five cents per voter, the candidate who spends 80 percent or more always wins.[50] But rarely does one party so dominate the

46. Morris P. Fiorina, *Congress: Keystone of the Washington Establishment* (Yale University Press, 1977); and Fiorina, "Some Problems in Studying the Effects of Resource Allocation in Congressional Elections," *American Journal of Political Science,* vol. 25 (August 1981), pp. 543–616.

47. See, for example, John P. Robinson, "The Press as King-Maker: What Surveys from the Last Five Campaigns Show," *Journalism Quarterly,* vol. 51 (Winter 1974), pp. 587–94; Thomas E. Mann and Raymond E. Wolfinger, "Candidates and Parties in Congressional Elections," *American Political Science Review,* vol. 74 (September 1980), pp. 617–32; Lyn Ragsdale, "Incumbent Popularity, Challenger Invisibility, and Congressional Voters," *Legislative Studies Quarterly,* vol. 6 (May 1981), pp. 201–18; and John A. Ferejohn, "On the Decline of Competition in Congressional Elections," *American Political Science Review,* vol. 71 (March 1977), pp. 166–76.

48. Alan I. Abramowitz, "A Comparison of Voting for U.S. Senator and Representative in 1978," *American Political Science Review,* vol. 74 (September 1980), pp. 633–40; Barbara Hinckley, "House Reelections and Senate Defeats: The Role of the Challenger," *British Journal of Political Science,* vol. 10 (October 1980), pp. 441–60; and Mark C. Westlye, "Competitiveness of Senate Seats and Voting Behavior in Senate Elections," *American Journal of Political Science,* vol. 27 (May 1983), pp. 253–83. See also Ragsdale, "Incumbent Popularity."

49. Thomas E. Mann, *Unsafe at Any Margin: Interpreting Congressional Elections* (Washington: American Enterprise Institute for Public Policy Research, 1978), p. 1.

50. David B. Magleby, "Campaign Spending in Ballot Proposition Elections," paper prepared for the 1986 annual meeting of the American Political Science Association.

spending competition in congressional elections. What happens when spending for House and Senate campaigns is less one-sided?

As we have shown, congressional incumbents rarely lose. At least part of their success stems from their ability to raise more money than their opponents. On the other side, according to Gary Jacobson, the amount nonincumbent candidates spend has a large effect on their probability of winning elections "even when the effects of other variables, such as the strength of the party in the district or national electoral tides are controlled." However, the more money incumbents spend on the campaign, "the worse they do on election day."[51] But heavy spending by incumbents usually comes as a result of a stiff challenge that may have more to do with losing than dollars spent. "In most House races, no matter how much money the challenger spends, the incumbent will probably be reelected," Alan Abramowitz has written; however, "the challenger's expenditures are the most important factor influencing an incumbent's vulnerability."[52]

Jacobson's findings have been challenged by Donald Green and Jonathan Krasno. They find that the political quality of the challenger has a significant direct effect on the vote and that the effect of incumbent spending on winning is much greater than previously estimated. Furthermore, the direct effect of a challenger's spending is lower than previously estimated and subject to diminishing marginal returns. Finally, how much a challenger spends changes "the structure of the House vote by increasing the importance of quality and decreasing the role of previous electoral outcome."[53]

In a study of the relationship between spending and voting in Senate elections, Abramowitz also found candidates' qualities important. But, like Jacobson, he concluded that "money is probably now more important than ever, especially for challengers and candidates for open seats."[54] Thus, while disagreement continues about the relative importance of money to challengers and incumbents, the conclusion of all is that

51. Jacobson, *Politics of Congressional Elections,* pp. 49, 52.

52. Alan I. Abramowitz, "The Spendthrift Incumbent Rebuffed: Campaign Spending and House Election Outcomes" (forthcoming).

53. Donald Philip Green and Jonathan S. Krasno, "Salvation for the Spendthrift Incumbent: Reestimating the Effects of Campaign Spending in House Elections," *American Journal of Political Science,* vol. 32 (November 1988), p. 898.

54. Alan I. Abramowitz, "Explaining Senate Election Outcomes," *American Political Science Review,* vol. 82 (June 1988), p. 387.

money matters in congressional elections. The only dispute is how much more important it is for nonincumbents than for incumbents.

Conclusions

Congressional candidates have increasingly turned to political action committees and to large numbers of wealthy individuals to finance campaigns. As the roles of these contributors expand, the importance of small individual contributions, including those from candidates' electoral constituents, is reduced. Those who make large donations probably assume that candidates will be more responsive to them when considering legislation or pursuing their legislative responsibilities. PACs often deny such motives, but the magnitude of their involvement suggests otherwise. Such interested money is most important to incumbent House Democrats, but in the 1980s it also became crucial in contested Senate elections in smaller states. While House Democrats lead the parade in accepting PAC money, incumbents in both parties and both houses do much better with PACs than their opponents.

These phenomena are at least partly the result of election reforms that made raising the enormous amounts of money needed more efficient by turning to PACs. These reforms also changed the way money is raised by reducing the role of a few very large contributors. Because new challengers can no longer turn to a small number of backers to finance their entry into politics, it is hard for them to mount a viable campaign. The pragmatic PACs stay away from them.

Candidates are not limited in how much they can give or loan to their own campaigns. Many challengers provide $25,000 or more from their own pockets; some spend much more. This places a premium on wealthy candidates and haunts others with the possibility that a rich opponent could write one check and equal all the funds they have raised in months or years. A similar oddity is the unrestricted nature of independent expenditures. While direct contributions from PACs and individuals are limited, both can spend unlimited amounts on independent activities supporting or opposing candidates.

Campaign funding by the parties continues to be important but constitutes a smaller share of candidates' total receipts than money from individuals or PACs. That party contributions, which are also limited by law, could become a more significant force is suggested by the Republicans' propensity to contribute the maximum amount allowed: if they could spend without limits, they would target more money to selected races.

The most important difference in how funds are raised and spent is not so much party affiliation as it is candidate status. Incumbents have access to more money in larger chunks than do most challengers, and the challengers must labor under their inability to become sufficiently visible to be seriously considered. Incumbents also have access to funds earlier in their campaign cycles. But if access to money is unequal, candidates use it in pretty much the same ways. The single most important campaign expense is advertising, especially broadcast advertising. For some House districts television spots are inefficient, but for the rest, and for all Senate races, television and radio advertising accounts for the largest share of candidate spending. Expenses for other forms of advertising and communication, including direct mail, are also significant and in some House districts may represent the largest part of the budget. Most campaigns also hire media consultants, pollsters, and professional campaign managers. Finally, fundraising itself is expensive.

Why do candidates raise and spend this much money? They understand that the price of admission to Congress is high and getting higher. And there is, thanks in part to the inadvertent effects of campaign finance laws, more money available, especially to incumbents. A strong demand and an expanding supply pushes and pulls the contestant into the fundraising marathon. For the congressional elections in the 1990s, the consequences of continuing as in the past are longer and longer campaigns, greater dependency on PAC money, and a higher premium on recruiting large numbers of wealthy candidates.

5

Political Action Committees

"Say what you will about the integrity of individual members of Congress, the lack of a precise correlation between campaign contributions and votes in committee or on the floor. All the qualifications are true, and none of them matters," a 1987 *Washington Post* editorial commented. "The math is too strong; we have, if not a bought, at least a paid-for Congress."[1] The editorial captures the crux of the concern about the influence that organized groups or, as they are more commonly referred to, "special interests" wield in Congress. While the statement is extreme, few knowledgeable observers would claim that special interest money has no influence on congressional behavior.

Two matters are important here: one is the role of special interest money in congressional elections, the other its role in congressional policymaking. In both instances it is the effect of money, rather than special interests per se, that is at issue. Organized interests have long participated in congressional elections, particularly through get-out-the-vote drives and information campaigns, and their efforts have provided ways to encourage participation in the electoral system. Similarly, these interests have, since the early days of the Republic, provided a collective means for citizens to exercise their constitutional rights to petition the government. However, the ever-greater amount of special interest money contributed to congressional candidates has serious implications for both elections and national policymaking.

The increasing presence of PACs has altered the mix of sources that finance congressional campaigns. Rather than seeking contributions primarily from individual constituents and party committees, candidates

---

1. "A Paid-For Congress," *Washington Post,* February 12, 1987, p. A26.

72

turn to PACs, which are more easily identified and have higher contribution limits than individuals, to fund their campaigns. For incumbents this strategy is successful; for others it generally is not. Incumbents have become increasingly dependent on PAC money, and other candidates must work much harder to raise less from individual contributors. The distorting effect of PACs may extend to the legislative process as well. PACs are interested parties in what Congress does, and they give money in ways that demonstrate that interest. Exactly how much influence they wield is open to dispute. What is clear, however, is that public perception of undue PAC influence is widespread.

Growth in Numbers

It is ironic that most of the growth in the number of PACs has occurred among those that are business-related, because the impetus for congressional legislation to establish these committees in their current form came from the AFL-CIO. Organized labor had long used political action committees to support its activities during elections, but believed these activities might be threatened by court rulings. To ensure the continuation of PAC activity, in 1971 the AFL-CIO sought legislation clarifying the legal status of the committees. The AFL-CIO recognized the calculated risk of backing legislation to legalize PACs, since any legislation allowing labor PACs would also allow corporate PACs, but organized labor did not expect business to establish them, since PACs had not historically been important vehicles for the political activities of corporations and trade associations.[2]

For a while the calculations proved correct: the Federal Election Campaign Act of 1971 did not spawn very much growth in nonlabor PACs. Not until passage of the 1974 amendments to the act, which established limits on individual contributions, did the growth begin. The amendments radically changed the rules of the electoral game for corporate interests. They could no longer depend on large contributions from individual members of the business community to provide access

2. Edwin M. Epstein, "Business and Labor under the Federal Election Campaign Act of 1971," in Michael J. Malbin, ed., *Parties, Interest Groups and Campaign Finance Laws* (Washington: American Enterprise Institute for Public Policy Research, 1980), p. 112. The National Association of Manufacturers and the American Medical Association, which established PACs in the early 1960s (BIPAC and AMPAC, respectively), accounted for most of the contributions from business-oriented PACs in the late 1960s and early 1970s. Larry J. Sabato, *PAC Power: Inside the World of Political Action Committees* (Norton, 1984), p. 6.

TABLE 5-1. *Registered PACs, by Type, 1976–88*

Type of PAC	1976	1978	1980	1982	1984	1986	1988
Corporate	433	825	1,251	1,557	1,806	1,906	2,008
Labor	224	280	331	420	438	417	401
Trade, membership, health	489	547	635	669	757	789	848
Cooperatives	n.a.	12	36	51	58	57	61
Nonconnected	n.a.	256	471	915	1,146	1,270	1,341
Corporations without stock	n.a.	29	61	110	139	157	169
Total	1,146	1,949	2,785	3,722	4,344	4,596	4,828

SOURCES: See appendix A.
n.a. Not available.

to congressional policymakers. Any one person could now contribute only $2,000 to a candidate, while a PAC could contribute $10,000. In contrast, W. Clement Stone had contributed $2 million to President Nixon's 1972 reelection campaign, and Gulf Oil, Ashland Oil, and Phillips Petroleum each contributed $100,000.[3] It did not take business long to decide that PACs had become an important way for corporations as well as labor unions to participate in the electoral process.

Between 1974 and 1976 the number of corporate PACs registered with the Federal Election Commission jumped from 89 to 433.[4] As table 5-1 shows, the numbers of PACs have since increased in all categories, but corporate PACs, and later nonconnected PACs—those with no parent organization—have grown most.[5] In 1976 there were 1,146 PACs; in

3. Robert E. Mutch, *Campaigns, Congress and Courts: The Making of Federal Campaign Finance Law* (Praeger, 1988), p. 46; and Herbert E. Alexander, *Financing Politics: Money, Elections and Political Reform* (Washington: Congressional Quarterly Press, 1976), p. 205.

4. Center for Responsive Politics, *Money and Politics: Campaign Spending Out of Control* (Washington, 1987); and Federal Election Commission, *Corporate-Related Political Committees Receipts and Expenditures,* FEC Disclosure Series no. 8 (September 1977), p. 7. A decision by the FEC in November 1975 also encouraged growth in the numbers of corporate PACs. The commission ruled that Sun Oil Company could use general treasury funds to establish and solicit contributions to SunPAC. It could also solicit contributions from both stockholders and employees and establish multiple political action committees, each with separate contribution limits, as long as contributions to the committees were voluntary. Federal Election Commission, "Advisory Opinion 1975-23," December 3, 1975.

5. The growth in the number of corporate PACs likely would have been even greater but for the 1976 amendments to the Federal Election Campaign Act, which established that all political action committees formed by a company or union would be treated as one PAC for purposes of contribution limits and restricted the categories of people who could be solicited for contributions. 90 Stat. 475 (1976). In essence the amendments overturned the SunPAC decision, but by the time they were passed, Pandora's box had already been opened.

1988 there were 4,828 of them, 42 percent corporate. Because so many labor unions had PACs before 1974, and because the 1976 amendments to the FECA prohibited an organization from forming more than one PAC, the number of labor PACs has increased relatively slowly. Nonconnected PACs, which are primarily ideological, such as the National Conservative Political Action Committee (NCPAC), had become major participants in congressional elections by 1988, when they contributed more than $19 million to House and Senate candidates (figure 5-1). It is, however, important to keep in mind that while some 2,000 corporations had PACs as of 1988, there are at least 50,000 corporations that could form them if they chose.[6] Corporate PAC contributions to congressional candidates almost tripled between 1978 and 1988 and those from trade, membership, and health association PACs, such as the National Association of Renters, the National Council of Senior Citizens, and the American Medical Association, nearly doubled. Contributions from labor have fallen well short of this growth.

PAC Money and Congressional Policymaking

One reason PACs are such a focal point in the debate about campaign finance reform is that people believe money from special interest groups has too much influence in congressional policymaking. A 1985 ABC News–*Washington Post* poll showed 70 percent of Americans agreed with the statement, "Most Members of Congress care more about special interests than they care about people like you." A 1985 Gallup poll found that 79 percent of those surveyed completely or mostly agreed that "Money is the most important factor influencing public policies."[7]

Supporters of PACs argue that there is nothing insidious about these organizations, that they are just another way for people to participate in the electoral and policy processes. They emphasize that PACs are made up of individual contributors who have banded together to take part in

6. Center for Responsive Politics, *Money and Politics,* p. 13.
7. Statement of Ellen S. Miller, executive director, and Herb K. Schultz, campaign finance project director, Center for Responsive Politics, *Campaign Finance,* Hearings before the Subcommittee on Elections of the Committee on House Administration, 100 Cong. 1 sess. (Government Printing Office, 1987), p. 496. What little support there is among the public varies with the type of PAC. A 1984 Harris survey found that 69 percent of likely voters thought "big company" political action committees were a bad influence on politics and government, and 57 percent thought the same about labor union PACs. However, 58 percent believed environmental PACs were a good influence on politics and government and 64 percent that women's PACs were a good influence.

FIGURE 5-1. *PAC Contributions to Congressional Candidates, by Type of PAC, 1978–88*

Millions of 1988 dollars

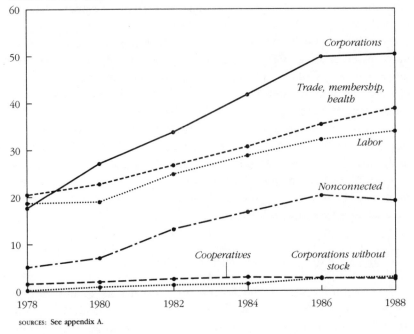

SOURCES: See appendix A.

the political system. As Ken Cole, president of the National Association of Business Political Action Committees, commented before the House Subcommittee on Elections in 1987, "Contrary to the belief of some, PACs are not mere check-writing machines. ... PACs motivate citizens to get involved in the political process. In fact, but for their participation in PACs, many citizens might play no active role in politics." And Joseph Fanelli, president of the Business-Industry Political Action Committee, wished that others "could know PACs as we do; surely they would recognize PACs as a legitimate avenue for political participation that allows ordinary citizens to pool their contributions with others of like mind and to take a more active and responsible role in political affairs through PAC involvement."[8]

Other participants in the political process consider PACs less benignly as yet another avenue for special interests to gain undue influence over

8. *Campaign Finance,* Hearings, p. 459.

congressional policymaking. PAC campaign contributions seem at best attempts to gain access to members, at worst attempts to influence their votes and actions. Representative Anthony Bielenson expressed a view shared by many on and off Capitol Hill: "It only takes a cursory look at the patterns of PAC donations to see our campaign finance system for what it really is: a system of buying and selling opportunities to influence legislative decisions."[9] Philip Stern, an opponent of PAC contributions to members of Congress, recalled that "during the Carter years, right in the middle of the hospital-cost-control vote—the hospitals and the AMA were just throwing money at the [House Commerce] Committee [which was handling the bill] as fast as they could. It was coming in wheelbarrows. The PACs took those 10 or 15 [swing] votes and they really went to work on 'em. It was just no secret."[10]

There is some truth in both points of view. PACs do encourage people to participate in the political system by soliciting campaign contributions from them. The organizations provide an additional, collective avenue of participation for those who wish their interests to be heard by lawmakers. As Richard Conlon, an advocate of congressional campaign finance reform, said, "I wouldn't for a minute like to see a system without PAC money. . . . PAC money is voluntary association money, and that is what our country is made up of. I think it should be part of the mix."[11] However, PACs typically do not make contributions to candidates for altruistic reasons: like individuals, they expect something in return—at a minimum that the issues they are interested in will get a fair hearing by a member and the committee on which he or she serves. PACs also make contributions to affect the partisan or ideological balance in the House and Senate. They hope that a Congress in which a majority of members shares their philosophy will be more receptive to their more specialized and individualistic concerns.

In the past ten years many political scientists have examined the relationship between PAC contributions and congressional voting. The results fall into three categories: studies that find a relationship between campaign contributions and legislative behavior; studies that find a relationship, but conclude that it is weak and that factors such as party,

9. Quoted by Fred Wertheimer, president of Common Cause, in *Campaign Finance*, Hearings, pp. 728–29.

10. Philip M. Stern, "The Tin Cup Congress: In between Fundraising, They Squeeze in a Few Hours to Govern," *Washington Monthly*, May 1988, pp. 27–28.

11. Interview with Richard Conlon, November 16, 1987.

ideology, and constituency are more important in understanding legislative behavior; and studies that find little or no relationship between campaign contributions and legislative behavior.[12]

When studies have found a relationship between campaign contributions and congressional voting, the issues under deliberation tended to be low-visibility, nonpartisan ones on which other voting cues were lacking. For example, John Frendreis and Richard Waterman found a connection between PAC contributions from the American Trucking Association and Senate voting on trucking deregulation in 1980, but concluded the relationship stemmed from weak partisan, ideological, or constituency voting cues.[13] On more visible issues and votes, where party interests, ideological positions, and constituency concerns are identifiable, PAC preferences are much less important.

However, these studies have some clear limitations. First, all of them focus on the relationship between PAC contributions and votes on the House, and in one case the Senate, floor; but key actions in both chambers often occur elsewhere. In one study that found no relationship between campaign contributions and votes, the author conceded, "Interest groups also attempt to influence decisions made in committee. During committee markup sessions, numbers of these decisions involve small wording changes that favor a particular interest. Undoubtedly it is easier to convince members to support a minor change on a committee draft of a bill that attracts little publicity than it is to influence their public roll call votes on an amendment to major legislation."[14]

12. For studies that find a relationship, see James A. Kau and Paul H. Rubin, *Congressmen, Constituents and Contributors: Determinants of Roll Call Voting in the House of Representatives* (Boston: Martinus Nijhoff Publishing, 1982); and Jonathan Silberman and Garey Durden, "Determining Legislative Preferences on the Minimum Wage: An Economic Approach," *Journal of Political Economy*, vol. 84 (April 1976), pp. 317–29. For studies that find a relationship but conclude other factors are more important, see John Wright, "PACs, Contributions and Roll Calls: An Organizational Perspective," *American Political Science Review,* vol. 79 (June 1985), pp. 400–14; and Benjamin Ginsberg, *The Consequences of Consent: Elections, Citizen Control and Popular Acquiescence* (Addison-Wesley, 1978). For studies finding little or no relationship, see Janet M. Grenzke, "PACs and the Congressional Supermarket: The Currency is Complex," *American Journal of Political Science,* vol. 33 (February 1989), pp. 1–24; W. P. Welch, "Campaign Contributions and Legislative Voting: Milk Money and Dairy Price Supports," *Western Political Quarterly,* vol. 35 (December 1982), pp. 478–95; and Henry W. Chappell, Jr., "Campaign Contributions and Congressional Voting: A Simultaneous Probit-Tobit Model," *Review of Economics and Statistics,* vol. 64 (February 1982), pp. 77–83.

13. John Frendreis and Richard Waterman, "PAC Contributions and Legislative Behavior: Senate Voting on Trucking Deregulation," paper prepared for the 1983 annual meeting of the Midwest Political Science Association.

14. Grenzke, "PACs and the Congressional Supermarket," p. 19.

A second and related point is that decisions about legislation are often made out of the public eye and off the public record. There is simply no way to measure the influence of PAC contributions in such instances—as when a member decides not to offer an amendment that would adversely affect an organization whose PAC made a contribution to his or her campaign.

Third, the kinds of votes on which scholars have found relationships to PAC contributions—on matters that are less visible and less clearly related to partisan, ideological, or constituent concerns—are those that may have little consequence for broad national policy but have very real results for particular special interests.[15] Even if such votes are the only type influenced by PAC contributions, they constitute a significant portion of what occurs on Capitol Hill.

Finally, as nearly everyone agrees, contributions ease access to congressional policymakers: "Money may facilitate an opportunity to present one's case, and in the absence of conflicting testimony, the member may change his or her position as a result of the meeting."[16] As one PAC director told the Center for Responsive Politics, "I discovered, after my best efforts of two or three years to visit with members of Congress, that those who made regular contributions had much easier access, and consequently I persuaded our organization to authorize a small PAC."[17]

The opportunity to present one's views to members or their staffs early in the legislative process may well shape their predisposition toward an issue. Moreover, the simple necessity of raising money to run for office makes contributions from special interests an important resource for members of Congress. While no one contribution from a PAC may be determinative, the general pervasiveness of money in Congress suggests that money does affect the legislative process.

Nevertheless, it is important to keep the role of special interests in perspective. First, as has been mentioned, they have long taken part in congressional elections and policymaking, and they will continue to do so, no matter what reforms are instituted. Just how much their part has increased is hard to know: there is no way to compare the amount of money contributed to congressional campaigns since 1972 with what

15. Frendreis and Waterman, "PAC Contributions and Legislative Behavior."
16. Grenzke, "PACs and the Congressional Supermarket," p. 19.
17. Center for Responsive Politics, *PACs on PACs: The View from the Inside* (Washington, 1988), pp. 6–7.

special interests contributed before the Federal Election Campaign Act was passed. It is known, however, that their activities have increased since the act was passed.

Second, aggregate figures on the total number of PACs and the total amount of money contributed by them oversimplify their possible influence in congressional elections. Of the 4,828 PACs that registered with the Federal Election Commission at some point during the 1987–88 election cycle, only 3,287 actually made contributions to congressional candidates. And although a few are big spenders, most make relatively small contributions. The top-ranking PAC in contributions to federal candidates in 1987–88, the National Association of Realtors PAC, contributed about $3 million to candidates, but the fiftieth in rank contributed only $460,000.[18]

Third, the public perceives congressional candidates as being besieged by contributions from political action committees anxious to gain favor, but candidates themselves openly lay siege to PAC money.[19] As one PAC director noted, the invitations "come in every day, probably five or six a day. Contributors' lists get passed around. Members call personally. It varies. When a race is tight, money is tough and the man is scared, he'll be on the phone personally. Staffers do it. ... It's tiresome, worrisome, difficult. ... It grows worse year by year."[20]

Therefore, before Congress entertains proposals that would further restrict the role of PACs, either by an aggregate limit on the amount a candidate could accept from them or by reducing the amount a PAC could contribute, it would be well to examine more closely the patterns of special interest contributions to congressional campaigns, to look at who currently benefits and who would be most affected by changing the law.

Patterns of Contributions

PAC contributions are not distributed equally: incumbents are the principal beneficiaries, a tendency more pronounced among these organizations than among individual contributors. In 1988 PACs con-

18. Federal Election Commission, "FEC Finds Slower Growth of PAC Activity during 1988 Election Cycle," press release, April 9, 1989.

19. Brooks Jackson, *Honest Graft: Big Money and the American Political Process* (Knopf, 1988).

20. Center for Responsive Politics, *PACs on PACs*, p. 39.

tributed $82.23 million to House incumbents but just $9.48 million to challengers (table 5-2).[21] Incumbent Senators received $28.67 million, challengers $7.67 million. Incumbents in both chambers have become increasingly dependent on PAC contributions. In 1978 House incumbents received 32 percent of their total campaign money from PACs; by 1988 these contributions made up almost half. Senate incumbents, while less dependent on PACs, nevertheless received 15 percent of their contributions from them in 1978 and 29 percent in 1988. Both House and Senate incumbents receive more money and a larger percentage of their total campaign contributions from PACs than do challengers and candidates for open seats. Because of this, incumbents, particularly in the House, would be most affected by an aggregate limit on the amount of money candidates could accept from PACs.

Table 5-3 shows PAC contributions to House and Senate general election candidates in more detail. House Democratic incumbents are bigger beneficiaries than Republican incumbents, and became even more dependent on special interest money between 1978 and 1988, as did the Republicans. By 1988 Democratic incumbents received slightly over half of all campaign contributions from PACs, Republican incumbents about two-fifths.

The patterns of PAC contributions to House challengers and candidates for open seats reflect the committees' expectations of electoral success for each party.[22] Both 1980 and 1984 were good years for the Republican party: it won the White House and gained and then kept control of the Senate. As a result, Republican challengers and candidates for open House seats received more money from PACs than did their Democratic counterparts, though Democratic challengers did receive a larger percentage of their campaign receipts from PACs in 1984 than did Republican challengers. In contrast, in 1982, a recession year, Democratic challengers received more from PACs than did Republican challengers. By 1988 PACs were clearly contributing to candidates in the party that would retain control of the House for the foreseeable future; Democratic challengers received three times more money from them than did Republican challengers. The most dramatic trend has been the virtual

21. Where FEC data allow, we have looked at contributions to candidates in general elections. However, in most cases the FEC reports only aggregate PAC receipts for all congressional candidates, including those who lose in the primaries.

22. Gary C. Jacobson and Samuel Kernell, *Strategy and Choice in Congressional Elections* (Yale University Press, 1981).

TABLE 5-2. *PAC Contributions to House and Senate General Election Campaigns, by Candidate Status, 1978–88*[a]
Amounts in millions of constant 1988 dollars

| | Incumbents | | | | Challengers | | | | Candidates for open seats | | | |
| | House | | Senate | | House | | Senate | | House | | Senate | |
Year	Amount	Percent	Amount	Percent	Amount	Percent	Amount	Percent	Amount	Percent	Amount	Percent
1978	26.18	32	7.91	15	7.79	17	4.91	13	7.49	20	3.31	12
1980	35.25	34	11.36	23	10.56	20	8.60	20	5.68	26	2.91	18
1982	48.90	37	17.50	26	12.67	23	5.88	14	9.36	25	3.34	11
1984	64.65	43	20.42	24	12.28	24	6.73	19	6.84	29	4.64	10
1986	70.95	44	25.57	26	9.44	21	10.49	18	11.63	28	12.06	24
1988	82.23	47	28.67	29	9.48	23	7.67	16	7.48	31	8.04	23

SOURCES: See appendix A.
a. Amounts are rounded. Percentages are share of total contributions received.

TABLE 5-3. *PAC Contributions to House and Senate General Election Campaigns, by Party and Candidate Status, 1978–88*[a]

Amounts in millions of constant 1988 dollars

| | Incumbents | | | | Challengers | | | | Candidates for open seats | | | |
| | Democrats | | Republicans | | Democrats | | Republicans | | Democrats | | Republicans | |
Year	Amount	Percent	Amount	Percent	Amount	Percent	Amount	Percent	Amount	Percent	Amount	Percent
						House						
1978	17.83	35	8.36	26	2.44	14	5.35	19	3.68	18	3.81	22
1980	23.02	37	12.23	30	2.75	17	7.81	21	2.21	22	3.47	29
1982	27.29	38	21.62	35	7.47	28	5.20	19	4.72	28	4.64	22
1984	42.78	47	21.88	38	5.35	30	6.92	20	2.92	25	3.92	33
1986	44.18	49	26.78	38	6.92	30	2.52	12	6.50	31	5.13	25
1988	53.56	52	28.70	40	7.32	33	2.16	11	4.65	38	2.83	22
						Senate						
1978	3.33	26	4.59	11	2.27	10	2.64	18	1.47	10	1.84	13
1980	8.47	22	2.89	23	1.00	8	7.60	25	1.08	14	1.82	22
1982	9.66	24	7.84	28	2.58	13	3.30	14	1.06	7	2.29	15
1984	7.36	29	13.06	22	4.98	19	1.75	19	2.44	9	2.20	11
1986	7.89	28	17.68	26	8.45	21	2.05	11	5.10	23	6.96	23
1988	15.24	30	13.42	28	4.55	17	3.12	13	3.38	17	4.67	30

SOURCES: See appendix A.

a. Amounts are rounded. Percentages are shares of total contributions received.

TABLE 5-4. *PAC Contributions to All Congressional Campaigns,*
by Party and Type of PAC, 1978–88
Millions of constant 1988 dollars

Type of PAC	1978		1980		1982		1984		1986		1988	
	Dem	*Rep*	*Dem*	*Rep*	*Dem*	*Rep*	*Dem*	*Rep*	*Dem*	*Rep*	*Dem*	*Rep*
Corporate	6.5	11.1	9.8	17.5	11.5	22.2	15.8	25.3	19.0	30.7	23.5	26.9
Labor	17.6	1.1	17.7	1.1	23.4	1.2	27.0	1.5	29.9	2.3	31.4	2.5
Nonconnected	1.3	3.4	2.0	4.9	6.7	6.4	8.9	7.7	11.7	8.5	12.2	6.9
Trade, membership, health	9.1	11.8	9.9	12.6	11.4	15.3	15.2	15.4	17.3	18.1	21.3	17.5
Cooperatives	1.1	0.4	1.1	0.6	1.6	0.9	1.7	1.0	1.5	1.1	1.5	0.9
Corporations without stock	0.2	0.1	0.4	0.4	0.7	0.5	0.9	0.6	1.2	1.2	1.6	1.2

SOURCES: See appendix A.

collapse of PAC support for House Republican challengers. In 1988 Democratic incumbents received almost twenty-five times more money than did Republican challengers.

Senate incumbents also benefit from PAC contributions. Democratic incumbents received three times as much as Democratic challengers in 1988. Republican incumbents received far more money than Republican challengers did in the four elections after 1980.[23] In 1988, for the first time since 1982, Democratic incumbents received more PAC money than Republican incumbents received. Senate Republicans as a whole got only slightly more money from PACs than Democrats did in 1984 and 1986. Unlike the dominant PAC funding of House Democrats, then, neither Senate party has a distinct advantage. Consequently, efforts to curb PAC contributions to congressional candidates may receive much more bipartisan support in the Senate than in the House.

Table 5-4 shows campaign contributions by party and type of PAC. There is a clear alliance between Democrats and labor PACs—almost no labor money goes to Republicans. Corporate PACs have contributed to candidates of both parties but more to Republicans. Although the ratio did not change between 1978 and 1986, by 1988 corporate PAC contributions had become more even. Trade, membership, and health association PACs contributed somewhat more to Republicans than to Democrats a decade ago, but by 1988 they were giving more to Democrats.

---

23. In 1980 there were eighteen Republican challengers and only six Republican incumbents, which likely explains the higher receipts for the challengers.

Incumbents again receive far more support than challengers, even when differences in PAC types are taken into account (table 5-5). PAC contributions to incumbents increased dramatically between 1978 and 1988, while support for challengers and candidates for open seats changed relatively little. Indeed, in real dollars corporate PAC support for challengers declined between 1980 and 1988. The overwhelming support for incumbents makes it all the more difficult for challengers to find sufficient funds to run competitive campaigns. As William Moore, president of the National Association of Realtors, told the Senate Rules Committee in 1987, "It's hard to argue with the notion that PACs themselves have become an 'incumbents' protection program.'"[24]

PACs also contribute to party committees. The national Democratic campaign committees have benefited far more than the national Republican campaign committees. While the National Republican Senatorial Committee received more money from PACs than the Democratic Senatorial Campaign Committee did in 1980 and 1982, the DSCC received a larger percentage of its receipts from them (table 5-6). For the Republican campaign committees, PAC contributions represent a negligible percentage of total receipts. The relationship between organized labor and the Democratic party is strong: for every year except 1980 the Democratic National Committee received half its PAC money from labor, and from 1982 to 1988 the Democratic congressional campaign committees received one-quarter to one-third of all PAC contributions from labor.

In addition to limits on aggregate PAC contributions to candidates, campaign finance reform proposals often recommend changing the limit on PAC contributions to individual candidates. Some reformers would raise the limit, but more often they seek to lower it. For example, Senator Bob Dole introduced legislation at the beginning of the 101st Congress to lower the limit on contributions from $5,000 to $1,000 per election.[25] To understand the effects these proposals would have, one needs to examine the average PAC contribution under the current laws.

The average PAC contribution is much less than the $10,000 per election cycle each is allowed under current law (table 5-7). However, reducing the limit to $1,000 per candidate would set a ceiling lower than the average contribution for almost every category of candidate. Some candidates receive the maximum amount of money they can from

24. Center for Responsive Politics, *PACs on PACs,* p. 25.
25. *Congressional Record,* daily ed., January 25, 1989, p. S209.

TABLE 5-5. PAC Contributions to All Congressional Campaigns, by Candidate Status and Type of PAC, 1978–88[a]
Millions of constant 1988 dollars

Type of PAC	1978			1980			1982			1984			1986			1988		
	I	C	OS	I	C	OS	I	C	OS	I	C	OS	I	C	OS	I	C	OS
Corporate	10.5	3.6	3.6	15.5	8.5	3.3	24.4	4.4	4.8	31.8	4.6	4.7	37.4	3.9	8.4	41.3	3.4	5.5
Labor	11.0	4.0	3.6	13.4	3.2	2.3	14.1	6.9	3.8	18.0	6.8	3.7	18.1	8.0	5.9	22.0	7.2	4.6
Nonconnected	1.3	2.0	1.3	2.2	3.5	1.3	5.9	4.5	2.5	8.3	5.7	2.6	9.9	5.2	5.1	11.4	4.1	3.5
Trade, membership, health	12.2	4.2	4.5	14.5	5.2	2.9	19.7	3.4	3.4	24.0	3.5	3.1	27.0	3.0	5.3	31.6	2.7	4.4
Cooperatives	1.1	0.2	0.4	1.6	0.1	0.1	2.1	0.1	0.3	2.4	0.1	0.1	2.2	0.1	0.2	2.1	0.1	0.2
Corporations without stock	0.13	0.04	0.05	0.7	0.1	0.1	1.0	0.1	0.1	1.1	0.1	0.1	1.8	0.2	0.3	2.5	0.2	0.3

SOURCES: See appendix A.
a. I = incumbents; C = challengers; OS = candidates for open seats.

TABLE 5-6. *PAC Contributions to Party Committees and Percentage of Total Contributions, 1978–88*

Amounts in thousands of constant 1988 dollars

Party committee	1978 Amount	1978 Percent from labor	1978 Percent of total	1980 Amount	1980 Percent from labor	1980 Percent of total	1982 Amount	1982 Percent from labor	1982 Percent of total	1984 Amount	1984 Percent from labor	1984 Percent of total	1986 Amount	1986 Percent from labor	1986 Percent of total	1988 Amount	1988 Percent from labor	1988 Percent of total
DNC	308	52	*	1,660	39	7	1,258	51	6	1,639	54	3	1,362	57	7	1,492	52	3
RNC	259	1	*	605	*	*	499	*	*	761	3	*	405	8	0.4	1,009	6	1
DCCC	83	3	14	240	18	8	983	39	12	1,677	35	14	2,567	34	19	3,268	27	26
NRCC	227	1	*	200	2	*	196	3	*	277	7	*	812	6	2	811	4	2
DSCC	183	20	37	149	1	6	262	27	4	2,027	29	20	3,047	30	21	3,577	28	22
NRSC	122	*	2	302	*	1	596	7	1	432	6	*	1,109	5	1	1,033	3	2

SOURCES: See appendix A.

* Less than 0.05 percent.

TABLE 5-7. *Average PAC Contribution to General Election House and Senate Campaigns, by Party and Candidate Status, 1978–88*
Constant 1988 dollars

	Incumbents		Challengers		Open seats	
Year	Democrats	Republicans	Democrats	Republicans	Democrats	Republicans
			House			
1978	1,058	907	1,689	1,388	1,640	1,410
1980	974	761	1,332	1,112	1,507	1,066
1982	991	840	1,554	1,062	1,442	1,047
1984	1,110	841	1,562	1,067	1,580	1,078
1986	1,155	937	1,909	1,044	1,651	1,084
1988	1,279	975	2,304	1,027	2,001	1,087
			Senate			
1978	2,114	1,680	2,504	1,751	2,199	1,577
1980	1,997	1,204	1,998	1,696	1,925	1,577
1982	1,924	1,496	2,449	1,552	2,349	1,982
1984	1,705	1,639	2,722	1,477	2,374	1,953
1986	1,904	1,891	2,663	1,825	2,739	2,143
1988	2,506	2,149	3,291	2,022	2,486	2,082

SOURCES: See appendix A.

a PAC, and the number of these has increased steadily. In the 1981–82 election cycle PACs contributed the maximum 597 times; in the 1987–88 cycle, 1,856 times.[26] In these eight years almost half of all maximum contributions came from labor PACs, and about one-quarter came from trade and health association PACs. Ninety-seven percent of labor's $10,000 contributions went to Democratic candidates; 55 percent of all those of trade and health associations went to Republicans, although they increased the proportion of maximum contributions to Democratic candidates from 31 percent in 1982 to 56 percent in 1988.

Because labor PACs are more likely than corporate and trade association PACs to contribute the limit, labor most opposes lowering it. As one labor representative commented,

If they limit the amount that a PAC can give from let's say $5,000 to $2,500 . . . and that's all they do, that would be a devastating blow to us. . . . The only reason that labor stays up with corporations in terms of being able to put the kind of money they need into having any influence is because the corporate PACs, while there are an abundance

26. Calculated from FEC data.

of them, don't do a very good job of raising money. So as a result, you have ... a bunch of corporations out there that have PACs but very few of them max out to a candidate, where all of the big international unions max out in all of the Senate races and almost all of the marginal House races.[27]

Still, of the thousands of PACs, just twenty-five or fewer contributed the maximum permitted to five or more candidates during the 1981–82 and 1983–84 election cycles. Those that contributed the limit to the most candidates—the United Auto Workers, the realtors, the American Medical Association, and the machinists—gave to between ten and forty House members. In the 1984 Senate election, several PACs gave the limit to both candidates for a seat.

While the average PAC contribution is considerably less than the maximum allowed under current law, $10,000 contributions are increasing with each election cycle. Moreover, the average contribution to almost all types of congressional candidates increased between 1978 and 1988. By 1988 the average PAC contribution to Senate Democratic candidates exceeded the total amount individuals could contribute.

Independent Expenditures

In addition to contributing money to candidates and parties, PACs also make independent expenditures. The Federal Election Campaign Act defines an independent expenditure as "an expenditure by a person expressly advocating the election or defeat of a clearly identified candidate which is made without cooperation or consultation with any candidate or any authorized committee or agent of such a candidate and which is not made in concert with, or at the request or suggestion of, any candidate, or any authorized committee or agent of such candidate."[28] When Congress passed the 1974 amendments to the act, independent expenditures by individuals and PACs were limited to $1,000 per candidate. However, the Supreme Court ruled in *Buckley* v. *Valeo* in 1976 that there could be no limits on independent expenditures because such limits violated the constitutionally protected right of free speech.

While independent expenditures represent only a small proportion of all PAC spending in congressional elections, they have the potential

27. Off-the-record telephone interview, January 27, 1989.
28. 2 U.S.C. 431 (P).

to increase significantly if further restrictions are placed on other types of PAC contributions. Between 1978 and 1986 PACs' independent expenditures in congressional elections rose from $515,000 (in 1988 dollars) to $11.1 million; in 1988 they declined to $6 million. The largest increase in independent expenditures occurred between 1978 and 1980, when they rose from 0.4 percent of all PAC expenditures to 10.3 percent. As table 5-8 shows, independent expenditures have been used primarily by nonconnected PACs, though trade, membership, and health association PACs have increased their use of them. Although the amounts have increased, the number of PACs using independent expenditures has not: 185 PACs made independent expenditures in 1980, and 161 in 1988.

Most independent expenditures are made in support of candidates (table 5-9). The only exception occurred in 1980 and 1982, when nonconnected PACs spent heavily against incumbents. In 1980 the National Conservative Political Action Committee spent more than $1 million dollars against six liberal Senate incumbents, four of whom were defeated.[29] In 1982 it again targeted incumbent liberals, but this time sixteen of seventeen were reelected. NCPAC was probably less successful because such targeted incumbents as Edward Kennedy and Robert Byrd had much safer seats and were much more ideologically attuned to their states than the senators defeated in 1980. In addition, a number of liberal PACs were formed following the 1980 elections and were active in supporting liberal incumbents and targeting conservative ones. Since 1984, PACs have concentrated their independent expenditures in support of candidates.

Spending on behalf of a candidate can mean that a PAC actually supports the candidate or that it simply wants to defeat the candidate's opponent. As table 5-10 shows, nonconnected PACs had more independent expenditures in support of Senate challengers in 1978, 1980, and 1982 and House challengers in 1978 and 1980 than they did in support of incumbents. In 1984 their independent spending became pro-incumbent and continued so through 1988. Trade, membership, and health association PACs, like all others except the nonconnected ones, used most of their independent expenditures to support incumbents. The exception was 1986, when a number of the trade association committees, such as the National Association of Realtors PAC and the

29. Federal Election Commission, *Index of Independent Expenditures, 1979–1980* (November 1981), p. 31.

TABLE 5-8. *PAC Independent Expenditures in Congressional Elections, 1978–88*
Amounts in thousands of constant 1988 dollars

Type of PAC	1978		1980		1982		1984		1986		1988	
	Amount	Percent[a]	Amount	Percent[a]	Amount	Percent[a]	Amount	Percent[a]	Amount	Percent[a]	Amount	Percent[a]
Corporate	31	*	29	*	25	*	38	*	29	*	8	*
Labor	44	*	125	*	13	*	349	0.6	105	*	7	*
Trade, membership, health	196	*	1,392	2.9	966	1.9	2,207	3.6	4,455	5.6	2,194	5.1
Cooperatives	2	*	0	0	2	*	16	*	8	*	0	0
Nonconnected	239	0.8	18,811	32.7	5,964	7.6	21,747	19.6	6,157	4.8	3,680	19
Corporations without stock	4	0.5	68	3.4	22	0.9	885	18.4	359	5.2	115	3.9
Total	516	0.4	20,425	10.3	6,992	3.0	25,242	8.3	11,113	3.0	6,004	4.0

SOURCES: See appendix A.
* Less than 0.5 percent.
a. Percent of total PAC expenditures.

TABLE 5-9. PAC Independent Expenditures for and against Congressional Candidates, 1980–88[a]

Thousands of constant 1988 dollars

Type of PAC	1980 For	1980 Against	1982 For	1982 Against	1984 For	1984 Against	1986 For	1986 Against	1988 For	1988 Against
Corporate	26	0	23	1	36	**	29	0	8	**
	(*)	(0)	(*)	(*)	(*)	(*)	(*)	(0)	(*)	(*)
Labor	24	7	13	0	333	16	104	1	7	0
	(*)	(*)	(*)	(0)	(0.6)	(*)	(*)	(*)	(*)	(0)
Trade, member-ship, health	898	16	957	10	2,043	163	4,376	78	2,148	45
	(2)	(*)	(1.9)	(*)	(3.3)	(*)	(5.5)	(*)	(5.4)	(*)
Cooperative	3	0	2	0	16	0	8	0	0	0
	(*)	(0)	(*)	(0)	(*)	(0)	(*)	(0)	(0)	(0)
Nonconnected	355	1,791	434	5,530	19,484	2,263	4,921	1,235	2,869	811
	(*)	(3)	(0.6)	(7.0)	(17.6)	(2.0)	(3.9)	(1.0)	(15)	(4.2)
Corporations without stock	4	62	21	1	744	141	119	153	53	61
	(*)	(3)	(0.8)	(*)	(15.5)	(2.9)	(2.9)	(2.2)	(1.7)	(2.0)
Total	1,310	1,876	1,550	5,542	22,656	2,583	9,557	1,467	5,085	917
	(*)	(*)	(0.6)	(2.4)	(7.5)	(0.9)	(2.6)	(4.0)	(3.3)	(*)

SOURCES: See appendix A.

* Less than 0.5 percent.

** Less than $500.

a. Percentages of total PAC expenditures shown in parentheses. Data for 1978 not included because independent expenditure activity was negligible.

TABLE 5-10. *PAC Independent Expenditures on Behalf of House and Senate Incumbents and Challengers, by Type of PAC, 1978–88*
Thousands of constant 1988 dollars

Type of PAC	1978	1980	1982	1984	1986	1988
			House			
Corporate						
Incumbents	5.1	9.6	8.7	21.1	17.2	3.5
Challengers	5.8	9.1	8.6	3.4	3.9	3.0
Labor						
Incumbents	19.1	6.8	19.4	27.0	36.0	2.2
Challengers	2.7	2.3	8.1	4.0	29.5	2.8
Nonconnected						
Incumbents	8.0	33.9	86.3	299.2	1,580.1	441.9
Challengers	199.0	87.8	14.6	163.8	239.6	43.9
Trade, membership, health						
Incumbents	83.2	340.3	560.8	412.6	242.9	1,014.9
Challengers	28.7	247.9	116.9	301.5	627.9	0.7
Cooperatives						
Incumbents	1.8	2.2	0	6.5	6.5	0
Challengers	0	0	0	0	0.05	0
Corporations without stock						
Incumbents	0.7	1.9	9.1	12.4	93.7	8.4
Challengers	1.3	0.1	11.9	5.4	31.0	3.7
			Senate			
Corporate						
Incumbents	10.3	4.5	4.2	1.6	1.7	0.9
Challengers	1.5	0.7	2.5	0	0	0
Labor						
Incumbents	3.6	10.2	3.3	0.5	3.5	0
Challengers	0.4	4.0	0.06	0	0	2.2
Nonconnected						
Incumbents	11.1	27.0	74.2	636.0	1,917.5	1,261.3
Challengers	15.8	171.4	122.7	123.5	155.7	274.2
Trade, membership, health						
Incumbents	46.1	134.9	165.2	456.5	754.1	469.9
Challengers	5.6	88.9	33.8	28.9	685.6	− 2.7[a]
Cooperatives						
Incumbents	0	0	4.9	5.7	0.5	0
Challengers	0	0	0	0	0	0
Corporations without stock						
Incumbents	0.9	0	0	8.2	23.1	14.0
Challengers	0	0	0	1.0	31.6	17.7

SOURCES: See appendix A.
a. A PAC that made a purchase, such as a media buy, late in the 1986 election, but did not actually get the purchase, would get a refund in 1987. That refund would be reported and would show up as a negative expenditure in the 1987–88 election cycle.

American Medical Association PAC, spent heavily on behalf of a number of challengers running against House incumbents with whom the organizations disagreed. However, only half of the candidates supported by AMPAC and only one of the six supported by the realtors were successful.[30] In 1988 all but $700 of the independent expenditures of trade, membership, and health association PACs supported incumbents.

Despite the constitutional protection that independent expenditures enjoy, they cause concern because PACs do not have to be accountable for them and because there is some question of how independent the expenditures actually are. When a PAC makes a direct contribution, a candidate is free to accept it or reject it, but a PAC may make independent expenditures without explanation or approval. Candidates are often not willing recipients. As one manager of a PAC that does not use independent expenditures said, "Basically . . . you're substituting your own judgment for the judgment of the candidate and his campaign managers." And a former campaign manager commented, "Independent expenditure scares the daylights out of me. A third party comes in that doesn't know my strategy or my budget and interjects itself. This could terribly jeopardize a campaign."[31] Thus even independent expenditures meant to help a candidate can be potentially harmful. The message or tone of a TV spot, for example, may be different from that of the campaign or may cause other complications, as happened in the 1982 Senate race in Maryland when NCPAC targeted Senator Paul Sarbanes and ran negative television spots that backfired; Sarbanes was able to raise money from liberal supporters precisely because of the ads.[32]

PACs making independent expenditures also have no accountability to voters. In the 1988 presidential campaign, for example, Americans for Bush made independent expenditures in support of their candidate. The organization had no connection with the Bush campaign, but most Americans did not know that. Unless voters know who is making independent expenditures and know that they are independent, they have no way of evaluating the message.

The second problem raised by independent expenditures is the extent to which they are truly independent. Candidates are concerned because

30. Viveca Novak and Jean Cobb, "The Kindness of Strangers," *Common Cause*, September–October 1987, pp. 32–37.

31. Both are quoted in Sabato, *PAC Power*, pp. 102–03.

32. Larry Boyle and John Hysom, "Independent Expenditures: Cutting through Barriers," *District Lawyer*, vol. 10 (May–June 1986), p. 41.

they assume such expenditures are in truth independent and thus could upset their campaigns. However, some observers suggest that it is virtually impossible for an independent expenditure to be just that. Larry Sabato argues that "the network of friends and associates among campaigns and PACs is so large and so informed that anyone seriously desiring to know a candidate's campaign needs or plans has very little trouble doing so. The news media may be the best source of all for campaign information, and it is supplemented by a candidate's own literature and advertising, which often clearly reveal his underlying strategy."[33] Roger Stone, a Republican political consultant, concurs: " 'In Washington, everyone talks.' Politics is a relatively small industry . . . and the world gets even smaller within a congressional district."[34] But although there have been numerous allegations of collusion between campaigns and organizations making independent expenditures, the FEC has seldom found that coordination occurred. In one of the few such instances, Senator Pat Moynihan charged that Bruce Caputo, his opponent in the 1982 Senate race in New York, and NCPAC, which spent $73,000 against Moynihan, used the same campaign consultant. The FEC ruled that NCPAC's expenditures were illegal; but still, the case has been by far the exception.[35] If independent expenditures are not independent of candidates and their campaigns, they become a way for PACs to circumvent restrictions on direct contributions.

Leadership PACs

Most PACs are formed by organizations to enhance their influence with Congress. There are, however, a small but important number that have been formed by members of Congress or candidates themselves. These are generally referred to as leadership PACs because they enable elected or potential officeholders to raise money to contribute to other candidates for office or to spend on their own election-related activities. In the 1985–86 election cycle thirty-nine members of Congress and one Senate challenger, Skip Humphrey, had leadership PACs. Alan Simpson was the only member of the Senate leadership without one; Robert Byrd, Alan Cranston, and Robert Dole all had their own. In the House, Speaker Tip O'Neill, Majority Leader Jim Wright, Majority Whip Tom Foley, and

33. Sabato, *PAC Power,* p. 184.
34. Quoted in Novak and Cobb, "Kindness of Strangers," p. 35.
35. Novak and Cobb, "Kindness of Strangers," p. 35.

Congressman Tony Coelho, chair of the DCCC, also had leadership PACs.[36]

Leadership PACs vary widely in their contributions: eight of the thirty active in the 1984 congressional elections gave more than $100,000 to other candidates, while an equal number gave less than $10,000. Many contribute a large portion of their money to candidates involved in close races, thus fostering competition. Contributions by party leaders have also seemed "targeted to increase the party's strength in Congress, and not to build legislative coalitions. No contributions by party leaders in 1984 went to committee chairmen, and over half of party leader contributions went to candidates involved in close contests."[37] Supporting competition and developing party strength are admirable goals.

But leadership PACs also have less admirable consequences. They provide a legal means for candidates to exceed the limits on individual and PAC contributions to candidates. By establishing PACs, candidates can accept an additional $10,000 from both individual contributors and from PACs, effectively doubling the amount they receive from PACs and increasing fivefold the amount they can accept from individuals. William Moore of the National Association of Realtors described leadership PACs as "nothing more than legal slush funds which allow PACs to contribute double the legal maximum to powerful members of Congress."[38] The PAC director for a small trade association commented, "We give to the Chairman's campaign and again to his PAC. We don't like doing it, but we feel that it is our only way of getting access."[39]

Many leadership PACs are run by lobbyists. Senator Bennett Johnston's PAC, for example, "has as its inner circle a set of lawyers and lobbyists whose clients frequently lobby the Energy and Natural Resources Committee."[40] Both the opportunity to increase special interests' contributions to members through contributions to their PACs and the involvement of representatives of special interests in running members' PACs are troublesome. Finally, while the proximate reason for contributing to congressional candidates may be to increase their likelihood of

36. Center for Responsive Politics, *Spending in Congressional Elections: A Never Ending Spiral* (Washington, 1988), pp. 30–35.

37. Clyde Wilcox, "Fundraising, Contributions, Power, and Decisionmaking in Congress," paper prepared for the Conference on Campaign Finance Reform and Representative Democracy, Marquette University, February 1989, p. 18.

38. Center for Responsive Politics, *PACs on PACs,* p. 42.

39. Wilcox, "Fundraising, Contributions, Power, and Decisionmaking," p. 25.

40. Wilcox, "Fundraising, Contributions, Power, and Decisionmaking," p. 25.

success, once they are in office the contributions could affect votes for party and committee leaders and votes on legislation.

Conclusions

PACs are important in financing congressional campaigns, but certainly not all campaigns or types of candidates. Democrats are more dependent on them than Republicans, House candidates more than Senate candidates, and House incumbents most of all. House Democratic incumbents also constitute the single largest group in Congress who would have to vote for campaign finance reform. Thus in discussing reform proposals that affect PACs, partisan and institutional differences must be taken into account.

Although PACs are not the root of all evil in the current congressional campaign finance system, congressional observers, lawmakers, and the public are increasingly aware that special interest money plays a significant role in congressional elections and perhaps in policymaking. Escalating campaign costs necessitate seeking funds from sources that can make relatively large contributions, and it is PACs more than political parties or individuals who are answering that need—mostly for incumbents. Limiting the function of PACs in financing congressional elections will not remove special interests from the legislative process. Such groups will continue to communicate their views, mobilize support or opposition, and pursue their public policy agendas. What should change is the dependence of Congress on PAC money.

6

Political Parties

Political parties figure prominently in the debate over congressional campaign finance reform. One reality that colors all discussions is that the Republican party raises and spends more money than the Democratic party. Although the discrepancy in fundraising ability has narrowed in recent years, it remains significant and affects the attitudes and calculations of both parties as they consider reform proposals. The discrepancy is not, however, as important in affecting election outcomes as it might be because parties are limited in what they can give, directly or indirectly, to any candidate. This is why raising ceilings on party expenditures is a staple of most Republican proposals and is almost uniformly objected to by Democrats.

The function of parties in campaign activities is limited by the structure of the U.S. electoral system and the tradition of candidate-centered politics. Unlike those in most other nations, political parties in America do not dominate candidate recruitment, campaign issues, or campaign financing.[1] Indeed, since the advent of direct primaries, they have only a peripheral role in the recruiting and nominating processes in most states. And candidates for Congress construct their own platforms and campaigns, which may differ dramatically from those of their party's presidential candidate or other candidates.

---

1. At least twenty-one countries have some form of direct public funding of elections, largely accomplished through the political parties. These countries are Argentina, Australia, Austria, Brazil, Canada, Costa Rica, Denmark, Finland, France, Israel, Italy, Japan, Mexico, Netherlands, Norway, Spain, Sweden, Turkey, United States, Venezuela, and West Germany. Other countries, like Great Britain, provide less direct aid in the form of free advertising and tax incentives for political contributions. See Herbert E. Alexander, ed., *Comparative Political Finance in the 1980s* (Cambridge University Press, 1989); Michael Pinto-Duschinsky, *British Political Finance, 1930–1980* (Washington: American Enterprise Institute for Public Policy Research, 1981); and Khayyam Z. Paltiel, "Campaign Finance: Contrasting Practices and Reforms," in David Butler and others, eds., *Democracy at the Polls: A Comparative Study of Competitive National Elections* (Washington: American Enterprise Institute for Public Policy Research, 1981), pp. 138–72.

American parties also are less important to financing campaigns than parties elsewhere. Adopting a party-centered campaign finance system like the ones found in most other democracies has never been seriously considered by Congress. Part of the reason campaign finance reform in the United States is focused on candidates is that they do the reforming. It is clearly in their interest to maintain a system in which they have maximum flexibility on their positions, campaign budgets, and fundraising strategies.[2] Although attempting to expand the functions of parties is part of a long-standing tradition of promoting more party-centered politics and greater party accountability and responsibility, the reality is that American congressional elections are likely to remain highly candidate-centered.[3]

Discussions of possible reform have often suggested that parties should be a more important force in financing campaigns. Recent proposals to strengthen them have suggested increasing the limits on party contributions to candidates, reestablishing at least a 50 percent federal income tax credit for small contributions to parties, and channeling money raised in public financing schemes through the parties, permitting them to keep a portion.[4] Others have suggested that, instead of restricting PACs, parties be strengthened by funds publicly appropriated from the U.S. Treasury and by public matching gifts.[5] Such proposals have never been very popular with legislators, who wish to preserve their independence and financial autonomy.

Before discussing various proposals thoroughly later in the book, it would be well to explore the structure of party committees and the functions they perform in congressional campaigns: raising money for candidates, providing other services, and possibly leading the effort to reform the campaign finance system.

2. Because congressional districts rarely coincide with other politically important boundaries for state parties, most members of Congress feel it is necessary to build their own organizations in their districts. Senate candidates, although they campaign throughout a state, also establish their own campaign organizations.

3. On expanding the functions of parties, see Austin Ranney, *The Doctrine of Responsible Party Government* (University of Illinois Press, 1962); and American Political Science Association, "Toward a More Responsible Two-Party System," *American Political Science Review,* vol. 44, Supplement (September 1950), pp. 1–96.

4. Chuck Alston and Glen Craney, "Bush Campaign Reform Plan Takes Aim at Incumbents," *Congressional Quarterly Weekly Report,* July 1, 1989, p. 1648; and Larry J. Sabato, *The Party's Just Begun* (Scott, Foresman, 1988), pp. 212, 216.

5. Herbert Alexander and Brian Haggerty, *PACS and Parties: Relationships and Interrelationships* (Los Angeles: Citizens Research Foundation, 1984), p. 69; and Philip M. Stern, *The Best Congress Money Can Buy* (Pantheon, 1988), pp. 186–87.

Committee Structure and Operation

Both national parties have a House committee, a Senate committee, and a national committee that directly or indirectly influence congressional campaigns. Democrats have the Democratic Congressional Campaign Committee (DCCC), Democratic Senatorial Campaign Committee (DSCC), and Democratic National Committee (DNC). Republican counterparts are the National Republican Congressional Committee (NRCC), National Republican Senatorial Committee (NRSC), and Republican National Committee (RNC).[6] The congressional campaign committees are made up entirely of Democratic or Republican members of the appropriate house of Congress. Typically, each committee is balanced regionally and ideologically. The National Republican Congressional Committee goes one step further and is composed of one Republican from each state with at least one Republican representative.

Each committee is chaired by a representative or senator appointed or elected by the party leadership and approved by the party caucus. Committee chairmen are chosen because of their fundraising abilities and their capacity to recruit able and attractive candidates; and they can be well rewarded for their efforts. Representative Tony Coelho, a powerful force in rejuvenating the Democratic party and its structure before being charged with ethics violations in 1989, chaired the DCCC from 1981 to 1987. Coelho was successful in expanding the committee's fundraising ability, which may have helped him become majority whip in 1987.[7] Similarly, Senator George Mitchell, who chaired the DSCC in 1985 and 1986, is given credit for building a successful strategy to regain party control of the Senate in 1986. He too entered the party leadership in 1987 as deputy president pro tempore of the Senate and then was elected to succeed Robert Byrd as majority leader in 1989. Republican committee chairmen have also been visible party leaders. Representative Guy Vander Jagt and Senators John Heinz and Richard Lugar chaired their respective party committees in the 1980s.

---

6. The Republicans were the first to organize a House campaign committee in 1866. The development of separate party committees for Congress stemmed from policy disagreements between President Andrew Johnson and Congress. Each of the groups held midterm conventions in 1866, and after the Union party meeting in Philadelphia the precursor to the NRCC was formed. In 1916, as the Senate became popularly elected, each party set up Senate committees as well. Robert J. Huckshorn, *Political Parties in America,* 2d ed. (Brooks-Cole, 1984), p. 73.

7. Brooks Jackson, *Honest Graft: Big Money and the American Political Process* (Knopf, 1988), pp. 286–88.

As recently as 1984 a scholar argued that "both of the party committees in the Senate are chiefly fundraising organizations, usually built around dinner speeches and direct mail and not furnishing any significant level of campaign services."[8] But this view is now disputed. According to Larry Sabato,

Each national party committee has been recruiting and training House and Senate candidates as never before, and devising common themes for all nominees in election seasons—work that may help to produce a consensual legislative agenda for each party. The carrot and stick of party money and campaign services, such as media advertising production and polling, is also being used to convert independent candidates into party team players.[9]

The growing involvement of parties in fundraising, recruitment, training, research on the opposition, polling, and producing television spots indicates that the committees have expanded their activities in congressional elections.

The House Democrats, who have long lagged behind the Republicans in party committee staff, reached parity with the NRCC in 1988.[10] The turning point came with the 1982 elections. As the Republicans talked openly about winning control of the House and raised even more money than in previous election cycles, the Democrats responded by enlarging their campaign committee operation. They established a more aggressive direct mail program and in other respects mirrored what the Republicans had been doing for more than a decade. In 1986 the Democrats opened a $3-million media center that includes a satellite dish, copying already established Republican services.[11]

One explanation for the surge in Democratic fundraising in 1982 was the fear Republicans stirred when they defeated prominent Democrats in the 1980 elections and won control of the Senate. The Democratic party's response was to increase its share of contributions from PACs, especially from business and trade associations. As Tony Coelho observed, "Business has to deal with us whether they want to or not. I tell them,

8. Huckshorn, *Political Parties in America,* p. 74.

9. Sabato, *Party's Just Begun,* p. 55.

10. Paul Herrnson, "Reemergent National Party Organizations," in L. Sandy Maisel, *The Parties Respond* (Westview Press, forthcoming).

11. The center was financed in part by a $550,000 grant from Pamela Harriman. See Sabato, *Party's Just Begun,* p. 87.

TABLE 6-1. *Share of Congressional Candidates' Total Receipts Coming from Party Committees, 1974–88*

Percent

Party	1974	1976	1978	1980	1982	1984	1986	1988
House								
Democrats	1	4	3	2	2	3	2	3
Republicans	7	13	11	9	10	11	6	6
All candidates	4	8	7	6	6	6	4	4
Senate								
Democrats	2	2	3	4	4	6	8	7
Republicans	13	6	8	15	15	8	9	11
All candidates	6	4	6	9	10	7	9	9

SOURCE: Norman J. Ornstein, Thomas E. Mann, and Michael J. Malbin, *Vital Statistics on Congress, 1989–90* (Washington: Congressional Quarterly, 1990), pp. 85–86.

'You're going to need to work with us.'"[12] Individual Democratic incumbents were also shaken. Martin Franks, then executive director of the DCCC, commented, "Panic is not too strong a word to describe it. Even people who were traditionally safe went out and really raised money in Washington and around the country in a way that they haven't before."[13] Many raised much more than they needed: thirty-two had more than $100,000 remaining in their accounts after the campaign. Ironically, the incumbents' efforts probably robbed Democratic challengers of the funds necessary to unseat Republicans in a year in which the Republican party was vulnerable.[14]

Financial Functions

Parties are less important than individuals and PACs in financing campaigns, partly because they have limited funds and, especially for the Republicans, because they have more money than they are permitted to give. On average, House Democrats have received 2.5 percent of their campaign funds from party sources since 1974; House Republicans have received 9.1 percent (table 6-1). Senate Democrats have received 4.5

12. Gregg Easterbrook, "Washington: The Business of Politics," *Atlantic Monthly,* October 1986, p. 30.

13. Quoted in Alan Clymer, "Campaign Costs Soar as Median Spending for Senate Hits $1.7 Million," *New York Times,* April 3, 1983, p. 20.

14. Thomas E. Mann and Norman J. Ornstein, "Sending a Message: Voters and Congress in 1982," in Thomas E. Mann and Norman J. Ornstein, eds., *The American Elections of 1982* (Washington: American Enterprise Institute for Public Policy Research, 1983), pp. 140–41.

percent; Republicans, 10.6 percent. However, the share for Senate Democrats nearly equaled that of the Republicans in 1986 before declining in 1988.

Congressional campaign committees provide financial resources in two ways: direct contributions and coordinated expenditures, which include services the party may provide or purchase for candidates, such as polling, mailings, production of broadcast advertisements, or in some cases buying television or radio air time.[15] When Congress amended the Federal Election Campaign Act in 1974, it limited direct contributions from party and nonparty committees (PACs) to $5,000 per candidate for each campaign (primary, general, and in some states runoff elections), or $10,000 each election cycle, assuming no runoff election. Congress also permitted parties to spend on behalf of candidates (the so-called coordinated expenditures) up to $10,000 for House races and, for Senate races, either two cents times the voting age population of the state or $20,000, whichever is greater. Unlike the contribution limitations, the coordinated expenditures are permitted to rise with inflation. The limit for House candidates had risen to $23,050 by 1988.

Technically, the party controls coordinated expenditures, whether for a poll, production assistance for advertising, or research. In reality, there is little difference between these expenditures and direct party contributions because candidates have a strong say as to how coordinated money is spent. In contested races in which the level of spending itself might be an issue, coordinated expenditures have the advantage that they do not show up on the candidate's receipt or expenditure disclosure statements.

The FECA amendments also permit state and local parties to contribute to federal candidates and to spend on their behalf. These organizations routinely cede such spending authority, through devices called agency agreements, to the congressional campaign committees, a practice begun in 1978 by the NRSC that has been upheld by the Supreme Court.[16] Nearly all state Republican committees have ceded authority extensively.

Overall, contributions and coordinated expenditures by congressional campaign committees rose from $28 million in 1978 (in constant 1988 dollars) to almost $36 million in 1982 and declined to $29 million in

15. Larry Sabato has reported that between 70 and 100 Republican House candidates received help with their media advertising in each election cycle from 1980 to 1986. See *Party's Just Begun,* p. 78.

16. See *Federal Election Commission* v. *Democratic Senatorial Campaign Committee,* 454 U.S. 27 (1981).

1988 (table 6-2). By comparison, PAC giving rose from $64 million in con-
tributions and independent expenditures in 1978 to $153 million in
1988. PACs, then, are in general much more important than parties as
sources of campaign funds. The parties' direct contributions actually
declined in both nominal and constant dollars, but coordinated expenditures increased. Republican coordinated expenditures rose from $13
million in 1978 to $21 million in 1982 and then declined to $14 million
in 1988. Democrats saw a more dramatic increase: coordinated expenditures rose from $723,000 in 1978 to $9 million in 1988. Yet even so,
Democrats remain well behind the Republicans in every category of
party support for congressional candidates. In the most vivid instances,
Senate Democrats' coordinated expenditures rose over a ten-year period
from zero in 1978 to $6.2 million in 1988, while House Republicans' ˜
total spending nearly doubled in just one election cycle. Between 1980
and 1982, Republican spending rose from $6.7 million to $11.2 million.

Party committees raise and spend much more than they are permitted
to contribute to candidates or use as coordinated expenditures. The
NRCC, for example, spent about $1 million in 1974 and almost $35
million in 1980, but it made only $2 million in direct contributions to
candidates in 1980 and just $1.2 million in coordinated expenditures,
together less than 10 percent of the committee's total budget. The
pattern has continued throughout the 1980s.

Republicans have used coordinated expenditures strategically. In the
1978 campaigns, for example, they emphasized spending on races for
open seats and on Republican challengers in the most competitive
districts. The aid more than offset the dollar advantage that Democratic
candidates, especially incumbents, had in PAC receipts from labor
unions.[17] Ben Ginsberg, counsel to the National Republican Senatorial
Committee, commented, "Certainly since ... the 1978 elections, we
have always been able to max out [that is, to spend up to the statutory
limit]," and Joe Gaylord, executive director of the NRCC, concurred:
"Any race that has been within 10 points, we've maxed out on ... anyone
that is even close to credible has received full funding from the Committee
since 1982."[18]

An additional indication of the Republican committees' financial edge

17. Edie N. Goldenberg and Michael W. Traugott, *Campaigning for Congress* (Washington: Congressional Quarterly Press, 1984), p. 71.
18. Interviews with Ben Ginsberg, November 11, 1987, and Joe Gaylord, November 17, 1987.

TABLE 6-2. *Party Committee Contributions and Coordinated Expenditures in Congressional Elections, 1978–88*[a]

Thousands of constant 1988 dollars

Committee	1978	1980	1982	1984	1986	1988
			Democrats			
DNC						
Contributions	102	42	102	119	1	138
Coordinated	125	798	47	6	378	30
Total	227	841	149	126	379	168
DCCC						
Contributions	1,769	1,267	847	991	712	665
Coordinated	0	72	296	1,460	1,801	2,426
Total	1,769	1,339	1,142	2,450	2,513	3,090
DSCC						
Contributions	1,405	993	756	546	680	421
Coordinated	0	1,216	2,823	5,127	7,069	6,206
Total	1,405	2,209	3,578	5,673	7,749	6,627
State and local committees						
Contributions	786	542	671	581	499	463
Coordinated	598	505	1,326	1,306	1,081	811
Total	1,384	1,046	1,997	1,888	1,580	1,274
Total Democrat	4,785	5,435	6,868	10,136	12,220	11,159
			Republicans			
RNC						
Contributions	1,642	1,201	2,085	967	0	325
Coordinated	611	1,218	286	8	2	21
Total	2,254	2,419	2,370	975	2	346
NRCC						
Contributions	5,982	4,138	3,842	3,352	1,929	1,584
Coordinated	2,763	2,536	7,433	8,134	4,776	4,108
Total	8,745	6,674	11,274	11,486	6,705	5,691
NRSC						
Contributions	1,501	856	840	731	734	760
Coordinated	8,555	10,369	13,093	8,742	11,605	10,251
Total	10,057	11,225	13,932	9,473	12,339	11,011
State and local committees						
Contributions	1,352	1,105	997	1,005	824	702
Coordinated	1,052	1,016	492	79	283	63
Total	2,404	2,121	1,489	1,083	1,107	765
Total Republican	23,459	22,439	29,066	23,017	20,153	17,814
Grand total	28,245	27,874	35,933	33,153	32,373	28,973

SOURCES: FEC data tapes; see appendix A; and FEC, "FEC Summarizes 1988 Political Party Activity," press release, March 27, 1989.

a. Includes all party committees—national, state, and local—involved in congressional campaigns. Totals may not add because of rounding.

TABLE 6-3. *Total Party Campaign Spending Permitted by Law and Actual Spending, 1980–88*[a]

Thousands of dollars

Chamber and party	1980	1982	1984	1986[b]	1988[b]
House—Contributions					
Democratic spending	1,023	1,051	1,299	984	1,198
Total permitted	12,750	12,990	13,020	17,080	17,080
Republican spending	3,490	4,715	4,082	2,522	2,651
Total permitted	12,000	11,790	11,520	15,320	15,280
House—Coordinated					
Democratic spending	256	694	1,793	1,860	2,880
Total permitted	12,512	15,969	17,534	18,539	19,685
Republican spending	2,204	5,293	6,204	4,162	4,163
Total permitted	11,776	14,494	15,514	16,663	17,610
Senate—Contributions					
Democratic spending	480	579	441	621	489
Total permitted	963	908	908	1,018	908
Republican spending	677	600	591	730	721
Total permitted	990	908	963	963	908
Senate—Coordinated					
Democratic spending	1,133	2,265	3,948	6,656	6,592
Total permitted	6,375	8,849	7,212	12,890	12,804
Republican spending	5,435	8,716	6,518	10,078	10,261
Total permitted	7,894	9,100	7,741	11,515	12,804

SOURCES: FEC data tapes; see appendix A; and FEC, "FEC Summarizes 1988 Political Party Activity."
a. Includes all party committees—national, state, and local—involved in congressional campaigns.
b. The FEC permitted $10,000 to be given by the congressional committees to candidates from the other house.

is a comparison of what they actually contributed and the maximum contribution allowed by law (table 6-3). The NRSC has spent more than 80 percent of its limit for coordinated expenditures on Republican Senate candidates in every campaign since 1982. The DSCC, however, has been spending about 50 percent since 1984, an improvement over the 18 to 26 percent it was spending in 1980 and 1982. The NRSC has reached the limit in direct contributions and coordinated expenditures in about half the races since 1978. All other party committees fall well below this level.

In large part because of their success in fundraising, the Republican congressional campaign committees have been a much more powerful presence than their Democratic counterparts. In particular, the Republicans have been able to have a larger and more stable national staff that successfully coordinates its activities from one election to another.[19]

19. Xandra Kayden, "The Nationalization of the Party System," in Michael J. Malbin, ed., *Parties, Interest Groups, and Campaign Finance Laws* (Washington: American Enterprise Institute for Public Policy Research, 1980), pp. 257–82.

"Some campaigns don't need us," said Scott Cottington, NRSC political director. "But the vast majority would not do as well without us in many areas—shaping a message, fund raising, opposition research, technical expertise and so on."[20] In many respects the DCCC is now modeled after its Republican counterpart. Although it still lags far behind in fundraising and committee infrastructure, it has made a commitment to using direct mail and seeking small contributions to help it catch up. Moreover, under the leadership of Tony Coelho, Democrats improved their marketing of candidates to PACs, admitting openly that they were "trying to do the best job [they could] of copying the Republicans."[21] The DCCC is, in fact, much more reliant on PACs than is the NRCC, receiving 14 percent of its funds from them in 1984, 19 percent in 1986, and 26 percent in 1988. The NRCC, in contrast, received virtually no money from PACs before 1986 and only 2 percent in 1986 and 1988.

The National Republican Senatorial Committee, like the NRCC, has been much more successful at fundraising than the Democratic Senatorial Campaign Committee. In the crucial 1980 Senate elections the NRSC raised $23 million, the DSCC $1.6 million. The gap had not narrowed much by 1988, when the NRSC raised $66 million and the DSCC $16 million.

The Republicans' success in raising money from individual donors has not been accompanied by similar success with PACs. As Jerry Lewis, former House Republican Policy Committee chairman, stated in a 1988 report, "To the extent PACs keep favoring incumbents, the PAC system of election financing serves House Democrats." He later added, "The fundamental task facing us as House Republicans is to challenge PACs to encourage more competition in House elections."[22] On September 22, 1988, Senate Republicans met with seventy-five PAC officials in Washington to encourage larger contributions to Republican candidates. During the first eighteen months of the 1987–88 election cycle, PAC contributions to Senate Democratic candidates had increased 58 percent while those to Republican candidates declined by 19.5 percent.[23] What particularly troubles Republicans is the lack of support they have received from business PACs. House Minority Leader Robert Michel even wrote a letter to them in 1988 saying that Republicans were dismayed at seeing

---

20. Richard E. Cohen, "Party Help," *National Journal,* August 16, 1986, p. 1999.
21. Interview with Martin Franks, November 17, 1987.
22. Jerry Lewis, House Republican Policy Committee, "Access or Competitiveness: What Do PACs Want?" (March 1, 1988), pp. 1, 10.
23. Congressional Quarterly, *Campaign Practices Reports,* October 3, 1988, p. 4.

so many contributions going to members who consistently oppose the interests that business leaders advocate.[24]

But business and trade PACs are driven by pragmatism rather than partisanship or ideology. Tony Coelho emphasized this when he explained why the DCCC had done well with them: "The thing to do with business men and women is to appeal to their business sense. You can't sell them H.R. 1236. You can't sell them a legislative program. People aren't interested in that. Business men and women want to be associated with success. If they see you are going to be successful they latch on to you."[25] Because contributions are more pragmatically placed with the majority party, Republican fundraising efforts have clearly been hampered. Again, during the first eighteen months of the 1987–88 election cycle, 53 percent of contributions from corporate PACs and 59 percent from trade association PACs went to Democrats. In a September 1988 meeting, Senator Robert Dole "pointed out that Republicans have taken politically nettlesome, pro-business positions . . . and yet business PACs give increasingly to Democrats." According to one PAC manager who was at the meeting, Dole's argument was "We've helped you. Now it's time for you to help us."[26] In the Senate as well as the House, PACs are pragmatic, giving disproportionately to incumbents. Thus at least part of the explanation for the recent growth in Senate Democrats' fundraising among PACs is their return to the majority after the 1986 elections.

The advantage enjoyed by Republicans in total fundraising has slipped recently but remains substantial, and most believe it will continue. Because Democrats assume that they will be outspent, they try to raise enough to get their message out and save enough to compete on an even footing during the critical last weeks of a campaign and in the most contested races. As David Johnson, executive director of the DSCC in 1985–86, recalled, "We were able to max out in every hot race in the country, and that was our goal."[27]

Republican strategy recognizes that Democrats enjoy some nonfinancial advantages that force Republicans to outspend them just to remain competitive. For example, Mark Braden, former general counsel to the RNC, commented that Republicans lack the resources "readily available to Democrats. . . . Many of the functions which we perform for Republican

---

24. Chuck Alston and Janet Hook, "An Election Lesson: Money Can Be Dangerous," *Congressional Quarterly Weekly Report,* November 19, 1988, pp. 3366–67.

25. Quoted in Easterbrook, "Washington: The Business of Politics," p. 30.

26. Congressional Quarterly, *Campaign Practices Reports,* October 3, 1988, p. 4.

27. Interview with David Johnson, November 26, 1987.

candidates here are performed for Democratic candidates down at the AFL-CIO."[28] Among the advantages the Democrats have that do not show up in disclosure reports are better party infrastructure and patronage at the state and local level; the greater opportunity to design House districts to their liking, which results from their control of most state legislatures and governorships; and more volunteer-intensive group support and partisan identifiers. Republicans' substitution of money for volunteer services was bemoaned by former U.S. Senator and RNC Chairman Paul Laxalt: "We've got way too much money, and too many political operatives. . . . We are substituting contributions and high technology for volunteers in the field. I've gone the sophisticate route, I've gone the television route, and there is no substitute for the volunteer route."[29]

Until the mid-1980s, receipts of party committees were rising. But in the 1986 election cycle the totals of the three national Democratic committees dropped to $43 million from $66 million in 1984, and those of the three Republican committees dropped to $208 million from $246 million. Receipts at the DNC and RNC declined more than those of the congressional campaign committees. Since 1986 the receipts of the NRCC, and to a lesser extent the NRSC, have also plummeted. Looking at off years only, the NRCC raised $29 million in 1981, $25 million in 1983, $18 million in 1985, $12 million in 1987, and $14 million in 1989. NRSC off-year receipts peaked in 1985 with $39 million and dropped to $24 million in 1987 before climbing back to $36 million in 1989. The Republican committees raised more than four times as much money as the Democrats in 1989.[30]

The idea that party committees serve as important fundraising organizations is comparatively new. As Mark Braden explained, "In the early sixties, up until Ray Bliss, the national committee received funds from the state party organization. We really functioned as a confederation, and there really wasn't any national fundraising, except for the presidential campaign."[31] Among the fundraising strategies of the committees has been the intensive use of direct mail. In the early 1960s the Republican party, using mailing lists borrowed from friendly groups and from publishers such as *Reader's Digest,* started a $10 Sustaining Members

28. Interview with Mark Braden, November 16, 1987.

29. Quoted in Thomas B. Edsall and Paul Taylor, "GOP Leaders Compose a New Song," *Washington Post,* January 24, 1987, p. A3.

30. Federal Election Commission, "Republican Lead Continues in 1989," February 6, 1990, report provided by Robert Biersack, supervisory statistician, Federal Election Commission.

31. Interview with Mark Braden, November 16, 1987.

program. Those who returned contributions were given a membership card and a subscription to a party publication. In 1963 the receipts from the program were $1.1 million; in 1964 they were almost $2.4 million.[32] The NRCC has led the way in large-scale, direct mail fundraising and still leads the field. The Republicans have taken particular advantage of reduced postage rates, which were part of the 1979 amendments to the FECA (2.7 cents a letter for the parties rather than the normal 8.4 cents for third-class mail). Reduced postage costs are especially important in the early stages of direct mail fundraising, when parties are still prospecting a large sample to sort out real donors. It is ironic that the Democrats proposed eliminating the subsidy in 1987, because they are still at the stage where they could benefit from increased prospecting.

In 1981–82 the Democratic campaign committees, especially the DCCC, followed the Republican lead by investing heavily in direct mail fundraising. The committee had a list of only 12,000 to 13,000 names before 1981, while the NRCC announced its millionth direct mail donor in the 1981–82 election cycle. Tony Coelho was instrumental in the DCCC's decision to establish a direct mail program. Because direct mail is very expensive in its initial stages, Coelho knew that Democrats would receive very little return on the investment in 1981–82, but he saw the effort as necessary for the party to remain competitive.[33] As Martin Franks summarized the strategy, "It wasn't going to be just enough for us to improve our own fundraising structure. We were also going to have to go out and at least try and put a dent in their fundraising."[34] Coelho reported that in 1981 "the average Democratic House contribution was about five hundred dollars, while the comparable Republican average was thirty-eight dollars. That told me very quickly something was wrong. Here we were the party of the little guy, yet the small contributors were going Republican."[35] Because of the heightened insecurity among House Democrats during the 1981–82 cycle, Coelho's decision to invest in direct mail becomes all the more impressive. It was also made with some opposition from incumbent House Democrats, who felt they needed the money for their campaigns more than the party needed such a long-term investment.

It should be noted that direct mail fundraising is restricted by limitations on individual contributions. As Rodney Smith, chief fundraiser

32. Huckshorn, *Political Parties in America,* pp. 166–67.
33. Jackson, *Honest Graft,* p. 100.
34. Interview with Martin Franks, November 17, 1987.
35. Quoted in Easterbrook, "Washington: The Business of Politics," p. 32.

for the National Republican Senatorial Committee, said, "When you impose a contribution limit . . . you cut the legs out [from under] a basic, critically important tenet of fundraising, which is resoliciting known donors; . . . once you get them to the limit, you have to go find a new donor."[36] This has not been a significant problem for Republicans, however, because most of their direct mail contributions are well below the individual limit.

Both parties depend heavily on individual contributions, yet there are important partisan differences. Much has been said about the smaller average Republican contribution, but while the Democrats' average contribution is higher, the Republicans still surpass them in the number of both small and large contributors. In a study of Californians who contributed more than $500, 75 percent were registered Republicans; only 22 percent aligned themselves with the Democrats.[37] Thus, according to Larry Sabato, "the Republican party has thoroughly outclassed its Democratic rival in almost every category of campaign service and fundraising."[38] And as Frank Sorauf concludes, "By any measure one wants to adopt, the average Democratic loyalist has less disposable income than the average Republican, and that is a crucial fact in a system of campaign finance that rests ultimately on the voluntary contributions of individuals."[39]

Another important difference is the level of support Democratic committees get from PACs. This dependence is most pronounced in the House and Senate committees. The Democrats also differ from Republicans in that "the party fields candidates with a far broader range of ideological positions and policy preferences."[40] As a result, Democratic contributors understandably want to pick and choose among candidates much more than do Republican contributors, and contributions to party committees suffer accordingly.

In addition to contributions from individuals and PACs, which are subject to FECA limits, both parties raise so-called soft money not subject to federal disclosure laws. As the Center for Responsive Politics has reported, "Once soft money distribution systems were created, national

36. Interview with Rodney Smith, December 2, 1987.
37. Larry L. Berg, Larry L. Eastland, and Sherry Bebitch Jeffe, "Characteristics of Large Campaign Contributors," *Social Science Quarterly,* vol. 62 (September 1981), p. 413.
38. Sabato, *Party's Just Begun,* p. 75.
39. Frank Sorauf, *Money in American Elections* (Scott, Foresman, 1988), p. 150.
40. Gary Jacobson, "Party Organization and Distribution of Campaign Resources: Republicans and Democrats in 1982," *Political Science Quarterly,* vol. 100 (Winter 1985–86), pp. 622–23.

parties were able to collect and transfer unlimited amounts of money to their state and local affiliates and in return, these affiliates could spend whatever other money they raised on election activity—especially those activities benefitting federal candidates." The report added that "the national parties also learned they could use their 'non-federal' money to support 'non-partisan' voter registration programs run by tax exempt organizations. . . . Groups can be set up to register only those voters who are likely to vote for one particular party or candidate."[41] Republicans used soft money to register evangelical Christians and servicemen, while Democrats backed organizations registering Hispanics, blacks, welfare recipients, and working mothers.[42] Depending on state requirements, soft-money contributions may be unlimited in both amount and source (that is, in some states corporations can make soft money contributions). Because the source is undisclosed, it is difficult to gauge how much soft money is raised and spent; but it seems to be contributed mostly in presidential elections, special elections for the House and Senate, and some contested congressional races. U.S. Federal District Court Judge Thomas Flannery has ordered the FEC to come up with clearer guidelines regarding the raising and spending of soft money.[43]

How Party Money Is Distributed

One of the key decisions the committees face is how to allocate resources. "Funds for a party and its candidates are finite, and some of them could go either to the party or [to] the incumbent candidates for reelection," Sorauf has noted. "In such a competition, of course, almost all advantages are on the side of the incumbents. . . . The party committees, whose purpose is to some degree redistributive, suffer in the competition, and so, therefore, do the party's needy challengers and open-seat candidates."[44] But the context for decisions is different for Democrats than it is for Republicans because of greater scarcity of funds for Democrats. For House races the party's allocation of funds between incumbents and nonincumbents varies considerably from year to year

41. Center for Responsive Politics, *Money and Politics: Soft Money—A Loophole for the '80s* (Washington, 1985), pp. 4, 15.

42. Maxwell Glen, "Republicans and Democrats Battling to Save Big Bucks for Voter Drives," *National Journal,* September 1, 1984, p. 1621; and Thomas Edsall, "Soft Money Will Finance Voter Signup," *Washington Post,* August 12, 1984, p. A4.

43. *Common Cause et al.* v. *Federal Election Commission,* Civ. A. No. 86-1838, U.S. District Court, District of Columbia, August 25, 1988, memorandum.

44. Sorauf, *Money in American Elections,* p. 137.

(table 6-4). In 1980 and 1984, for instance, Democrats gave more than half their money to incumbents; in midterm years it was closer to one-third. The pattern appears to hold for both direct contributions and coordinated expenditures.

Republican wealth means the party can target more of its money to challengers and candidates in races for open seats. In other words, it can contribute the maximum allowed to incumbents and still have enough to fund other candidates who are competitive. Democrats have not had as much money and have thus been forced to choose a different strategy. Before 1982 the DCCC gave each candidate the same amount, usually $1,000, regardless of campaign circumstances. When Tony Coelho became chairman in 1982, he decided to pass by candidates in safe seats and invest in competitive races. As Gregg Easterbrook has written, "Many in the party old guard were furious. Senior incumbents who had served faithfully found themselves rewarded with no party funds; green or little-known candidates got the legal maximum of $50,000 in intra-party help." He quotes Coelho as admitting, "I still have enemies in Congress because of it."[45] Nevertheless, as Al Jackson, director of the National Committee for an Effective Congress (a consortium of liberal PACs), has said, "The DCCC is a lot better than it used to be, but it is still mainly an incumbents' committee. Its first obligation is to see that Democratic incumbents get re-elected."[46]

Since the early 1980s, Democrats have channeled their campaign resources more effectively to incumbents in electoral trouble. In 1983–84, for instance, the average incumbent Democrat in a district with little or no opposition got a $53 contribution. The average Republican in such a virtually uncontested district got more than $8,000 (table 6-5). The discrepancy in coordinated expenditures is not nearly as great, but a substantial difference still exists. In contested districts, Democrats still receive less party support, but the gap between the parties has narrowed. This strongly suggests that with fewer resources Democrats have become even more selective in the allocation of party funds.

The difficult decision now for the DCCC is how to allocate funds among incumbents and challengers. First, "any redistribution of resources from stronger to weaker candidates must ... come almost entirely at the expense of incumbents."[47] But letting incumbents fend for themselves

45. Easterbrook, "Washington: The Business of Politics," p. 32.
46. Quoted in Robert Kuttner, "Getting There: It's Worse Than Being There," *New Republic,* February 15, 1988, p. 23.
47. Jacobson, "Party Organization and Distribution of Campaign Resources," p. 605.

TABLE 6-4. *Democratic and Republican Party Actual and Permitted Spending by Congressional Candidate Status, 1980–88*

Thousands of dollars

Candidate status	1980		1982		1984		1986[a]		1988[a]	
	Direct	Coordinated	Direct	Coordinated	Direct	Coordinated	Direct	Coordinated	Direct	Coordinated
House										
Democrats										
Incumbents	596	133	396	263	660	936	336	583	432	1,404
Permitted	7,500	7,360	6,450	7,928	7,620	10,262	9,400	10,246	9,920	11,433
Challengers	254	83	497	319	411	522	423	821	495	1,016
Permitted	4,170	4,092	5,010	6,158	4,500	6,060	5,880	6,409	6,120	7,053
Open seats	173	40	159	113	228	335	210	431	270	461
Permitted	1,080	1,058	1,530	1,880	900	1,212	1,800	1,962	1,040	1,199
Republicans										
Incumbents	1,220	347	2,222	2,059	1,518	1,543	1,076	1,467	1,015	1,340
Permitted	4,290	4,208	5,040	6,194	4,620	6,220	6,400	6,976	6,560	7,560
Challengers	1,703	1,344	1,565	1,958	2,040	3,747	847	7,935	1,065	1,839
Permitted	6,630	6,506	5,190	6,380	6,090	8,200	7,280	7,852	7,720	8,897
Open seats	5,668	5,131	928	1,277	5,237	9,145	597	1,320	571	984
Permitted	1,080	1,058	1,560	1,916	810	1,090	1,640	1,787	1,000	1,153

Senate

Democrats										
Incumbents	260	659	317	1,099	121	594	146	1,891	169	2,055
Permitted	522	3,712	522	5,455	330	2,672	247	4,108	413	6,109
Challengers	147	365	209	704	240	1,945	307	3,271	218	3,017
Permitted	302	603	302	2,036	467	3,173	495	5,528	330	4,528
Open seats	73	109	53	462	943	1,616	167	1,494	101	1,520
Permitted	137	2,659	82	2,008	137	1,886	192	1,786	165	2,167
Republicans										
Incumbents	110	452	207	2,033	323	3,037	356	4,897	245	3,576
Permitted	192	603	302	2,036	467	3,173	495	5,528	330	4,528
Challengers	443	3,708	323	4,673	182	1,825	193	3,494	324	4,580
Permitted	660	3,712	522	5,455	357	2,672	275	4,108	413	6,109
Open seats	124	1,274	70	2,009[b]	109	1,898[c]	181	1,678	152	2,105
Permitted	137	2,659	82	2,008	137	1,886	192	1,786	165	2,167

SOURCES: FEC data tapes; see appendix A; and FEC, "FEC Summarizes 1988 Political Party Activity."

a. The FEC permitted $10,000 to be given by the congressional committees to candidates from the other house.
b. The overspending occurred in Virginia.
c. The overspending occurred in West Virginia and Texas.

TABLE 6-5. *Average House and Senate Party Committee Support for Incumbents, by Competitiveness of Election Outcome, 1980–88*

Dollars

Party and percentage of vote	1980 Direct	1980 Coordinated	1982 Direct	1982 Coordinated	1984 Direct	1984 Coordinated	1986[a] Direct	1986[a] Coordinated	1988[a] Direct	1988[a] Coordinated
House										
Democrats										
71–100	505	48	297	240	53	150	460	832	420	1,533
61–70	1,258	446	1,902	564	655	1,231	1,674	2,880	1,453	6,578
51–60	4,981	883	5,583	4,672	6,309	6,361	6,396	11,022	6,527	16,586
41–50	5,952	1,764	10,333	4,382	9,763	21,483	1,294	2,020	79	3,678
Republicans										
71–100	7,206	205	8,525	91	8,270	1,298	2,806	−109 [b]	3,607	350
61–70	9,218	1,278	9,903	3,104	10,616	13,519	5,993	4,452	5,146	5,338
51–60	10,622	9,316	14,458	14,645	12,451	28,086	12,394	25,398	11,778	27,070
41–50	12,818	6,872	21,866	36,593	16,700	38,767	15,896	39,973	13,296	45,742
Senate										
Democrats										
71–100	0	0	17,500	0	2,500	325	17,999	1,991	2,620	50
61–70	13,707	19,266	15,416	47,449	277	1,409	14,522	13,226	12,107	14,747
51–60	6,015	16,460	19,410	91,145	18,532	74,645	17,749	125,277	11,968	367,794
41–50	17,808	50,782	17,500	73,715	18,500	216,220	19,523	1,695,875	17,500	82,630
Republicans										
71–100	16,048	30,284	...	...	18,736	85,987	15,754	9,790	0	0
61–70	15,000	105,788	...	...	18,897	197,300	15,964	62,415	16,138	166,415
51–60	15,923	56,671	19,533	209,029	18,117	199,723	22,936	446,086	21,632	577,981
41–50	16,879	96,803	15,834	76,095	22,019	423,738	19,783	287,595	22,350	143,710

SOURCES: FEC data tapes; see appendix A.

a. The FEC permitted $10,000 to be given by the congressional committees to candidates from the other house.

b. A negative number results from offsets to or refunds of contributions or coordinated expenditures in the previous election cycle.

can have unwanted consequences. When House Democratic incumbents pursued fundraising more aggressively than usual in 1981–82, they effectively reduced the pool of campaign dollars available to Democratic challengers. The result was a less successful election year for the challengers than might have otherwise been the case.[48] Furthermore, much of the money was not really needed since "thirty-two House Democrats had more than $100,000 left over after the campaign; their unspent funds alone amounted to more than $6.3 million."[49]

Party committees usually avoid choosing sides in contested primaries.[50] But they do often assist the winning candidates in retiring debt after the primaries are over. Once the nominee is known, the party can then give its full contribution and coordinated expenditure. A hands-off policy in the primaries does not, however, preclude efforts to identify, recruit, and train potential candidates.

Other Committee Functions

Parties are important to congressional campaign finance in ways less obvious than supplying candidates with money. The House and Senate campaign committees serve as liaisons between candidates and prospective contributors, both individuals and PACs. They also consider part of their mission to be identifying and marketing targeted races to contributors. This process begins when the parties bring the candidates to Washington for training seminars. Included in the two- or three-day sessions are one or more social gatherings, which Martin Franks has described as

the campaign equivalent of your freshman college mixer where we would have a cocktail hour or a breakfast hour, or whatever, where we would invite the PACs to just literally come in and meet candidates, not with any expectation that anybody was going to raise any money, but at least as an icebreaker. But if candidates could come into town, we would help them set up appointments and help them see the

48. Edward Tufte's model of midterm seat loss would have predicted a loss of forty-five seats. Before the election Tufte scaled that back to forty seats because of the "potency of Republican financing and organization," but the Republicans lost only twenty-six seats. See Larry J. Sabato, "Parties, PACs, and Interest Groups," in Mann and Ornstein, eds., *The American Elections of 1982,* p. 80.

49. Jacobson, "Party Organization and Distribution of Campaign Resources," p. 615.

50. John F. Bibby, *Politics, Parties, and Elections in America* (Chicago: Nelson-Hall, 1987), p. 145.

PACs, and we also played kind of an honest broker role in the sense of supplying our own information to the PACs regularly.[51]

Not every candidate receives such a personal introduction to those who help fund congressional campaigns, but candidates fortunate enough to be in contests targeted by the party generally do. According to Ben Ginsberg, the NRSC works the PAC community "pretty hard. The difference between us and the Democrats is that the committees, by and large, don't get any money out of it, but we will try and raise as much money as possible ... we will help them coordinate events, put on events, give them our facilities if they want to send people over to make calls. [We] keep a list of all the PACs in Washington to make available to the candidates."[52] The committees also assist candidates in developing fundraising strategies in Washington, in their districts, and in other hunting grounds around the country—New York, Texas, Florida, and California.

As the election approaches, the committees identify key races that they can pitch to Washington contributors as being competitive and needing support. Committees regularly hold briefings in which these races are highlighted. Television spots are shown, the campaigns' pollsters summarize recent surveys, and on some occasions the candidates themselves make short presentations. It is expected that word of which races have been highlighted will spread among Washington PACs and individual contributors. If contests are not highlighted, potential contributors can assume that money donated to them would not be as useful: every party committee is sensitive to the need to maintain a reputation as an honest broker, since it wants to tap the contributors again and again, and defeated candidates cannot help in this effort.

In highlighting key races, the party committees' first priority is to protect incumbents. Tony Coelho vowed that "not a single Democratic incumbent would be defeated in 1986."[53] But parties also play an important role in assisting challengers and especially candidates for open seats. Here, their liaison role is important both in the early stages of the campaign when candidates need sufficient funds to be credible and in the final stages when the campaign committees attempt to channel money to races where it might make the difference. "The candidates

51. Interview with Martin Franks, November 17, 1987.
52. Interview with Ben Ginsberg, November 16, 1987.
53. Jackson, *Honest Graft,* p. 167.

and the parties do not wait passively for an AMPAC or R-PAC to make its selections. Rather, the contenders and their party sponsors energetically seek to reach and impress the PAC decision makers."[54]

Sometimes the party committee steps beyond being liaison and becomes a conduit for transferring funds from individuals to candidates. The NRSC used this process, called earmarking, to solicit funds from individual donors for five Senate races it had targeted in the 1986 elections. Individuals sent their money to the NRSC, with checks made out either to the committee or to the targeted candidates. The checks were then sent on to the relevant campaigns as if they had been sent directly to the candidate. By raising the money this way, the NRSC could contribute the maximum and still channel more money to candidates, arguing that the checks were individual contributions to candidates and not to the party. As Ben Ginsberg explains, contributors "didn't know who they were donating the money to. . . . The way the solicitation pieces work is, 'We want you to give to the campaigns in these states, South Dakota, Nevada, three others,' and the [contributors] would then send back the money, checking the box saying, 'Yes, I agree with who I am giving the money to.'"[55] After the 1986 election, Common Cause filed a complaint with the FEC, questioning the legality of the NRSC's actions, but the commission deadlocked 3–3 along partisan lines over whether the contributions should be applied to party contribution limits. The Republican members of the commission concluded that the NRSC had no "direction or control" over the contributions; the three Democratic commissioners reached the opposite conclusion.[56]

The Republicans' ability to raise more money than they can legally spend on behalf of individual candidates enables them to conduct generic national campaigns such as those used in 1980 ("Vote Republican. For a Change") or in 1982 ("Stay the Course"). Joe Gaylord, NRCC director, recalled that "two-thirds of all our money was spent on the mail, and the other third was roughly television."[57] Republicans also explored independent party spending on behalf of candidates in 1983, when

54. Sabato, "Parties, PACS, and Interest Groups," in Mann and Ornstein, eds., *The American Elections of 1982*, pp. 96–97.

55. Interview with Ben Ginsberg, November 16, 1987.

56. FEC Statements of Reasons, MUR 2282, January 30, 1989, and June 2, 1989. In January 1990 the U.S. District Court for the District of Columbia reversed the commission's decision, finding the 3–3 deadlock, and thus dismissal of the complaint, "arbitrary, capricious and contrary to law." The court remanded the matter to the commission, which subsequently reopened enforcement proceedings. FEC, *Record* (March 1990), pp. 11–12.

57. Interview with Joe Gaylord, November 17, 1987.

Senator John Heinz organized a "Republican National Independent Expenditure Committee." The "independence" of party committees was never addressed in the courts, but there is an assumption that they cannot be independent.

Parties are also active in recruiting candidates. Of crucial importance is the potential candidate's fundraising ability. Thomas Griscom, former executive director of the NRSC, used to tell prospective Senate candidates two things: "First, you need to have a game plan of why you should get elected, and why you want to be a Senator. And number two, almost at the same time, is can you raise the money, where is it going to come from, and how much are you willing to put in?"[58] The committees assume prospective congressional candidates know that funding their races will be time consuming, difficult, and will likely cost them some of their own money. J. Kenneth Klinge, the national campaign director of the NRCC, tells candidates "that $20,000 seed money can be critical."[59] Potential candidates who do not have this skill and desire are systematically discouraged from running.

Parties may also provide such campaign-related services as research, production of broadcast spots, and purchasing. They routinely track incumbents' voting records, positions, and speeches to provide ammunition for prospective challengers. They also provide candidates with materials on issues likely to arise in a campaign. The NRCC has led the way in services related to advertising. It has in-house production facilities permitting it to produce television and radio spots for a fraction of what they would cost if contracted to outside specialists. The committee has also often purchased broadcast time slots, thus saving the candidates the usual fee. In the 1980 campaign the NRCC produced more than 300 commercials.[60] It also took the lead in generic party advertising in the 1980, 1982, and 1984 campaigns. In 1987–88 the DCCC produced 660 commercials for 125 candidates; the NRCC produced 300. However, the NRCC "arranged for many candidates to receive professional assistance [with media production] at its expense."[61]

The other party committees have recognized the importance of the NRCC's broadcast communications efforts and have begun to provide their candidates with media production assistance, satellite dishes, and so forth. As former committee chairman Coelho observed, "Politics has

58. Interview with Thomas Griscom, November 16, 1987.
59. Interviews with J. Kenneth Klinge, November 11 and November 18, 1987.
60. Sabato, *Party's Just Begun,* p. 78.
61. Herrnson, "Reemergent National Party Organizations."

become the business of communication. If I make a sale, they react by voting for us. I still think you ought to do what is legislatively right, but the way you package your idea has become just as important."[62]

Conclusions

The Republican campaign committees began the 1980s with a tremendous fundraising advantage, and that advantage, while not as pronounced as it was, remains. The Democratic campaign committees, particularly the DCCC, have tried to develop long-term programs to enable them to approach the capabilities of the Republicans. Nevertheless, because of the nature of each party's supporters and its position in Congress, their donor bases remain very different.

Parties help foster electoral competition in congressional elections. They recruit candidates, train them and their staffs, provide research on issues and information on the opposition, and give money. More than individual donors, and especially more than PACs, party committees contribute to challengers and candidates in contests for open seats. They carefully target their resources to contests in which the money will make the greatest difference. Enhancing or enlarging the functions of parties would thus likely expand these positive activities.

But parties face political difficulties in helping effect reform. Because of election laws—most notably single-member-district, winner-takes-all electoral rules—and a preference for letting voters decide the nominees, American congressional elections are and will remain candidate-centered. Candidates who have built political careers out of establishing their own electoral and fundraising organizations are not likely to reduce them voluntarily for the possibility of party support. Parties will probably not become the principal means for reform because it is the candidates who will do the reforming, and they have shown little interest in expanding the role of the parties.

An analysis of the prospects for reform, either incremental or comprehensive, must understand both the specific and more general implications of change. This is clearly true of political parties. The Republican party's fundraising advantage among individual contributors is, in this sense, like the House Democratic incumbents' advantage among political

---

62. Quoted in Easterbrook, "Washington: The Business of Politics," p. 32.

action committees. Those who benefit from the present rules are not likely to give away that advantage without a corresponding reduction of some advantage enjoyed by the other participants. Changing the rules on the functions of political parties will, of necessity, also require changes in the rules for PACs, individual contributors, and candidates themselves.

7

The Federal Election Commission

In 1985 the Federal Election Commission was described as an agency "with no constituency, little money and few friends . . . an agency whose administrative decisions are vilified by politicians, ridiculed by lawyers and overturned by courts."[1] Yet the FEC is the federal agency responsible for implementing and enforcing campaign finance laws. It is only when the causes for the widespread criticism of the commission are understood that ways can be found to improve its functioning under either the current system of congressional campaign finance or proposed reforms.

History

The Federal Election Campaign Act, as amended in 1974, took effect January 1, 1975. A day later Senator James Buckley and others filed suit challenging the constitutionality of the act's provisions. That case, *Buckley* v. *Valeo,* was decided by the Supreme Court in January 1976. In the interim, the Federal Election Commission, created by the 1974 amendments, began its work.

The FEC's first year was extremely difficult by any measure. The agency was not popular with the members of Congress, whose elections it was charged with overseeing. It seemed clear from the outset that Congress did not intend for it to be a strong, independent agency. Four of the first six commissioners—Robert Tiernan, Thomas Curtis, Neil Staebler, and Vernon Thompson—were former members of Congress, two Republicans and two Democrats. A fifth, Joan Aikens, had strong ties to the Republican party, and a sixth, Thomas Harris, was former

---

1. Congressional Quarterly, *Campaign Practices Reports,* February 11, 1985, p. 1.

associate general counsel for the AFL-CIO.[2] In addition to appointing commissioners who were expected to be responsive to their views, members of Congress took early action to assert their authority over FEC activities. The commission's first appropriation request was cut from $20 million for two years to $7.78 million for eighteen months. Using the one provision for a legislative veto that was part of the act, Congress rejected the first two regulations promulgated by the commission.[3]

When the Supreme Court handed down its ruling in *Buckley* v. *Valeo*, it declared the commission as constituted under the 1974 amendments to the FECA to be unconstitutional. The Court allowed thirty days for the commission to be reconstituted, with all members to be appointed by the president and confirmed by the Senate. (The act had originally provided for two of the six commissioners to be appointed by the Speaker of the House and two by the president pro tempore of the Senate, with the remaining two appointed by the president.) But reestablishing the commission proved more difficult than the Court might have anticipated. It took three months for Congress to pass new legislation, and it was not until May 11, 1976, that President Ford signed legislation bringing the act into compliance with *Buckley* v. *Valeo*.[4]

The newly constituted commission had six voting members—three Democrats and three Republicans—and two nonvoting members, the clerk of the House and the secretary of the Senate. Five of the six original members of the commission were reappointed by President Ford. The sixth, Thomas Curtis, resigned because he thought the commission, as it was evolving, could no longer be independent of Congress. For the commission to be independent, he argued, commissioners should be part time, deriving their incomes from sources other than congressional appropriations, and the commission's authorization should be multiyear rather than annual.[5] Curtis's action had been precipitated when Wayne Hays, chairman of the House Administration Committee, learning that

2. Common Cause, *Stalled from the Start* (Washington, March 1981), pp. 7–8; and Herbert Alexander, *Financing Politics: Money, Elections and Political Reform* (Washington: Congressional Quarterly Press, 1976), pp. 142–43.

3. The first regulation would have required that so-called office slush funds maintained by some members to supplement congressional office expenses be disclosed at regular intervals and be subject to contribution and expenditure limits. The second would have changed the initial point of entry for reports of candidates and political committees from the clerk of the House and secretary of the Senate to the FEC. In both cases Congress believed the commission was interfering unduly in established congressional practices. Alexander, *Financing Politics*, pp. 145–48.

4. Alexander, *Financing Politics*, pp. 153–54.

5. Alexander, *Financing Politics*, p. 155.

he could possibly be the subject of a random audit, told Curtis, "You're not going to set the ground rules. The [House Administration] Committee is. As Chairman, I'll tell you. You're coming back every year for an authorization."[6] Curtis was replaced by William Springer, a former Republican member of Congress.

The first appointments of former members of Congress, coupled with reduced appropriations and legislative vetoes, sent clear signals that the agency was not to stray very far from the interests of the people it was charged with regulating. Even after the commission was reestablished, Congress was not hesitant in curbing its powers. When the 1979 amendments to the FECA were enacted, Congress prohibited the commission from conducting random audits of congressional campaign reports, which the commission had begun in 1976. The commission had argued that "random selection was 'the most nonpartisan and evenhanded approach'" and that audits would "verify and, where necessary, correct the public record . . . would be educational for those audited [and] would gauge the general level of compliance with the act."[7] In comparing the FEC with other regulatory agencies that often become captives of the industries they are supposed to regulate, one observer has said, "The FEC was not so much captured as it was kidnapped and held hostage."[8]

Structure

The criticisms of the FEC's structure and functioning have not abated. For some, the commission does not move swiftly enough in enforcing the law; for others, it engages in trivial and inconsequential enforcement procedures. One observer described it as "wielding a lash as stinging as a wet noodle."[9] However, the commission operates as it was designed to by Congress. Both its structure and the enforcement procedures established by statute hinder its ability to be an effective regulatory

6. Robert E. Mutch, *Campaigns, Congress and Courts: The Making of Federal Campaign Finance Law* (Praeger, 1988), p. 89. Opposition to the FEC was not limited to the House. In 1981 conservative Senate Republicans led a six-month effort to cut off commission funding entirely; Brooks Jackson, *Broken Promise: Why the Federal Election Commission Failed* (New York: Priority Press, 1990), p. 13.

7. Mutch, *Campaigns, Congress, and Courts*, p. 96.

8. Jackson, *Broken Promise*, p. 23.

9. Steve Goldberg, "FEC Lash Often Stinging as a Wet Noodle," *Richmond Times Dispatch*, May 6, 1984, p. A3.

agency.[10] Its structure encourages partisanship and inaction; the enforcement procedures make prompt action almost impossible. Although members of Congress may become frustrated when the commission is slow to act in cases in which they feel they have been wronged, they are also unwilling to change the statute to allow the commission to act more expeditiously.[11]

The structure of the FEC—the number of commissioners, the responsibilities of the chairman, the statutory provisions for and limitations on its activity, and the budget constraints under which it operates—sets it apart from other regulatory agencies.

The first unusual characteristic is its three voting members from each party. The Securities and Exchange Commission, the Federal Trade Commission, the Interstate Commerce Commission, and most other regulatory agencies have five voting members. The FEC is a partisan rather than a bipartisan or nonpartisan commission. In light of its history, it is commonly believed that the appointed members are expected to represent and protect fellow partisans when they come before the commission. Furthermore, "Congress wants more than the statutory balance between Republicans and Democrats on the Commission— Congress wants the right kinds of Republicans and Democrats, preferably ones who are both partisan and closely tied to congressional party leaders."[12]

Some who have watched the commission from its inception believe it has increasingly adopted this role. Not only did its first chairman, Thomas Curtis, not seek reappointment because he did not think the commission could be independent of partisan politics, but another initial

10. Most state election commissions, in contrast, are much more effective in carrying out their responsibilities. The differences between the state commissions and the FEC stem from both the bipartisanship of the state commissions and their lack of major enforcement responsibilities. State election commissions either have an uneven number of members, as in California and Maine, or, in states with even numbers, the commissions' activities do not split along partisan lines. And because most state commissions are responsible only for disclosure, there is less reason for their activities to result in partisan deadlock. Interviews with Sandra Michioku, media director, California Fair Political Practices Commission, May 26, 1988; Marilyn Canavan, administrative assistant to the Maine Governmental Ethics and Election Practices Commission, May 26, 1988; Jeanne Olson, fiscal manager of the Minnesota Ethical Practices Board, May 26, 1988; Donald J. McCarthy, Jr., counselor of the New York State Board of Elections, May 26, 1988; and Gail Shea, Wisconsin campaign finance and elections administrator, May 26, 1988.

11. For example, in hearings before the Senate Rules Committee in 1987 Senators Daniel Patrick Moynihan and Harry Reid both criticized the FEC for its slowness in acting on complaints. Congressional Quarterly, *Campaign Practices Reports,* December 14, 1987, p. 5.

12. Mutch, *Campaigns, Congress, and Courts,* p. 105.

appointee, Neil Staebler, was turned down for reappointment largely because of his vote in the SunPAC decision.[13] Staebler, a liberal Democrat, had voted with the three Republican commissioners. Both organized labor and congressional Democrats thought the decision gave corporate PACs an advantage over labor PACs, and thus they saw Staebler as a probusiness commissioner.[14] Thus Congress's desire to have a partisan commission quickly became clear.

Daniel Swillinger, a former FEC assistant general counsel, thinks that the commission today is much more partisan than in its early years.[15] Among the current commissioners, Thomas Josefiak was special deputy to the secretary of the Senate before his appointment, and John Warren McGarry was special counsel on elections to the Committee on House Administration. The only criticism occasionally made of a potential commissioner's qualifications is that he or she is not partisan enough. When Frank Reiche of New Jersey was nominated in 1979, Senate Republicans were concerned that he might not pay enough heed to Republican interests.[16] Reiche believes that "Congress views the FEC as a partisan body. There is no question that [a commissioner's] votes will be scrutinized as the time for reappointment approaches."[17] Additionally, the attendance of the two ex officio members, responsible to the House and Senate leadership, ensures that congressional presence, and presumably partisanship, is never very far removed from commission deliberations.

The commission needs four votes to take any action, be it a routine administrative decision or an enforcement decision. Consequently, any decision must be either truly bipartisan, or a member of one party must be willing to side with the three members of the other. Thus more difficult questions are rarely resolved in a timely manner. In 1986, for example, the Democratic Congressional Campaign Committee filed a complaint alleging that the National Republican Congressional Committee violated the FECA by not counting a $10,000 expenditure for a mailing in Rhode Island against its limit on coordinated expenditures. Despite the recommendation of the commission's general counsel that it find "reason to believe," and despite the precedent set in an advisory

13. See chap. 5, note 4, for a description of the SunPAC decision.
14. Mutch, *Campaigns, Congress and Courts,* p. 104.
15. Interview with Daniel Swillinger, April 29, 1988. Swillinger dates the increasing partisanship to Lee Ann Elliott's appointment to the commission. Elliott was the first PAC representative to become a commissioner.
16. Common Cause, *Stalled from the Start,* p. 27.
17. Jackson, *Broken Promise,* p. 34.

opinion in 1985, the vote split 3–3. Consequently, the commissioners closed the file, without explanation of the decision.[18] More recently, the National Republican Senatorial Committee was accused of having failed to report almost $3 million in earmarked contributions to twelve Senate campaign committees. Despite its general counsel's recommendation to find the NRSC in violation of the campaign act, the commission vote again split along party lines.[19]

However, estimates are that only 10 percent of all commission decisions raise controversial, and presumably partisan, issues. One reason may be that candidates may take potentially controversial actions without seeking an advisory opinion and risk an investigation at some point in the future, most likely after the campaign is over.[20] Daniel Swillinger believes people take the attitude that "the Commission is never going to get four votes, so they can do anything they want. . . . It is undercutting what was anyway a rather weak enforcement system and making it even more toothless."[21]

The commission is further hampered because its chairman serves for only one year, and the chairmanship alternates between parties. Such a provision reduces the chairman to a figurehead whose major responsibility is to preside over meetings. The chairmen of other regulatory agencies are appointed by the president and serve at the pleasure of the president; the chairman of the FEC is selected by the commissioners themselves. The chairman has no power to appoint the staff director or give overall direction to commission actions; the appointment of the staff director is a commission decision. Yet, were the chairman to have powers comparable to those of the chairmen of other regulatory agencies, the partisan balance on the commission would be disturbed. Giving

18. After the commission's action the DCCC filed suit. The commission responded by arguing that the dismissal of the case was not justiciable because, since it did not have four affirmative votes, "Commission action [constituted] neither a 'dismissal' nor a 'failure to act'. . . but rather [amounted] to a 'no-action' middle ground." Judge Stanley Sporkin overruled it, stating that there was "absolutely no articulation of a rationale for the FEC's actions." *Democratic Congressional Campaign Committee* v. *Federal Election Commission,* U.S. District Court for the District of Columbia, Civil Action 86-2075, p. 5. The FEC appealed, and the court of appeals ordered the commissioners to provide written explanations of their vote. They did, and the case was then dismissed. Anne Bedlington, "Abuses and Loopholes in the Congressional Campaign Finance System," paper prepared for the Conference on Campaign Finance Reform and Representative Democracy, Marquette University, February 1989, note 10.

19. Congressional Quarterly, *Campaign Practices Reports,* February 20, 1989, p. 10.

20. Off-the-record interview, January 25, 1988.

21. Quoted in Brooks Jackson, "Election Commission, Set up as a Watchdog, Has Become a Pussycat," *Wall Street Journal,* October 19, 1987, p. 1.

more authority to the chairman would make sense only in conjunction with other changes in the FEC's structure.

The FEC also suffers under budget limitations far greater than those of other regulatory agencies. In 1984 the *Washington Post* described the budget as "chicken feed."[22] For fiscal year 1989 its appropriation was $16 million, compared with $43 million for the Interstate Commerce Commission, $66 million for the Federal Trade Commission, $99.6 million for the Federal Communications Commission, and $143 million for the Securities and Exchange Commission.[23]

Each of these structural limitations has repercussions for the commission's effectiveness. Without adequate funding, a chairman with more power, or the willingness to deal with controversial partisan issues, the FEC is reduced to handling little more than minor infractions of campaign finance law. In 1976, for example, the Central Long Island Tax Reform Immediately Committee (CLITRIM) raised $135 to pay for printing a pamphlet that outlined an incumbent congressman's voting record on issues of interest to the committee. The FEC ruled there was "reason to believe" that CLITRIM violated the campaign act because it had not filed a financial disclosure report. The commission then spent four years and thousands of dollars in a losing court battle against CLITRIM. In dismissing the case, U.S. Court of Appeals Chief Judge Irving Kaufman said the FEC had "failed abysmally" in carrying out "its obligation to exercise its powers in ... harmony with a system of free expression."[24] The FEC's actions in the CLITRIM case illustrate Brooks Jackson's contention that "the commission has consistently taken an unrelentingly strict line on minor violations and an astonishingly relaxed attitude about big ones."[25]

Responsibilities and Procedures

The major responsibilities of the Federal Election Commission are to disclose campaign finance reports, interpret and enforce the Federal Election Campaign Act, and implement public funding of presidential elections. Of the three, the most difficult, and the one for which the FEC has received the most criticism, is enforcement.

22. "The FEC on the Rack," *Washington Post*, May 14, 1984, p. A18.
23. *Budget of the United States Government, Fiscal Year 1990*, pp. A259, A260, A262, A263, A271.
24. Common Cause, *Stalled from the Start*, p. 47; and Congressional Quarterly, *Campaign Practices Reports*, February 11, 1985.
25. Jackson, *Broken Promise*, p. 14.

Enforcement

The commission's enforcement procedures involve a series of steps, each determined by statute. Proceedings can begin either as a result of complaints or through cases generated within the commission, and they are roughly divided between the two.[26] Most internally generated cases come from the Reports Analysis Division, from audits of campaign filings, or as a result of failures to file finance reports. The Reports Analysis Division is responsible for analyzing reports filed by candidates and multicandidate committees and for reporting irregularities to the commission's general counsel. The FECA mandates that audits be conducted of all campaigns receiving federal funds. Candidates and committees who do not file are usually minor candidates with little chance of winning an election. The commission has the power to investigate allegations raised by the media or other external entities, but it has been reluctant to do so for fear of wasting precious time and resources on charges that may have no basis.[27]

Figure 7-1 illustrates the FEC's enforcement process. When a complaint is brought to the attention of the commission, the general counsel's office first determines whether it is valid under the provisions of the FECA or commission regulations. If the counsel determines that it is valid—many are not—the complaint becomes a "matter under review." The person or entity that is the subject of the complaint then has fifteen days to respond. At the end of fifteen days the general counsel determines whether there is "reason to believe" a violation has occurred and makes a recommendation to the commission. If four commissioners vote that there is indeed reason to believe, an investigation begins. The investigation can take anywhere from several months to years, depending on the complexity of the case.

During the investigatory stage, cases can be settled by what is called "preprobable cause to believe." About half of all cases are settled at this point. If the case proceeds, the general counsel decides whether there is probable cause to believe a violation of the FECA has occurred. If such a determination is made, the general counsel prepares a brief, which is given to the respondent and the commission at the same time. Again, the person or entity charged has fifteen days to respond. Then

26. Interview with Lawrence Noble, April 20, 1988.
27. Mutch, *Campaigns, Congress and Courts,* p. 100.

FIGURE 7-1. *Federal Election Commission Enforcement Process*

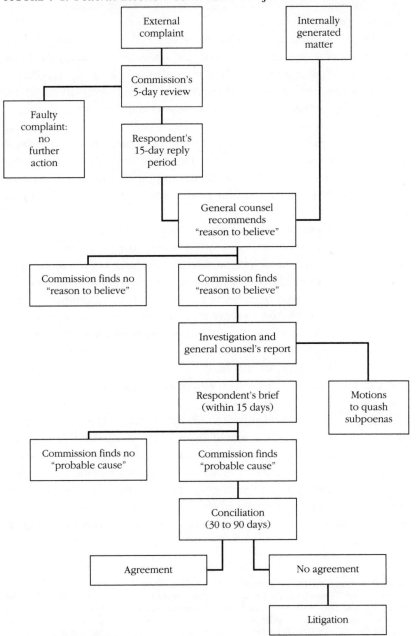

SOURCE: Adapted from Orlando B. Potter, "The Disposition of Compliance Cases and Penalties Incurred in the Enforcement of the Federal Election Campaign Act: An Analysis of Persuasion and Punitive Action," *Campaigns and Elections*, vol. 3 (Summer 1982), p. 11.

the commission must by a simple majority decide whether there is probable cause to believe.

If the commission votes for probable cause, it must by statute enter into conciliation negotiations, which last a minimum of thirty days and a maximum of ninety, though if the commission believes an agreement is near at the end of ninety days, it may extend negotiations. If no agreement is reached, the commission commences litigation proceedings.

Although investigations can drag on for months or even years, most complaints do not reach that stage. Of the 311 complaints filed in fiscal 1989, 258 were dismissed because they were improper, because the commission lacked jurisdiction, or because there was no finding of reason to believe. Of the remaining 53 cases, 35 were still pending as of April 1990.[28]

The commission is often criticized for the time it takes to resolve cases, but the general counsel's office argues that it is the statutory provisions that are most responsible for delayed enforcement. The statutory time limits effectively prohibit any complaint filed during the general election period from being resolved before the campaign ends. Respondents have 15 days to reply to a "matter under review," another 15 to reply to the general counsel's brief, and 90 days to engage in conciliation negotiations, so any respondent who wishes can delay litigation for 120 days. Moreover, if a respondent refuses to cooperate and the commission must get a subpoena, investigations are delayed even longer.

Each year in its annual report to Congress, the commission suggests changes in the statutes that would improve its functioning. Among the recommendations are that it be given the power to seek injunctions in enforcement cases to enable it to act swiftly when a violation of the law is about to occur, and that the language of the statutes be changed from "reason to believe a violation of the Act has occurred" to "reason to believe a violation of the Act may have occurred."[29] Thus far, Congress

---

28. Data provided by the Federal Election Commission.

29. In the commission's own words, "The statutory phrase 'reason to believe' is misleading and does a disservice to both the Commission and the respondent. It implies that the Commission has evaluated the evidence and concluded that the respondent has violated the Act. In fact, however, a 'reason to believe' finding simply means that the Commission believes a violation may have occurred if the facts as described in the complaint are true. . . . It would be helpful to substitute words that sound less accusatory and that more accurately reflect what, in fact, the Commission is doing at this early stage of enforcement." Federal Election Commission, *Annual Report 1986,* pp. 46–47.

has been unwilling to amend the act to reflect the suggestions. Consequently, the delay in enforcement cannot be placed entirely at the door of the commission.

Another change in the FECA that the commission has proposed for years is to eliminate state spending limits in the presidential nominating period. The limits remain, and they still seem to be regularly exceeded or circumvented by the candidates and their committees. In a *Harper's* magazine simulation of the 1988 presidential election held late in 1987, Robert Beckel, Walter Mondale's 1984 campaign manager, and Harrison Hickman, a Washington pollster, agreed that they would ignore state spending limits if necessary to win a primary for their candidates. Both believed it was worth exceeding the limits and then paying a fine months later, given the lack of timely FEC enforcement proceedings and the small amount of the fines.[30]

Their comments epitomize the commission's dilemma. Prompt enforcement and heavy fines would likely draw criticism from candidates who believed due process protections were being ignored or that the commission was being insensitive to the already strapped financial situation of many campaigns. Commission staff have also said that, in addition to the statutory restrictions on prompt enforcement, campaigns are often unwilling to cooperate with an investigation during the course of the campaign because it would mean assigning valuable campaign staff to answer the commission's inquiries.[31] The commission claims that its fines are not higher because it considers its role to be educational more than punitive. Moreover, it knows that often campaign treasurers or the candidates themselves will have to pay the fines out of their own pockets.

Thus the FEC is criticized for slow investigation and enforcement and for imposing relatively inconsequential penalties, at least for most candidates. Yet is is quite possible that swifter enforcement procedures and stiffer penalties would bring even greater criticism, and Congress has shown no interest in giving the commission such latitude. As Mark Braden, former general counsel of the Republican National Committee, has observed, "If we had an efficient commission, then we might have them having an impact on elections, which I don't think, at least from my perspective ... I would be real happy with. In some ways I sort of

30. "Manufacturing the Next President," *Harper's*, December 1987, pp. 43–54.
31. Interview with Lawrence Noble, April 20, 1988.

like the snail's pace that you have now, so that they never get anything done, so it does not affect any election."[32]

Policy Decisions

In addition to enforcing violations of the Federal Election Campaign Act, the commission is asked to interpret its statutes. Interpretation may take two forms: issuing advisory opinions and making regulations. Advisory opinions must be restricted to the specific situation presented to the commission. The scope of these opinions was restricted when Congress amended the act in 1976, largely in reaction to the SunPAC advisory opinion in 1975. The complaints about delay that plague the commission with respect to its enforcement procedures do not seem to be a problem with advisory opinions. The commission has, by statute, sixty days to issue opinions; its average time is about forty days.[33]

Broader policy pronouncements must be made by regulation. Before 1983 all regulations promulgated by the commission had to be submitted to Congress because the FECA included a one-house legislative veto provision. Despite the fact that the Supreme Court decision in *INS* v. *Chada* ruled that legislative veto provisions were unconstitutional, the commission still submits proposed regulations to Congress out of courtesy.[34]

Disclosure Activities

In addition to enforcement and policymaking, the commission is responsible for disclosing campaign finance reports and implementing public financing in presidential elections. While there is substantial criticism of the commission's enforcement activities, there is also the recognition that much more is known about campaign finance practices as a result of the FECA's disclosure provisions. To the extent that budgetary constraints allow, the commission has gone beyond the statutory requirements to make contribution and expenditure data available to the public in a useful format. However, when it was forced to cut back its activities as a result of the Gramm-Rudman-Hollings budget reductions in 1986, the disclosure activities, not its enforcement actions, suffered. In other words, the commission's most widely accepted

32. Interview with Mark Braden, November 16, 1987.
33. Interview with Lawrence Noble, April 20, 1988.
34. Interview with Lawrence Noble, April 20, 1988. For *INS* v. *Chada*, see 462 U.S. 919 (1983).

activity was reduced, while its more controversial and perhaps less effective ones were not.

The FEC has also received high marks for its implementation of public funding for presidential elections. Certifications of eligibility are made in a timely manner, and checks flow to candidates as they qualify. Thus in its work in disclosure and implementation the commission seems to be handling its responsibilities without much problem, at least to the limits of its financial abilities.

Conclusions

The dilemma the FEC and Congress currently face is how to have an enforcement agency that can enforce campaign laws without offending the members of Congress who must campaign under those laws. When asked what changes could be made to make the commission more effective, Mark Braden said, "The reason that nobody could come up with a theory on how to do it is no one is really sure that they want one that works. Because they are afraid of what would happen if it works."[35] Jan Baran, an attorney who has had extensive experience with the commission, shares Braden's view. "A lot of people ... complain that it's not a terribly efficient agency ... because it's an even-numbered commission, with three Republicans and three Democrats. I like that a whole lot better than a czar of politics—you know, some administrator, some chairman, that can actually do things—because for every good thing that that person will do, they will do a bad thing."[36]

For the FEC to become an effective and independent regulatory agency, its structure and funding would have to be changed, and it would have to be given the power to act quickly. A commission with six members equally divided between parties and appointed because of their partisanship and congressional connections can never be nonpartisan and independent unless the commissioners are distanced from Congress and expectations of partisanship cease. Similarly, a commission that must depend on annual authorization and appropriations cannot be independent. If the commission did not have to turn to Congress every twelve months to reestablish its existence and funding, it would be better able to act without partisan concerns. Finally, although protecting the rights of candidates and committees is important, so is the necessity

35. Interview with Mark Braden, November 16, 1987.
36. Interview with Jan Baran, February 17, 1987.

to move quickly to stop violations of the FECA. Changes in the statute to allow the commission to seek injunctions and increases in funding to allow it to expand the staff to process complaints quickly would improve the timeliness of its actions.

However, unless Congress is willing to extend to the FEC the financial and statutory authority necessary for it to perform its functions, the commission will continue to be little more than a necessary evil in the eye of its creator. Thus far lawmakers on both sides of the aisle seem unwilling to expand its authority. But any changes in the campaign finance system that occur without serious reconsideration of the role of the Federal Election Commission in administering and enforcing new campaign finance laws risk undermining the success of reform efforts.

Part II
Proposals for Reform

8

Changing Limitations on Contributions

The current congressional campaign finance system has created a mix of funding sources. Candidates raise money from individual donors, political action committees, and parties, and many nonincumbents contribute or loan their own money to their campaigns. The mix of sources varies for incumbents and nonincumbents, Democrats and Republicans, House and Senate candidates (see chapter 4). Incumbents, particularly House incumbents, rely on PACs for a substantial portion of their funds. Nonincumbents are much more dependent on self-financing and contributions from individuals. Democrats, because they are the majority party in both houses, receive more money from PACs than do Republicans and less from their party because the Democratic party committees have less to give. Senate candidates, because they need more campaign money than House members do, raise more money from all sources.

The enactment of contribution limits in 1974 changed the way the money is raised, introducing some serious problems. But by adjusting the current limits—raising some and lowering others—the funding methods and their consequences could be improved. This chapter examines the contribution limits now in place, their effects on campaign finance, and the reforms Congress could make. The objectives of changing contribution limits ought to be to increase competition by reducing the current advantages enjoyed by incumbents, reducing the dependence of candidates—especially incumbents—on PAC money, strengthening the role of the political parties, and decreasing the time candidates must spend fundraising.

Consequences of Current Limitations

Before the 1974 amendments to the Federal Election Campaign Act, candidates could turn to backers with deep pockets who were willing to contribute large sums. In 1968, for example, Stewart Mott contributed $18,000 ($61,000 in 1988 dollars) to Paul O'Dwyer, a Senate candidate in New York.[1] But the 1974 limits on such contributions, both to individual candidates and to candidates in the aggregate, have removed the opportunity to raise large amounts of money from the wealthy few, so candidates have had to expand their contributor base.

There have been both positive and negative consequences of the limits. By restricting the amounts that can be given to a maximum of $2,000 per election cycle, the act has removed large contributors, with expectations of influence in return for their contributions, from being powers in congressional elections. Contribution limits have had the effect of replacing large contributors with large fundraisers, people who are able to successfully raise money from several individuals. As campaign costs rise, candidates become increasingly dependent on these large fundraisers. Forcing candidates to raise money in smaller amounts from larger numbers of people makes candidates less beholden to any one contributor. In addition, a larger contributor base presumably demonstrates broader support for a candidacy. However, raising money in smaller amounts takes time away from other electoral activities and, in the case of incumbents, from legislative duties. Half of all senators surveyed by the Center for Responsive Politics and almost one-quarter of the House members said that the demands of fundraising cut *significantly* into the time they devoted to legislative work. Another 12 percent of the senators and 20 percent of the House members said fundraising had some effect on legislative time.[2]

In addition, most candidates cannot raise within their districts or states the amounts of money they need. Consequently, many find themselves appealing to outside individuals and PACs. As Linda Fowler and Robert McClure conclude:

The need for money and organizational help from political groups outside the district is increasingly significant in modern congressional

---

1. Herbert E. Alexander, *Financing the 1968 Election* (Lexington, Mass.: D.C. Heath, 1971), p. 255.
2. Center for Responsive Politics, *Congressional Operations: Congress Speaks—A Survey of the 100th Congress* (Washington, 1988), p. 91.

elections. Politicians ... who have not established the necessary relationship with the "Washington crowd" or who lack a local or state mentor influential with national power brokers soon find themselves stymied in their quest for a seat in Congress.[3]

But Washington is not the only place candidates go to raise money outside their districts or states. Democratic Congressman Stephen Solarz of New York, for example, raises most of his money from Asian-American communities in Chicago, Los Angeles, New Orleans, San Francisco, and Detroit.[4] And in 1988 Senator Quentin Burdick of North Dakota raised 99 percent of his contributions of more than $500 from out of state. Between 1980 and 1988 eight Senate candidates raised more than 90 percent of their large contributions from out of state.[5] These members thus have two constituencies, their electoral one and their financial one. This nationalization of campaign finance raises an important question of representation. To what extent are members of Congress beholden to their financial constituency at the expense of their electoral constituency?

Because it is also more time consuming to raise such large sums in small increments, candidates have turned to PACs, which can contribute larger amounts than any individual can, thus making PAC funds comparatively inexpensive to raise. But contributions from PACs entail their own problems. Because these organizations give disproportionately to incumbents, other candidates, particularly challengers, find it difficult to raise the money necessary to run competitive campaigns. Furthermore, when confronted with limits on what they can give to any one candidate, PACs have in some cases bundled individual contributions, a tactic that may be illegal. Bundling is what ALIGNPAC, a political action committee of independent insurance agents, did when it gave Senator Robert Packwood more than $250,000 in individual contributions in 1986.[6] Another option open to PACs is to spend independently (see chapter 5). The potential of unlimited independent expenditures made by

3. Linda L. Fowler and Robert D. McClure, *Political Ambition: Who Decides to Run for Congress* (Yale University Press, 1989), p. 37.

4. Chuck Alston, "Solarz Looks Abroad to Find Election Cash at Home," *Congressional Quarterly Weekly Report,* March 11, 1989, pp. 501–04.

5. David B. Magleby, "More Bang for the Buck: Campaign Spending in Small-State U.S. Senate Elections," paper prepared for the 1989 annual meeting of the Western Political Science Association.

6. Brooks Jackson, *Honest Graft: Big Money and the American Political Process* (Knopf, 1988), p. 131.

individuals and groups on behalf of opponents has further spurred candidates to raise large war chests to fend off attack.

Current contribution limits do not apply to personal funds candidates can spend on their own campaigns; thus wealthy candidates have inherent advantages. The capacity to commit millions of dollars of personal funds to a Senate race or hundreds of thousands to a House race is substantial: a John Heinz or a Jay Rockefeller can match in one moment what may have taken his opponent years to raise. Spending personal wealth does not guarantee electoral victory, as candidates such as Mark Dayton have discovered, but it gives wealthy candidates a distinct head start.

Finally, limits on party contributions restrict the importance and value of parties in congressional elections. Because the elections are candidate-centered, the parties' primary function is financial, either through direct or in-kind contributions. But party contributions can account for only a small part of what a campaign needs, and candidates must make up whatever shortfall there is by turning to individuals and, for those who are able, to PACs.

Because of these limitations, current campaign laws need to be changed. One way to increase competition in congressional elections and reduce candidates' dependency on political action committees would be to increase the amount individual donors can contribute and lower the amount PACs can contribute. Raising the aggregate annual limit on individual contributions would also reduce the competition between parties and candidates for funds. Strengthening the function of parties in congressional elections could also be accomplished by increasing the limit on what they can give and, depending on what changes were made in PAC limits, would perhaps make PACs less important. Allowing parties to contribute more would also increase competition, since they are much more likely than PACs to contribute to challengers.

New Rules for Individual Contributions

The largest proportion of funds for congressional candidates, except for House Democratic incumbents, comes from individual donors. While individuals and PACs both give disproportionately to incumbents, individuals are more likely to support nonincumbents for House and Senate seats. In both the 1986 and 1988 election cycles the proportion of individual contributions received by House challengers was twice that received from PACs, and in 1984 one-quarter of challengers' contributions came from individuals, compared with only 15 percent from PACs. In all three years, individual donors also contributed a larger proportion of funds to candidates for open seats than did PACs. Similarly, in the Senate a larger proportion of individual contributions went to nonincumbents. Thus for nonincumbents, individual donors are a more likely source of campaign funds than PACS are. Raising individual contribution limits would allow more money from them to flow into the political system, thus helping nonincumbents raise much-needed campaign dollars. And being able to raise more from individuals would perhaps lower the amount candidates would raise from PACs.[7]

Raising the ceilings on individual contributions or at least permitting them to rise with inflation is the reform discussed most frequently in Congress. As part of S.7, the campaign finance reform bill introduced at the start of the 101st Congress, Senators Dole, McConnell, and other Republicans included a provision to increase the limit on individual contributions from $1,000 to $2,000 per election ($4,000 per election cycle). Had the limits been allowed to rise with inflation, in 1988 they would have been $2,400 per candidate per election ($4,800 per election cycle).[8] In addition to encouraging candidates to concentrate more of their fundraising efforts on individual donors, thus perhaps reducing their dependence on special-interest money, the higher limits would enable challengers to raise money in larger amounts, increasing competition in congressional elections.[9]

Raising the limit on contributions by any one donor to any one candidate is not the only adjustment that could be made for individual contributions. The aggregate annual contribution limit of $25,000 could also be increased. To increase the contribution limit for giving to one candidate without increasing the aggregate limit would mean that those who wished to contribute the maximum could contribute more money but to fewer candidates. Raising both limits at the same time would

7. Although many advocates of further restrictions on PACs assume that more stringent contribution limits will reduce candidates' dependence on special interests, it is equally possible that such limits could drive special-interest contributions underground, that is, organizations would do more bundling of individual contributions.

8. Similarly, limits on individual contributions to national party committees would have been $48,000 in 1988, and on individual contributions to any other committee, $12,000. For PACs, inflation-adjusted limits on contributions to candidates and other committees would have been $12,000 each in 1988, and on contributions to the national party committees, $36,000.

9. It is also possible that increasing the contribution limits for individuals will only increase overall expenditure levels, because PACs will continue to give at present and increasing rates and there will be more money in the pool from individuals. This is one example of the consequence of incremental, rather than comprehensive, change in campaign finance laws.

enable individual donors to give the maximum to as many candidates as under current law, but at a higher level.

Because challengers rarely can raise much money from PACs (see chapters 4 and 5), they must rely on individual contributions to fund most of their campaign costs. But raising the $200,000 or so to begin to mount a credible campaign means that hundreds of individuals must be willing to invest in what is widely perceived as a very long shot. One way to permit challengers to obtain this early seed money would be to create a higher personal contribution limit for individual contributions to candidates' early campaign accounts, which could be capped at $200,000 or $250,000. Raising the individual contribution limit for this purpose from $2,000 to $10,000 would mean challengers could attempt to raise the start-up money for their campaign from a group of twenty to twenty-five individuals. Once a candidate reached the ceiling in start-up money, he or she would revert to the current or existing limits on individual contributions. To ease administration, this plan might be limited to the first eighteen months of the campaign cycle for the House and the first five and one-half years of a senator's term. It would follow that if individual contributions to candidates were raised for this campaign start-up purpose, total individual contribution limits would be adjusted as well.

Individual contributors' early seed money would be used by incumbents first and perhaps most. But, as we have demonstrated, the competition problem results more from underspending by challengers than from overspending by incumbents. Incumbents under current law have little difficulty hitting the first $200,000 in contributions from individuals, PACs, and parties. That is not the case for challengers.

Another change would be to exempt the limits on contributions to parties from a donor's aggregate annual limit; that is, the aggregate limit would apply only to individual and PAC contributions made directly to candidates. While there is no way to calculate how many donors actually give the limit now allowed, those who wish to contribute the maximum must divide their contributions between individuals, the party committees, and, for some, PACs.[10] This system means that the parties and candidates must compete for many of the same donors. Allowing

10. Candidates and party committees must identify contributors who make contributions of $100 or more, but individuals may identify themselves using slightly different versions of a name—for example, John Smith and Jack Smith. Consequently, it is impossible for even the Federal Election Commission to identify individual donors who give the maximum allowed in a calendar year.

individual donors to give, say, $20,000 to the national parties, in addition to $25,000 or $50,000 or whatever is the individual aggregate annual limit on contributions to candidates and PACs, would also potentially strengthen the political parties by helping them raise more money.

As with most reforms, there are partisan differences over the benefits of increasing the amounts individuals can give. Such proposals face opposition from Democrats, who think Republicans would benefit more. They believe that most of their backers could not contribute more than the present limit, so there would be no advantage in raising it. In fact, Democrats feel they would be handicapped because Republicans would be better able to raise money from their partisan supporters. Republicans suspect that the Democrats are right: they *would* be able to raise more money. For Republican candidates this would be a much appreciated advantage because they believe they need to spend more to run competitive races, and those who are challengers for House seats, at least, get very little money from PACs. For Republicans, higher individual contribution limits, in conjunction with their wealthier and better-defined contributor base, would increase their competitiveness.

New Rules for PAC Contributions

As pressure for reform mounts, the first reform to come to some members' minds will deal with PACs.[11] Contributions from political action committees can be limited in at least three ways: the amount a PAC can give to any one candidate; the aggregate amount any one candidate can receive from PACs; and the aggregate amount any one PAC can give to candidates. The first of these is the focus of the present law.

In the 1987–88 Senate debate on congressional campaign finance, several attempts were made to reduce from $10,000 to $6,000 or $5,000 the maximum amount any PAC could contribute to a candidate in an election cycle. In the McConnell-Packwood bill the limit was $5,000, and in the original version of the Boren-Byrd bill it was $6,000. As part of S. 7, Senator Dole and his cosponsors proposed reducing the amount to $2,000 in any one election cycle. Depending on where the limit is set, reducing the amount a PAC can give might appear to reduce the

11. Michelle Gardner, "Interpretations of the Senate Election Campaign Act of 1987: Editorial Opinion and the Cobb/Elder Agenda-Setting Model," honors thesis, Brigham Young University, March 1988.

influence of special interests without really changing things very much, because most PACs do not give the maximum allowed (see chapter 5). A limit of $5,000 or $6,000 in an election cycle would change present giving patterns very little. In contrast, Senator Dole's proposal would reduce PAC contributions to most types of candidates. Understandably, opposition to lowering the limits comes from those political action committees that now routinely make maximum donations—disproportionately labor and large corporate PACs.

A far more consequential reform would be an aggregate limit on what any one candidate could receive from PACs. An aggregate limit on contributions to House candidates passed the House in 1979, and one on contributions to both House and Senate candidates passed the Senate in 1985.[12] Such a limit would reduce the opportunities for PACs to contribute to candidates of their choice and would likely lead those who wished to contribute to particular candidates to do so early in the election cycle to ensure the contribution was received before the candidates reached their aggregate.[13] Another potential consequence would be increased independent expenditures by PACs who wanted to influence a race but could not because the candidate had reached the aggregate limit.

Less frequently considered is an aggregate annual or cycle limit on the amount any one PAC could contribute, similar to the aggregate limit on individual contributions. The motivation for such a rule would be to limit the role of large or dominant PACs. In fact an aggregate limit exists today; it is the total number of major-party general election candidates multiplied by the $10,000 PAC cycle limit. For 1988 a PAC would have contributed $8,790,000 if it had given the maximum allowed to all general election candidates.

Still another reform would be to restrict the activity of PACs of foreign-held corporations or interests. Senator Lloyd Bentsen of Texas

---

12. The Obey-Railsback amendment prohibited House candidates from accepting more than $70,000 from PACs in any two-year election cycle. See *Congressional Quarterly Almanac, 1979*, vol. 35 (1980), p. 556. The Boren-Goldwater amendment limited the total amount House candidates could take from PACs to $100,000 and limited Senate candidates to between $175,000 and $750,000, depending on the size of the state. For a discussion of the consideration of the amendment, see Jackson, *Honest Graft*, pp. 236–61.

13. There is no way to know what kinds of PACs would be most likely to act this way. While larger ones with greater cash resources might be best able to contribute money early in the cycle, it is also possible that a small PAC, but one with a strong interest in supporting a particular candidate, would want to be certain that its contributions were received before a candidate reached his or her PAC limit.

proposed this idea in the 100th Congress, as he had several years before. The problem, according to Bentsen and others, was the potential involvement of foreign interests or governments in the American electoral process. A *National Journal* survey in 1986 found there were ninety-two PACs sponsored by corporations in which a foreign investor held 10 percent or more of the stock.[14] While very few have played a significant role in campaign finance, concern about any foreign involvement in U.S. elections remains.

One problem with restricting foreign corporate PACs is defining them. How much foreign ownership is necessary to remove a PAC from participation—20 percent, 30 percent, more? What about Washington law firms that have several foreign clients and also a PAC for the firm? Is it the cumulative total of foreign clients that would make a firm's PAC illegal, or are law and public relations firms to be excluded? Then there is the issue of First Amendment rights. Is it constitutional to restrict the American employees of a foreign-held corporation from expressing their collective views when Americans working for American-owned firms have no such restriction? Because PACs are presumably the expression of corporate employees rather than the corporation itself, how can American citizens, regardless of their employer, be excluded from participation?

Finally, there has been some interest in banning PACs altogether: in June 1989 President Bush proposed eliminating corporate, labor, and trade association PACs.[15] However, such proposals probably would not pass constitutional review. As long as PACs are voluntary associations, they presumably are protected under the First Amendment.

Discussions of further restrictions on PAC contributions, either in the aggregate or for an individual candidate, inevitably lead to speculation as to where the money they now give directly to candidates would go. Some observers think that organizations would encourage their members or senior management to contribute money directly to candidates, much as corporations did before 1972.[16] As one business PAC director told

14. Maxwell Glen, "The Foreign Connection," *National Journal,* July 26, 1986, pp. 1832–38. The survey found that through the first eighteen months of the 1985–86 election cycle only eighteen of the ninety-two PACs contributed $25,000 or more to federal candidates, and thirty-five contributed no more than $1,000 during the period.

15. Chuck Alston and Glen Craney, "Bush Campaign-Reform Plan Takes Aim at Incumbents," *Congressional Quarterly Weekly Report,* July 1, 1989, p. 1648.

16. Edwin M. Epstein, "Business and Labor under the Federal Election Campaign Act of 1971," in Michael J. Malbin, ed., *Parties, Interest Groups and Campaign Finance Laws* (Washington: American Enterprise Institute for Public Policy Research, 1980), p. 111.

the Center for Responsive Politics, "If PACs were put out of business, we would give ... it through personal contributions, or if a state took corporate contributions we would give it that way. We have a network, we have people all over the country." Contributions made by individual donors on behalf of particular special interests would be difficult to identify as special interest money. Another PAC director warned, "I think [a thousand-dollar contribution to a candidate from an individual] is more corrupting than a PAC contribution. If you take money from us, you know where we are ... and you know what we stand for, but you don't know what that other guy supports."[17] Consequently, it is possible that less would be known about the interests of those who give money in congressional elections than is known today.

Additional limitations on organization contributions could also lead PACs to increase their use of independent expenditures. Because independent expenditures are constitutionally protected from limitation under the Supreme Court's decision in *Buckley* v. *Valeo,* they provide an option for special interest campaign spending under any campaign finance reform scheme.[18] Lowering the limit that a PAC could contribute to a given candidate might mean that it would choose independent expenditures. The same result could occur if a PAC were unable to contribute to candidates it supported because the candidates had reached the aggregate limit they could accept. During the debate on S. 2 in 1987, the director of a PAC that used independent expenditures found increased interest in them from other PACs: "It has been rather striking, the number of groups that have asked our people to come and talk to them about the process of independent expenditures. ... I do know that what it says is that they're now starting to look at it."[19]

Still, most PACs do not use independent expenditures, and how much that would change under campaign finance reform is not clear. Although a spokesperson for the National Association of Realtors said, "Independent expenditures are an attractive alternative [to direct contributions] for PACs that can afford to engage in the legally complicated and politically sensitive activity," few have either the sophistication or the resources

17. Center for Responsive Politics, *PACs on PACs: The View from the Inside* (Washington, 1988), p. 55.

18. The Court subsequently drew a distinction between independent expenditures made by PACs and those made from corporate funds. The former are permissible, but the latter may be legally limited or banned. *Austin* v. *Michigan State Chamber of Commerce,* 110 S. Ct. 21 (1990).

19. Center for Responsive Politics, *PACs on PACs,* p. 57.

to conduct such activity.[20] However, it is possible that a consortium of smaller PACs could work together. If severe limits were imposed, such as those in the 1987 Dole bill, they might consider pooling resources in selected races and conducting parallel but independent campaigns.

If direct contributions to candidates were curtailed, the largest PACs would be the ones most likely to increase independent expenditures. For example, in 1986 the Auto Dealers and Drivers for Free Trade made $1.3 million in direct contributions to candidates but still found itself with $1.6 million in additional funds. Of the $1.6 million, $1.2 million was used for independent expenditures.[21] Other large PACs might behave similarly if campaign finance reforms restricted direct contributions.

Although increases in individual contributions from people associated with special interests and increases in independent expenditures are two possible consequences of further restrictions on PAC contributions, they are not the only ones. As one PAC director said, "One of the quickest ways to find out more creative ways to spend political money would be to put PACs out of business. I guarantee it. And the alternatives are independent expenditures, 501(c)3 foundations, issue advocacy operations, which are generally ways of supporting not only causes but individuals. I do think the demands by politicians on business will continue, and business will then be forced to find some other way to respond. And so we'll probably go back to some sort of bundling system."[22] The problem reformers face is how to anticipate the consequences of further restrictions. We will return to this problem in chapter 11.

One other place PAC money could go under a system of tighter limits would be to the parties. As noted in chapter 5, party committees already count on PACs for some money and, in the case of the DCCC and DSCC, over 20 percent of receipts. Moreover, candidates, especially incumbents, would lead the parade to raise PAC money through the parties once they reach their PAC limits. How responsive PACs would be to this enlarged channel of fundraising is uncertain, but if it were driven by candidates important to PACs, as it almost certainly would be, then more PAC money would be likely to flow in this direction. The negative consequence of such a redirection of PAC money from candidates to

20. Edward Zuckerman, *PACs and Lobbies* (newsletter), Washington, January 7, 1987, p. 7.
21. Zuckerman, *PACs and Lobbies*, p. 8.
22. Center for Responsive Politics, *PACS on PACs*, p. 57.

parties is that the ability to trace the flow of PAC money would be lost, but the influence that comes with the contributions would remain. The positive result of such a change would be more money going to nonincumbents. Even if the party limits were raised, those most able to help the party raise PAC money would soon contribute the maximum allowed, and any PAC money they helped raise could be distributed among other candidates. Because parties have been much more likely than PACs to give to nonincumbents, this would likely facilitate greater competition.

New Rules for Party Contributions

Although parties contribute less than individual donors or PACs to most campaigns, they too are frequently the subject of proposed reforms.[23] The one most often mentioned is to increase the amounts they can contribute directly or through coordinated expenditures or both. Raising these limits would have a number of advantages. It could decrease candidates' dependence on PACs, and because parties are more likely than PACs to contribute money to challengers, it could increase competition. Higher limits could also make parties more important forces in congressional elections and thus make candidates more responsive to partisan interests and less responsive to special interests. Finally, because party money does not have to be raised by candidates, larger party contributions would decrease the time spent fundraising.

However, raising party contribution limits has serious partisan implications. The Republican party has more money than the Democratic party to spend in congressional races. In the 1987–88 election cycle, for example, the Republicans raised $263 million, the Democrats about $128 million.[24] Although the gap has been closing, Republicans are still in a much better position to contribute more money than allowed under current law. Democrats have been able to raise and spend what they have needed to compete successfully in targeted Senate races, but Republicans have generally been able to contribute more and have been

23. See for example, Jackson, *Honest Graft*, pp. 301–04; and Michael J. Malbin, "Looking Back at the Future of Campaign Finance Reform: Interest Groups and American Elections," in Malbin, ed., *Money and Politics in the United States* (Washington: American Enterprise Institute for Public Policy Research, 1984).

24. "GOP Spent Twice as Much as Democrats in 1987–88," *Washington Post*, March 27, 1989, p. A4.

close to the maximum coordinated expenditure limits in Senate races.[25] Both parties think that increased contribution limits would disproportionately benefit Republicans—thus the reason for Republican support for such a proposal and Democratic opposition to it.[26]

Finally, a further problem is that congressional campaigns are largely candidate-centered, which is what candidates prefer. Although they would probably welcome more money from their party committees, candidates would resist any party efforts to exert more direction and control over campaigns.

Conclusions

Limits on what individual donors and groups can give campaigns are designed to restrict the influence of any one person or interest. The existing rules have encouraged candidates to reach out to more and more individual donors and groups to fund their campaigns. However, the levels at which contributions are set have other important consequences for campaigns and for fundraising. Lower limits for individual giving than for PAC contributions make PACs more attractive as funding sources because of the opportunity to raise money in larger blocs. The current mix of funding sources encourages a greater role for special interests vis-à-vis individuals and parties. Raising individual and party contribution limits and lowering PAC limits would change the mix and make individual donors and parties more important forces in congressional campaign funding.

25. The Republicans have seriously considered challenging the constitutionality of limits on coordinated party activity, and in any system that limits more severely what candidates and parties spend, they are almost certain to do so. The basis on which the Republicans would challenge the coordinated expenditure limits is that other expenditures, such as candidates' expenditures and independent expenditures, are not limited. Most party money now spent on congressional campaigns is in the form of coordinated expenditures. If there were no limits on these expenditures, the Republican advantage in total party receipts would be readily transferred to candidates.

26. S. 7, introduced by Senators Dole, McConnell, and others in the 101st Congress, would change the figures on which coordinated expenditures are based from two cents multiplied by the voting age population of a state to five cents for Senate candidates and at-large House candidates and from $10,000 to $25,000 for House candidates; *Congressional Record,* daily ed., January 25, 1989, p. S212. S. 137, introduced by Senators Boren, Mitchell, and others at the start of the 101st Congress, makes no change in party contribution limits (pp. S466–S474).

9

Public Financing and Spending Limitations

There are many ways to remedy the problems of rising campaign costs and uneven spending by candidates, but the two crucial components are public financing and limitations on spending. The issues are often discussed together. One reason is the policy prescription required by the Supreme Court in *Buckley* v. *Valeo*—that limitations on spending are unconstitutional unless they are part of a system of voluntary public financing. A second reason is that limitations without public financing almost certainly will not help challengers or foster competition, especially if ceilings are set too low.[1] Similarly, public financing without spending limits, although more likely to foster competition, will not reduce the costs of campaigns. Indeed, costs would probably increase.

Spending limitations combined with public financing can improve competition and reduce candidates' dependence on interested money as well as moderate the general preoccupation with money that now characterizes congressional campaigns. Reforms or new rules could, however, make things worse. If spending ceilings were set too low, they would reduce competition. And public financing could encourage frivolous or artificial challenges.

Whatever changes are proposed, public financing and limitations on spending will continue to be contentious subjects because of political calculations made by both parties, differing partisan philosophies on the appropriate role of government in regulating political matters, and the costs associated with these reforms.

---

1. Gary Jacobson, *The Politics of Congressional Elections,* 2d ed. (Little Brown, 1987).

Public Financing

One of the most contentious issues in discussions of campaign finance reform is how to create a system that is fair to all candidates—the so-called level playing field. Public financing is one answer. Those who support public financing argue that it would allow candidates to have enough money to wage a competitive race and would reduce the burden of raising money, a task that is typically most difficult for challengers but that also has important consequences for incumbents. Opponents of public financing argue that it is not the responsibility of government to pay for congressional campaigns nor is public financing something the government can afford in an era of triple-digit budget deficits.

Public opinion is mixed and seems to depend on how the question is phrased. At frequent intervals since June 1973, a Gallup poll has asked, "It has been suggested that the federal government provide a fixed amount of money for the election campaigns of candidates for Congress and that all private contributions from other sources be prohibited. Do you think this is a good idea or a poor idea?" The proportion of Americans favoring public financing has varied from 67 percent in 1974 to 46 percent in December 1982. With the exception of the latter survey, there have always been more who favored the idea than opposed it. When those with no opinion are removed, support has been as high as 74 percent.[2] Support for public financing of congressional elections peaked in 1973–74.[3] Support does not, however, carry over to earmarking tax dollars through a voluntary tax checkoff on the federal income tax

2. Longitudinal surveys conducted for the American Medical Association between 1977 and 1985 found that between 64 percent and 68 percent of those surveyed opposed public funding of congressional campaigns. The AMA surveys asked the question as follows: "It has been proposed in Congress that the federal government provide public financing for congressional campaigns for the U.S. House of Representatives and Senate. Would you approve or disapprove of the proposal to use public funds, federal money, to pay the costs of congressional campaigns and how strongly do you feel?" Civic Service, "Attitudes toward Campaign Financing" (St. Louis, Mo., February 1, 1985), pp. 2–3.

3. A poll conducted by Greenberg-Lake illustrates public ambivalence toward public financing of congressional campaigns. When the question was phrased similarly to the Gallup poll's query, 58 percent of those surveyed thought public financing was a good idea. However, when the question was asked with the following qualifier, "Now, some people say, if campaigns are publicly funded, taxpayers will end up paying for all the negative campaigning and mudslinging on T.V. today," only 29 percent favored public financing of campaigns. Given this lack of strong opinion, public funding is not likely to be enacted in response to public demand. However, this same difference means that if public funding does come to pass, members of Congress are unlikely to face disapproval from their constituents. *Money and Politics: A Survey of National Opinion* (Washington: Greenberg-Lake, March 1990), pp. 3, 9.

form. Participation in this system for funding presidential campaigns has been declining in recent years and reached a low of 21 percent in 1987.

Under the present campaign finance system, direct public funding occurs only in presidential election campaigns and combines matching funds, used in the primary campaigns, and direct public grants, used in the general elections.[4] Under the system of matching funds, money raised by candidates is matched by the federal government up to a certain amount. The qualifying mechanism requires candidates to demonstrate support for their candidacy by raising $5,000 in each of twenty states from individual contributors in amounts of $250 or less. Once candidates qualify, contributions of $250 or less from individual donors are matched by federal funds. Because public funds are tied to spending limits, the amount of money candidates can spend in the prenomination period is limited, and consequently the amount of matching funds is also limited: in 1988, candidates for president could spend no more than $27,600,000 to seek the nomination. In addition, there were individual state spending limits, ranging from a low of $461,000 in states with voting age populations of 1.2 million or fewer to $7,509,505 in California, the most populous state.[5] In the general election the major-party candidates receive a set amount of money from the federal treasury on the condition that they accept no private contributions. In 1988 Governor Michael Dukakis and Vice President George Bush each received $46,100,000.

Until the 1988 election cycle, public funding was successful in controlling the costs of presidential elections.[6] Spending in the 1972 general elections was $91.4 million, more than double the $37 million spent in 1968; in 1976, the first election with public financing, spending

4. Public funding of presidential elections, provided for by the 1971 Federal Election Campaign Act, was first introduced in the 1976 presidential election. Since then all candidates, except John Connally in 1980, have received public funds. Connally's decision to refuse such funding was not to his advantage; he spent $14 million and won only one delegate to the Republican convention. Stephen J. Wayne, *The Road to the White House: The Politics of Presidential Elections,* 2d ed. (St. Martin's Press, 1984), p. 33.

5. There is general agreement that the state spending limits should be removed. The limits were instituted to prevent presidential candidates with vast financial resources from coming into a state with an early primary or caucus and overwhelming opponents by spending heavily. However, as the 1988 election showed, state spending limits are honored more in the breach than in the observance. In the days just before the Iowa caucuses and New Hampshire primary, there were numerous press accounts of ways candidates sought to evade the limits.

6. The number of major-party candidates—fourteen—coupled with the amount of soft money raised and spent by both national party committees, accounts for the increase in presidential spending in 1988.

in the general election was only $43.6 million.[7] However, it is one thing to have a publicly financed system with, at most, a dozen or so presidential candidates and quite another to consider one that supports campaigns for the 435 House seats and 33 or 34 Senate seats that are up every election.

Public financing of House and Senate elections, both primary and general, was proposed in the consideration of the 1976 amendments to the Federal Election Campaign Act. But since then Congress has shown little support even for partial public financing of congressional primary elections and substantial opposition to such financing of general elections. It is possible to provide public funds in only the general election but limit spending in both the primary and general elections.[8] A condition of accepting public funds could be accepting cycle (primary and general) limits. If this is not done, a predictable front-loading of spending in primaries would occur, especially in the states with late primaries.

However, even if public funding is discussed only for general elections, there is no agreement on the form it should take. Both matching funds and a grant system have been proposed, and each has advantages and disadvantages. However, before these alternatives are discussed, qualifying mechanisms must be considered.

Qualifying Mechanisms

Either a direct grant or a matching system would require that candidates first qualify for public funds. The qualifying mechanism is essentially a means of screening out fringe candidates with little public support. Most proponents of public financing favor a qualifying system that requires candidates to raise a certain amount of money in small contributions, generally less than $250, from individual donors, just as in the presidential system. One proposal introduced in the 100th Congress set a qualifying mechanism for Senate candidates of ten cents times the voting age population of their states, but no less than $150,000 and no more than $650,000, in contributions of $250 or less, with 80 percent from within the candidate's state. Legislation introduced by former Representative Tony Coelho, also in the 100th Congress, set a qualifying

7. Herbert Alexander, *Financing Politics: Money, Elections and Political Reform,* 3d ed. (Washington: Congressional Quarterly Press, 1984), p. 7.
8. Because such a system has not been tried, it is likely that spending limits without public funding in the primary election would lead to a constitutional challenge.

mechanism for public financing of House elections at 10 percent of the spending limit, in amounts of $250 or less, with 80 percent of the contributions coming from within the candidate's state. Ten percent of the spending limit may be too low a threshold, allowing almost anyone to qualify for public funds. However, the threshold needs to be set low enough to enable a serious but relatively unknown major-party candidate to qualify for public funds and high enough to discourage artificial competition from candidates who are not serious.

Such mechanisms assume that a certain amount of money raised in small contributions demonstrates broad-based support for a candidate. Requiring that 80 percent of the qualification funds be raised within a candidate's state or district ensures that the candidate demonstrates support among those who have the opportunity to vote for him or her and who would be the constituents.

A second qualifying mechanism, which has not generated much political support, is to assume candidates qualify for public funds once they receive the nomination of one of the two major parties. This is the system used in presidential general elections. The lack of support for it in congressional elections seems to come from a resistance to hand over federal dollars to candidates without first ensuring that they can attract either campaign contributions or votes.

Unlike presidential contenders, congressional candidates do not have to run in numerous caucuses and primaries to get their party's nomination. Indeed, in safe congressional districts the party that does not hold the seat often runs only token candidates. Dan Rostenkowski, the powerful chairman of the House Ways and Means Committee, for example, has served in Congress thirty years and routinely wins reelection with more than 70 percent of the vote. Nevertheless, the Republican party continues to field candidates against him. If a major-party nomination qualified a congressional candidate for substantial public funds, the dynamics of congressional campaigns likely would change. Perfunctory party candidates would disappear because both parties, knowing they would have public funds to support their candidates, would recruit more competitive challengers and candidates for open seats.

Allowing automatic qualification for major-party nominees raises the question of how to handle third-party and independent candidates. There would have to be some qualifying mechanism beyond getting on the ballot. The most logical system would provide funds to a candidate whose party had received a certain percentage of the vote in one or more previous elections or would provide funds retroactively if a candidate received a certain percentage of the vote in the general election. The latter was the system used in the presidential election in 1980, when Representative John Anderson ran as an independent candidate. The FEC ruled that if he received 5 percent or more of the general election vote he would be eligible for retroactive public funds. He got 6.6 percent and received $4.16 million.[9] Because of his showing in 1980, had Anderson chosen to run again in 1984, he would have been eligible for a grant of $5.7 million at the start of the general election period.[10] Qualification procedures for third parties in publicly financed congressional elections could work in much the same way.

Grants or Matching Funds?

Once a qualifying mechanism is established, the form public financing should take has to be decided. Two systems are usually proposed: an outright grant or matching funds. With an outright grant, once candidates qualify they receive a check from the federal treasury. The grant could be made in one lump sum or in a series of payments. While a grant system is usually tied to spending limits, it does not have to be. Public funds could provide a floor, a base of funds for a candidate to use to get a campaign started. Although incumbents have no problem raising seed money, challengers and candidates for open seats often do. Direct grants without spending limits would thus probably increase competition, which is of course one goal of reform, but they would not necessarily restrain the costs of congressional elections. Candidates would still tend to spend as much as they could raise.

An outright grant system in combination with spending limits has several advantages. If the grant were for the entire spending limit, as in the current presidential general election system, candidates would no longer have to spend more than 50 percent of their time raising funds. Even if the grant covered only part of the spending limit, fundraising time would still be cut significantly. An outright grant would also be much easier to administer. The FEC would be responsible for authorizing payments by the federal treasury, and given 800 or more congressional candidates in each general election, making one or two payments to each candidate would be much simpler than authorizing multiple payments.

---

9. Herbert Alexander, *Financing the 1980 Election* (Lexington, Mass.: D.C. Heath, 1983), p. 110.

10. Data provided by the Federal Election Commission.

The arguments against outright grants and in favor of matching funds are that grants do not require candidates to continue to demonstrate support throughout the general election period, that such a system locks out private contributors (particularly individuals) who want to participate in the electoral process by making campaign contributions, and that grants could be more expensive than a matching system. A matching system similar to that currently used in presidential primaries would encourage candidates who receive federal funds to continue to find support among a broad base of small contributors. It would also allow individual donors and, if the law was so written, PACs to continue to participate in the campaign finance process.

However, a matching system poses administrative problems. The FEC would need far more personnel to authenticate and process requests for matching funds. And for such a system to be feasible, candidates would have to be assured of receiving funds quickly, especially in the closing weeks of a closely contested campaign. A matching system would also require candidates to continue fundraising, to the detriment of other campaign activities, although the amount of time spent fundraising probably would not increase.

One likely consequence of a matching system would be greater reliance on direct mail fundraising. Direct mail is an efficient way to reach individuals who contribute small amounts of money. To try to raise small contributions in person, despite the desirability of such face-to-face contact between candidates and constituents, would be too time-consuming. If a matching system required contributions from citizens within a candidate's state or congressional district, direct mail would be even more attractive because it could be easily targeted. In addition, in a matching system, direct mail appeals do not have to be self-sustaining to be profitable. In the presidential system, as Gregg Easterbrook points out, "A direct mailer may spend $1.99 to reel in $1, and come out ahead when the matching federal dollar is added."[11]

Cost of Public Financing

There is substantial opposition, primarily from Republicans but also from conservative Democrats, to public financing of congressional campaigns. Part of the opposition rests on ideological grounds, part on dislike of spending federal money to finance campaigns, especially when there is such a large federal budget deficit. Public funding in presidential

---

11. Gregg Easterbrook, "Junk-Mail Politics," *New Republic,* April 25, 1988, p. 21.

campaigns is financed by the $1 tax checkoff on income tax returns ($2 if a joint return). Since 1976 about one-quarter of all tax returns have designated a checkoff. In the past ten years, an average of $36 million a year has been generated.[12] Thus far the amount of money designated by the tax checkoff has been more than enough for the presidential campaigns.[13] The size of the tax checkoff would almost certainly have to be increased if congressional campaigns were added. The amount would depend on whether a grant or a matching system were used and on the total funds allocable to candidates. Since every public financing proposal introduced in recent years has tied public financing to a spending limit, the amount of the limit and the proportion provided in public funds would determine the costs.

Four bills introduced in the 100th Congress provide examples of what the federal payments might be. H.R. 295, introduced by Tony Bielenson, would have provided full public financing in House races, with a spending ceiling of $200,000. H.R. 573, introduced by Mel Levine, and H.R. 2717, introduced by Tony Coelho, would have provided for partial public financing of House campaigns. In both bills, contributions of $100 or less would be matched by federal funds, up to 50 percent of the spending limit. However, Levine's bill set a spending limit of $200,000, Coelho's a limit of $400,000. In the Senate, S. 2, as reported by the Rules Committee, provided for almost full public funding of Senate campaigns; public funds would make up the difference between the qualifying threshold and the spending limits.

The Bielenson or Coelho bills, in combination with S. 2, would have meant a federal payout for House and Senate races of $259 million in 1988. A combination of the Levine bill and S. 2 would have meant a payout of $172 million. However, these estimates are only approximate because all four bills would have provided additional public funds if one candidate exceeded the spending limit or if independent expenditures against a candidate exceeded $5,000 or $10,000. As the comparison of

12. Federal Election Commission, "Presidential Fund—Income Tax Check-Off Status," press release, March 1988. It is possible that more taxpayers would check off if they understood that in so doing they did not incur an additional tax liability. The FEC asked Congress to appropriate $250,000 in fiscal year 1990 for the commission to use to conduct an educational campaign explaining to taxpayers the purpose of the checkoff and how it works. Congress refused to appropriate the funds.

13. However, the FEC warned Congress in 1989 that continued funding of presidential campaigns through the checkoff was in serious jeopardy unless changes were made in the system. In a letter to Senator Wendell Ford, chairman of the Senate Rules Committee, the FEC stated that under the current system there would be insufficient funds to cover the 1996 presidential election. Federal Election Commission, *Record,* May 1989, p. 2.

these four bills indicates, the formulas used to determine the amount of federal money paid out greatly affect the cost. A matching system is less costly than a grant system if grants are for the entire allowable amount of money to be spent. But if grants were to be for less than the full amount, say 50 percent of the limit, a grant system would be no more expensive than a matching system, would still allow private contributions in the general election, would provide money at the beginning of a campaign, and would be much easier to administer. When considering a matching system, it is also important to remember the higher administrative costs associated with it.

Compensatory Public Funds

Although limitations on spending are usually tied to public funding, they do not have to be. Under current law, adherence to spending limits must be voluntary. But a system of voluntary ceilings raises the question of what to do if one candidate accepts the limit and another does not. To encourage both candidates to accept, there must be an incentive to stay under the ceiling. One incentive would be to compensate the candidate abiding by the limit with public funds if an opponent exceeded it. Although some candidates with unlimited funds might not care, most would probably think twice about having to raise money that an opponent would be given from the federal treasury. Similarly, short of challenging the *Buckley* v. *Valeo* decision directly by barring independent expenditures, the only way to try to limit such spending against a candidate or on behalf of an opponent would be to provide the candidate with public funds equivalent to independent expenditures above a certain amount.

Challenging the part of *Buckley* v. *Valeo* that applies to independent expenditures by PACs associated with incorporated entities—corporations, labor unions, and trade associations—was recommended by the 1990 Senate campaign finance reform panel.

Many of the large corporations and unions establishing and financing PACs have substantial, ongoing legislative interests, and their programs for pursuing these interests are conducted in many instances by large lobbying staffs headquartered in the Nation's Capital who maintain continuous relationships with Members of Congress and their staffs. It strains public credibility to assume that on one level, lobbying relationships may be maintained while, on another, the PAC "connected" to the corporation or union can instantly fabricate "independence" in campaign seasons and proceed to make hundreds of thousands of dollars in independent expenditures for the benefit of the same Members running for reelection. The danger of illicit *quid pro quos* in these circumstances is very real and immediate. The same rationale for the imposition of contribution limits has no less force here and supports an outright prohibition on "independent expenditures" by these PACs.[14]

The Supreme Court in 1990 also distinguished among types of independent expenditures, but in this case the independent spending was to have been corporate treasury money and not PAC money.[15]

The idea of compensatory public funds may encourage some candidates to accept spending limits, but it is not without problems. Although compensatory funds likely would encourage candidates with limited financial resources to accept spending limits, they might not be sufficient to encourage candidates with large fortunes to accept. A second problem would be getting the funds to candidates in a timely fashion. If one candidate decided to violate the spending limit in the final days or weeks of a campaign, getting compensatory funds to the complying opponent in time to allow him or her to use them effectively could be difficult. The FEC would have to monitor candidates' spending almost daily, which would be extremely difficult and would impose severe reporting requirements on campaigns. The quick turnaround time necessary and the reporting and monitoring requirements should raise serious questions about the practicality of compensatory public funds.

Implementation

One of the most difficult questions about a publicly financed system is how to administer and enforce it. The current presidential campaign finance system illustrates how such a system works, but in several respects it is very different. In the presidential system, administration and compliance are primarily the responsibility of the Federal Election Commission, with the Treasury Department actually issuing the checks. However, presidential elections are held only every four years, and there are a limited number of candidates seeking public funds—the 1988

14. Campaign Finance Reform Panel, "Campaign Finance Reform: A Report to the Majority Leader and Minority Leader, United States Senate," March 6, 1990, p. 22.
15. *Austin* v. *Michigan State Chamber of Commerce,* 110 S. Ct. 21 (1990).

presidential election saw the most major-party candidates since public financing was instituted in 1976. To administer a system for 14 candidates is much simpler than administering one with potentially 900 or more.[16]

Under the presidential campaign system, once candidates submit the proper documentation, it takes the FEC two to three weeks to certify them for federal funds. After the initial certification, candidates who remain eligible submit requests for matching funds every two weeks during the nominating period. It takes the commission about a week to approve these additional funds.

If the FEC were to administer a publicly funded congressional campaign finance system, the very nature of the commission would change. Currently, certifying candidates is a task that takes seven months every four years. Certifying candidates for congressional funds would be a task for seven months every two years, and the number of candidates would be much greater. Getting funds to candidates in a timely fashion would also pose problems. A grant system would be much simpler to administer and would not leave candidates pushing for funds in the final days of a campaign. A matching system would place much greater demands on the FEC, especially in the final weeks before the elections. The commission and the Treasury Department would have to be able to turn requests around quickly enough to ensure that all qualified candidates received their funds well before the election.

Spending Limitations

Another important issue in the debate over campaign finance reform is the imposition of spending limitations. Proponents strongly maintain that campaigns are excessively expensive and that without ceilings costs will continue to rise. They argue that the need to raise and spend larger and larger amounts of money discourages otherwise qualified candidates from seeking office and fosters a growing reliance on PACs. Opponents of spending limits counter by arguing that spending encourages participation and that, when compared with the marketing of consumer products, political campaigns cost very little. They also argue that challengers need to be able to spend large sums of money to offset the advantages of incumbency.

Beyond the philosophical disagreement over the need for spending

16. A fifteenth candidate, Lola Fulani, who ran as an independent, also received public funds in 1988. Federal Election Commission, *Record,* February 1989, p. 7.

caps, there is a deep division along partisan lines. In both the 1977 and 1987–88 Senate filibusters on campaign finance reform, limits were the most important partisan issue. As Richard E. Cohen summarized, "Amid the rhetorical hype and the playground antics, the issues sometimes were submerged. The cutting issue became the Democrats' efforts to impose spending limits on Senate races."[17] Republican opposition to limits stems in part from self-interest: the Republican party has been much more successful than the Democratic party in raising money. Any effort to limit spending reduces this advantage, unless the ceilings are set very high. An alternative, which might be more acceptable to Republicans, would be to increase party spending limits as part of a package of caps on candidate spending.

Republican aversion to ceilings is also based on a sense that in many states and districts they need to spend more than Democrats to win because they have fewer incumbents and less grass-roots support. Democrats enjoy a stronger local party infrastructure, more partisan identifiers, and access to volunteers from organized labor and other groups. Republicans fear that spending limits would hurt their chances of winning and of becoming the majority party in the House and Senate.

Spending limitations, like other proposed reforms, can have very different consequences, depending on how they are structured. Should the limits apply only to the general election period or to the entire election cycle? Should there be a constitutional amendment that would permit Congress to set limits without a system of public financing? Should spending limits be part of a comprehensive package of reform that includes public financing, limitations on independent expenditures, and aggregate PAC receipt limitations?

Issues in Setting Spending Limitations

Limitations, if effectively implemented, would stop or reduce the rate of increase in campaign spending. This result is evident from their imposition in presidential campaigns, where the rate of growth has been restrained. Imposing limits would have the same effect on disclosed spending in congressional elections, even if the limits were set at present levels. There are, however, two caveats. One is the number of candidates who would choose to accept limits. Under a constitutional amendment they would be forced to, but under statutory reform, they would have the option of refusing. If the presidential system is any guide, and we

17. Richard E. Cohen, "Protecting the Ins," *National Journal,* March 5, 1988, p. 636.

think it is, the vast majority of candidates would accept spending limits. The second caveat is that this does not take account of the increasing levels of soft money, which grew significantly in the 1988 election. Because soft money is undisclosed, its magnitude is uncertain.

Under a system of public financing with spending limitations, few incumbents would go unchallenged, and challengers' campaigns would be on a more even financial footing with incumbents. Although incumbents would retain many of the other advantages of incumbency, sufficiently high spending limits coupled with public financing would make challengers more competitive.

A first issue in setting limitations is what kinds of spending to limit. As discussed earlier, candidates can get funding from four sources: themselves, parties, PACs, and individual donors. Parties, PACs, and individuals are limited in what they can contribute, but neither overall candidate spending nor personal spending by candidates on their own behalf is limited. And parties, PACs, and individuals are not limited in how much they can spend independently to further a candidate's cause. If overall spending limits were imposed on candidates, any other spending to influence the outcome of an election would become even more important because candidates would be limited in their ability to respond. For example, independent expenditures could have even more effect under a system of limits than they do under the present system.

One possible solution would be to provide candidates with funds that they could use to counter independent spending. For example, if an independent group or an individual spent $100,000 to oppose a participating candidate, that candidate could receive a grant of $100,000 from the federal treasury.[18] This remedy would impose additional costs on the system, however, and could conceivably result in mischief. A group could pretend to oppose a candidate, but do so in a way that actually helped him or her and in the process get the additional public funds transferred to the candidate's campaign. The late Terry Dolan said that NCPAC would welcome compensation for independent expenditures: he would "simply run $100,000 in ads 'attacking' a favored candidate and urging that he be defeated for 'lowering taxes, opposing busing and standing for a strong defense.'"[19]

An alternative way of dealing with independent expenditures would

---

18. A 1983 House bill would have granted victims of independent expenditure free air time to respond if the independent expenditure were $500 or more.

19. Quoted in Larry Sabato, *PAC Power: Inside the World of Political Action Committees* (Norton, 1984), p. 185.

be to raise the spending limits for participating candidates by the amount spent independently against them or for their opponents. This would not impose additional costs on the system, but it would increase the uncertainty of participating candidates because they would have to raise additional funds on short notice. It would be very difficult, for instance, for a candidate to counter an independent expenditure made in the last few days before an election. Moreover, administering such a system would be very difficult. The FEC would have to monitor all advertisements paid for with independent expenditures to determine whether they were made against a candidate or for his or her opponent. Alternatively, anyone making an independent expenditure could be required to notify the FEC when broadcast time was purchased, but such a provision would still require FEC enforcement. In short, compensation, in whatever form, for independent expenditures against a candidate or for an opponent raises serious administrative problems.

Unrestricted use of personal wealth by candidates would also be a problem in a system of spending limitations. At present, candidates can spend as much as they wish of their own money, including loans they take out to give their campaigns. Unrestricted spending of personal wealth is important in the context of spending limitations because if the law did not limit use of personal funds, wealthy candidates would have an even greater advantage than they do today. Where to set these limits and how to enforce them are both important issues. One simple way to do it under a system of spending limits would be to limit personal wealth to the cycle spending limit. In other words, candidates could substitute personal funds for PAC and individual contributions up to the level of the spending limit.

Independent activities conducted for candidates by friendly groups or state parties could potentially mushroom under a system of spending limitations. At present, private foundations conduct registration and get-out-the-vote campaigns, which are often intended to aid or oppose particular candidates. With spending limitations in place, such activity would become even more valuable, permitting candidates to use funds for other activities.

Republicans often raise the issue of the volunteer help Democrats receive from organized labor and other groups for working telephone banks, walking precincts, and driving voters to the polls. Republicans argue that their candidates have to buy with disclosed and presumably regulated dollars what the Democrats get free. Again, under a system of spending limitations, volunteer activities become even more valuable.

This problem is difficult to remedy with legislation. To require candidates to put a price tag on such activities would likely result in their turning away volunteers, something hardly consistent with American electoral tradition. Yet to ignore this matter would appear to perpetuate a Democratic advantage.

In a system of regulated campaign spending, the national party committees would also try to spend more soft money, strengthening the state parties and thus indirectly helping federal candidates. One way to avoid this would be to require disclosure of soft money and state-party spending and to increase what the national parties could spend in congressional elections.

A second major issue in setting limitations is whether they should be constitutional or statutory. The prohibitions of the decision in *Buckley* v. *Valeo* could be overcome through a constitutional amendment giving Congress the power to set spending limits. This reform is popular with some members of Congress because limits could be enacted without public financing. Hearings on the amendment were held in the 100th Congress, yet when the bill went to the Senate floor for a vote, Republicans filibustered and there were insufficient votes for cloture. Many advocates of spending limits are not enthusiastic about a constitutional amendment because they fear it could be stalled in the states, thereby effectively precluding reform. Furthermore, if the amendment were enacted, Congress could set limits on any type of spending wherever it wanted, without concern for First Amendment rights or the need to foster competition. This same charge could be leveled against statutory reform, but under statutory rules a candidate who challenges an incumbent could go to court, arguing that the limits were too low. A group desiring to spend independently could also go to court. Under a constitutional amendment, both would be effectively denied legal recourse.

A third reform involves voluntary spending limits that could be statutorily based or negotiated between two or more candidates. The bill introduced by Senator Boren at the start of the 101st Congress had spending limits but no public financing unless one of the candidates exceeded the limit. A variant on the idea is for contestants to negotiate among themselves a spending limit for their campaigns. This offers a way to avoid legislation or a constitutional amendment, but in practice such an approach has not worked. For example, Representative Peter Kostmayer has repeatedly suggested that his opponents join him in an agreement to voluntarily limit spending in congressional elections in his district. Until 1990 no opponent was willing to do so, but Kostmayer's

Republican opponent in 1990 accepted his challenge and proposed a $400,000 limitation on spending. Kostmayer, in turn, refused to accept a limit.[20]

A fourth way to establish spending limits, which appears to get around the partisan deadlock over the issue, is to make them flexible. This idea, originally proposed by the 1990 campaign finance reform panel, exempts from the candidates' spending limit money raised in small in-state individual contributions.[21] Participating candidates would have spending limits for every other category of money—PACs, out-of-state individual contributions, and in-state individual contributions above the threshold.

Flexible spending limits have the advantage of establishing limits on the most "interested" kinds of money—PAC contributions and large individual contributions—while at the same time encouraging candidates to raise money from their electoral constituents. Flexible spending limits were quickly endorsed by prominent Republicans in the Senate as a way to get around the partisan deadlock over spending limits.[22]

Flexible spending limits would further elevate the importance of direct mail fundraising, the most efficient way to raise money in amounts of $100 or less from targeted populations. They would also place a premium on large in-state contributors because part of their contribution would not count against the spending limit, while all of a large out-of-state contribution would. If, for example, the exempted in-state contribution was $100, only $900 of an in-state contribution of $1,000 would count against the spending limit while all of a $1,000 contribution from out of state would count.

How much money would be raised in this separate category is hard to know. However, there is presumably a finite small-donor base in any given state. Projections of the amount to be raised in this way will become part of any calculation of the state or district spending limit.

Another issue is whether limitations should apply to the general election only or to the election cycle. Until the 100th Congress, proposed congressional campaign finance legislation would have imposed spending limits only on general election campaigns. Reformers had always tied spending limits to public financing and believed that it was politically impractical to propose a system of public financing for primary campaigns.

20. Kim Mattingly, "Kostmayer Hypocrisy?" *Roll Call,* April 9, 1990, p. 1.
21. Campaign Finance Reform Panel, "Campaign Finance Reform."
22. David S. Broder, "Campaign Finance Reform: Keep It on Track," *Washington Post,* March 14, 1990, p. A17; and Helen Dewar, "Finally, Campaign Fund Reform?" *Washington Post,* March 12, 1990, p. A13.

Incumbents would have enough competition from publicly financed opponents in the general election. But S. 2 included a new provision that imposed a limit on spending in the primaries as a condition for receiving public funds in the general election.

Proponents argued that there were two important reasons for the provision. If spending were limited only in general election campaigns, there would be a tremendous temptation for candidates to spend early in an election cycle when there would be no limits. Significant early expenditures could eliminate any competitive balance in spending that had been constructed for general election campaigns. Proponents also noted that seventeen states have late primaries (after September 1), which pose additional problems because spending in August and September, while still in the primary period, clearly has consequences for general election campaigns. And whatever formula were used to arrive at the spending limit, strategic considerations would be far different in states that have late primaries than in states that have early ones.

The state best known for late primaries is Louisiana, but Washington, Massachusetts, Hawaii, and Oklahoma also have primaries or runoff primaries on or after September 15. In several states it can take weeks for primary winners to be certified as the general election candidates. Because certification is normally required by proposals for public campaign financing, candidates in these states would not receive federal funds until well into the general election period. And if one candidate accepted public funds while the other did not, the candidate who accepted would be at a serious disadvantage, perhaps enough to ensure that in these states both candidates would either accept spending limits and public funds or refuse them. The late election dates underscore the need to limit spending in both primary and general election campaigns.

A further matter is whether there should be separate spending limits for the primary and general election campaigns or simply a cycle limit, with candidates free to divide their spending however they see fit. Separate limits for primary and general election campaigns may well have consequences for competition very different from cycle limits, depending on the type of primary. It would make sense for a candidate in the party that does not hold a given congressional seat to spend as much as possible to win the primary. But under cycle limits, after the primary a winner may have little beyond the public grant left to spend to challenge an incumbent. Incumbents who have had no primary challenge likely would have spent very little and would be able to spend most of their money in the general election campaign. If there were separate primary and general election campaign spending limits, the candidates in the out party might spend less in the primary than they would with cycle limits but would have more money to run against the incumbent in the general election. But candidates who challenge incumbents in the primary would be better off with cycle limits, because they probably would have to spend more money than the primary limit might allow. Such a situation would be especially likely in one-party districts and states, where the primary election essentially is the general election.

Similarly, in states with late primaries it makes more sense to have cycle limits, since spending in the primary campaigns has obvious consequences for the general election. It makes little sense to impose an artificial limit on primary campaign spending in these states. In states with early primaries, such spending has less obvious consequences for the general election campaign. If candidates in states with early primaries have competitive races, as candidates from an out party might expect, a good deal of money might be spent in the primary campaign, with little residual benefit for the general election campaign.

Given the different incentives to spend early or late, it makes sense to leave as much of the decision to the candidates as possible. If the system has public money for the general election campaign, there is a general election limit built in. However, if there are no public funds involved, candidates ought to be free to choose when to spend within the overall cycle limit.

Whatever limitations might be set in place, should they be adjusted for inflation? Because campaign costs rise, it makes sense to index to inflation. Most of the contribution limits in the FECA are not indexed, but indexing is essential for proposed new limits or they would become increasingly unacceptable to candidates and more likely to protect incumbents from competition. Using a projected inflation rate, a campaign contribution worth $1,000 in 1978 would be worth, in real terms, only $519 in 1990.

What index should be used? Proposals have most frequently resorted to the consumer price index, but it includes commodities, services, and products that are not typically part of campaign budgets. Some observers have recommended using a "campaign cost index" that would exclude housing, food, and other parts of the CPI and emphasize such items as broadcast advertising rates, printing costs, and postal rates.

Compliance

One of the concerns candidates will have with any regime of spending limitations is compliance. What if their opponent spends beyond the limits near the end of the general election, too late for a response? This concern has been intensified by the way several presidential candidates have disregarded state spending limits in primary campaigns.[23] For House and Senate campaigns there would also be a strong temptation to spend beyond the limits if that might ensure victory and if the only penalty would be a small fine. Participants will understandably weigh the consequences of noncompliance against the chances of defeat. It is therefore important to design the limits with an eye to ensuring compliance by building in requirements for frequent reporting and providing stiff penalties for knowingly exceeding spending limits. The disincentives considered in proposed Senate legislation in the 100th Congress included a grant to complying candidates when opponents exceeded the limit. The legislation also included a provision for a quick decision at the Federal Election Commission and a fast payout by the Treasury Department so that the candidate campaigning within the limits could respond in time in the last two weeks.

As the discussion of compensatory public funds noted, however, there are serious administrative problems with these proposals. And one important assumption about compliance is that the electoral process itself will serve as a corrective, that when candidates say they will campaign within spending limits and then do not, the opponents will be able to make noncompliance a campaign issue. The extent to which this issue carries any weight in a campaign, however, is debatable. When campaign spending has been raised as an issue in candidates' campaigns or in campaigns concerned with ballot referendums, it has often not been very important.[24]

Because any system that is serious about congressional campaign spending limits will require significant additional reporting to the FEC, legislation should include provisions for a compliance cost account in candidates' budgets, as the presidential system does.

23. See "Manufacturing the Next President," *Harper's,* December 1987, pp. 43–54.

24. David B. Magleby, "Campaign Spending in Ballot Proposition and Candidate Elections: A Preliminary Analysis," paper prepared for the 1986 annual meeting of the American Political Science Association; and interview with Geoffrey Garin, a Democratic party pollster, January 27, 1988.

Spending Limits and Electoral Competition

If spending ceilings are set too low, the system becomes an incumbent protection plan. This is the most frequently cited problem political scientists have with such legislation. Fred Wertheimer of Common Cause has conceded that "the struggle in the House is always to make sure you have a high enough spending limit."[25] Low spending limits make it more difficult for challengers to gain enough visibility to be competitive. Richard E. Cohen criticized the 1987–88 reform legislation from this very perspective: "The Common Cause inspired drive for campaign spending limits may be a well-intentioned effort to deal with an obvious problem. But the proposed cure is wrong-headed and more likely to entrench the arrogance of incumbency."[26]

In congressional campaigns, candidates who wish to be taken seriously have to become visible. House and Senate incumbents are typically much better known than their challengers. For challengers to be competitive they must reach a certain threshold. As Tom O'Donnell, former political director of the Democratic Congressional Campaign Committee, has said, "Somebody has got to raise $300,000 just to sit at the table ... to hope to be competitive. And then they have got to run a good race."[27] Some challengers may have a lower competitiveness threshold—because of simple notoriety, because they come from famous political families, or because they have held public office before—but most find the threshold very expensive to reach. Unfortunately, many challengers cannot compete because they are essentially invisible.

One way to see the importance of money is to look at how much successful challengers and candidates for open seats spent between 1980 and 1988. We selected all instances in which the challenger won or was within five points of winning and all races for open seats in which the margin of victory was ten points or fewer. We then averaged what the losing and winning candidates spent. In constant 1988 dollars, costs rose from about $397,000 in 1980 to $583,000 in 1988 for House candidates (table 9-1). The range in competitive races in a given year is substantial. Excluding incumbents, competitive House candidates have had average expenditures of about $450,000 in real 1988 dollars since 1980. For the Senate, spending per voter has averaged at least $1 in all years, but shows more variability than House spending.

25. Interview with Fred Wertheimer, March 22, 1988.
26. Cohen, "Protecting the Ins," p. 636.
27. Interview with Tom O'Donnell, March 21, 1988.

TABLE 9-1. *Spending in Competitive Races by House and Senate Candidates, 1980–88*[a]

Constant 1988 dollars

Year	Mean	Minimum	Maximum
House			
1980	397,126	60,058	1,149,601
1982	350,888	46,971	1,162,486
1984	475,727	61,310	1,165,715
1986	486,251	127,470	1,619,788
1988	582,700	183,957	1,110,126
Senate[b]			
1980	1.46	0.11	5.33
1982	1.03	0.27	2.95
1984	2.03	0.30	9.60
1986	1.87	0.40	7.49
1988	1.00	0.39	3.75

SOURCES: FEC data tapes; see appendix A.
a. Includes open-seat winners, open-seat competitive challengers, and competitive challengers. See text for details.
b. Dollars per member of voting age population.

Another way to look at the effect of spending on competition is to estimate the effect of different levels of public funding on electoral outcomes. Alan Abramowitz has estimated that public financing could dramatically increase competition in House elections, but only at very high levels of funding. At low levels, coupled with spending limits, public funding would further decrease competition: in 1984 as many as seventy-six House incumbents could have been defeated, but only with a public grant of $800,000 to each challenger.[28] However, Abramowitz's analysis attempts to predict the point at which spending will result in victory for challengers, while our purpose is to identify the level challengers need to get 45 percent or more of the vote. If we use Abramowitz's equation to find the amount of spending needed to reach 45 percent of the vote, the amount would be very close to the $450,000 we have reported.

It is important to remember that the expenditures shown in table 9-1 include the costs of fundraising, normally between 20 and 30 percent of the total. If spending limits were part of a package of public financing, then the costs of raising money would decrease. Excluding the cost of fundraising, the competitiveness threshold in constant dollars has been about $360,000 for the past eight years for the House. In competitive

28. Alan I. Abramowitz, "Incumbency, Campaign Spending and Competition in U.S. House Elections," Emory University, Department of Political Science, August 1989.

Senate races since 1980, candidates have averaged $0.48 per person of voting age for states with voting age populations greater than 4 million and $1.80 for smaller states.[29]

Another way to set spending limits so that they would not unduly benefit incumbents would be to make them approximate the current spending levels of winning candidates, less the costs of fundraising, and to establish a system of public financing that would permit challengers to gain visibility. Such a system would not significantly reduce costs: it would only cap them at present levels. Still, given increases in campaign expenditures that have averaged more than 30 percent since 1974, putting a cap in place would be no small accomplishment. If such a plan were part of a system of public financing, however, it would increase the cost of the system and make the reform politically vulnerable.

Setting spending limits too low would improve the reelection prospects of incumbents, but setting them at the competitive threshold or higher and providing public financing would almost certainly increase competition. Candidate recruitment would be easier, especially for the out party. Although fundraising is only one part of the decision to seek office, it can be an important element. At present, challengers understand that incumbents can raise and spend more than challengers can. With spending limits, challengers would know what their opponents could spend and, if the limits were combined with public financing and other reform elements, the challengers' ability to compete would be improved. Knowing that partial public funding will be available in the general election campaign might encourage those who now are reluctant to challenge a well-funded incumbent to seek congressional office.

Variance in Costs

One feature of Senate elections in the 1980s has been the concentration of spending in small states (see chapter 3). With the balance of power between the parties depending on only a few seats for most of the decade, it is understandable that both parties, as well as interested groups and individuals, would see the small states as the battleground for control of the Senate. Less populated states tend to have considerably higher spending per voter than the more populated states. There is also a point of diminishing returns in spending per voter in very populous states such as New York and California.

29. We include here, as in table 9-1, winners of open seats, competitive losers for open seats, and competitive challengers.

As a result of this differential, legislation proposed to limit campaign spending has frequently provided both a floor and a ceiling. The floor elevates the spending limit in small states to a level more in keeping with the reality that more will be spent per voter in them. Without the floor, candidates, parties, and groups might forgo accepting spending limits and public funds and instead fund their campaigns with private money. There is less agreement on the need for a ceiling. As one Congress watcher has said, "We can't have change without a floor. We can't have a floor without a ceiling. And a ceiling is not politically feasible."[30]

Another difference is the economies of scale that can be achieved in more populous states. The application of a simple rule allowing so many cents per eligible voter may result in a limit higher than what is now spent. A solution is to build into the legislation a ceiling or declining scale. For example, in states with populations up to 4 million, candidates could receive twenty-five cents per person of voting age. For states with populations between 4 and 7 million, candidates could receive twenty-five cents per person of voting age for the first 4 million and twenty cents each for the number over 4 million. For states with more than 7 million, candidates could receive twenty-five cents per person of voting age for the first 4 million, twenty cents each for the next 3 million, and fifteen cents each for the number over 7 million.

A second important difference between states is television markets. Senate candidates in states with similar populations can have dramatically different campaign costs. New Jersey, for example, has about the same population as Michigan, but, unlike Michigan, which has twelve network affiliate television stations, New Jersey has none. Candidates who run for the Senate in New Jersey must buy television time in Philadelphia and New York City. Such a strategy is inefficient because they are reaching approximately 13.2 million voters who live outside the state. A similar problem exists for New Hampshire, which has only one commercial VHF station and depends heavily on Boston television stations. As a result, legislation that sets spending limits must also consider that in some states it simply costs more to run because of the nature of the media markets.

The problem faced in New Jersey for the Senate also exists for many House districts. In some places there are as many as thirty House districts in the same media market. In others, such as Wyoming, districts have more than one media market. There is also substantial variation in

---

30. Off-the-record discussion with the authors.

television costs for similarly situated congressional districts. When the costs of television advertising are high because of the problem of overreaching, candidates usually use direct mail, radio, or other means of communication. A dollar spent in one district will not necessarily buy the same market basket of services in other districts. For example, Wyoming's sole House member represents the entire state and often has to rent an airplane to campaign effectively, while one district in New York City has an area of only seven square miles.

It would be possible to design a formula that would take into account differences among House districts in broadcast and newspaper advertising costs, the degree of fit between media markets and districts, the costs of transportation within a district, and the costs of printing, labor, and telephones. But such a formula would be complex to construct, difficult to explain, and even more difficult to administer. For this reason, spending limits for the House need to be set high enough for candidates to launch viable campaigns in all but the most expensive districts, and in these most House candidates already adjust their campaign strategies to reflect the unusual circumstances. For instance, few candidates for the House in New York or Los Angeles run television spots. The solution is to provide candidates with sufficiently large blocks of money and let them spend it in the most efficient way, given the realities of their districts. Such a block grant is readily understood by candidates and the public. Administration of a more complicated allocation formula would almost certainly be very difficult. If a campaign cost index were created for each district, how would the relevant "market basket" of services be determined and how would current data on those services be gathered for 435 electoral districts? Ease of administration alone dictates a single spending limit for House districts.

Conclusions

Public funding and limitations on spending are probably the two most contentious issues in the debate over campaign finance reform. Public funding, coupled with spending limits, would bring the costs of individual congressional campaigns under greater control and provide a financial foundation for serious contenders. Public funding without spending limits would provide money to candidates and potentially reduce the time spent fundraising but would not limit the costs of running for office.

Spending limits without public funding would further dampen competition in congressional elections. A system of public funding and limits on spending would probably increase the total amount spent in congressional election campaigns. Spending limits would reduce the amount spent in the most expensive races, but public funding would increase what was spent, particularly by House challengers, in races that are presently underfunded.

Public financing coupled with spending limits stands the greatest chance of reducing the problems of the current system. Rising costs, declining competition, the preoccupation of candidates with fundraising, the large and growing role of special interest money, and the advantages enjoyed by wealthy candidates are all directly addressed. If combined with limitations on expenditures of soft money, this approach would put a meaningful ceiling on spending.

Public financing and limitations on spending would foster increased competition only if the limitations were set high enough to permit challengers to become visible. Spending limits with partial public financing would reduce the current arms race mentality toward spending. Candidates would become less preoccupied with it, and potential candidates would be more willing to consider running.

Public financing combined with spending limits would also reduce the now powerful role played by special interests because a cap would be placed on how much candidates could raise from them. The vacuum created by this limitation would be filled in part by public dollars, which would come with no strings attached. Although such a reform would not eliminate the influence of corporations, labor unions, trade associations, and the like, it would shift the locus of interest group activity from financing campaigns to issue advocacy and political mobilization. PACs would not be excluded from participating under a system of partial public financing, but their functions would be balanced against those of individual donors and political parties.

Spending limitations and public financing would also assist candidates unable to give their own campaigns large sums of money by providing enough to launch a credible campaign and permitting them to argue that the wealthy candidate is exceeding reasonable limits and attempting to purchase the election.

All these are possible benefits of high spending limits and partial public financing, but there are also some potential problems. Although we believe the parties will take an active role in recruiting well-qualified candidates to cash in on the greater probability of success, such a system might encourage frivolous candidates to seek office. The qualification standard needs to be strict enough to discourage artificial challengers but not so strict that it discourages real ones.

Low spending limits and incumbent protection are synonymous to most political scientists, but they are certain to be attractive to many if not most incumbents. Those who set the limits are themselves incumbents and they can cite the popular argument that costs should be kept down. Persuading them to overlook their own electoral self-interest and to ignore public pressure to control costs may be unduly optimistic. Reform could make matters worse rather than better if it establishes spending limits that are too low.

Public financing and limitations on spending have caused deep partisan differences in the past. Republican ideology dictates that the size of government ought not to grow, costs ought to be constrained, and bureaucratic power is dangerous. Republicans' self-interest for much of this period has been based on the hope that their party's success in raising money would be transferable to candidates and that the business community, most notably corporate PACs, would side heavily with them. Both hopes have been unfulfilled. The Republican partisan advantage in fundraising is muted by the limits on party spending, and corporate PACs are pragmatic—they give to both Democratic and Republican incumbents. Whether Republicans will come to consider spending limitations and partial public financing as the means to assist their underfinanced House challengers remains to be seen.

Democrats are caught between their philosophy and self-interest. Long identified as the party pushing this set of reforms, they will find it difficult to reject such proposals in the future. But many Democrats now have doubts about the wisdom of the reforms for their party. They would be taking a large risk in supporting spending limits and partial public financing, assuming the limits were set at high levels.

One additional problem with public financing and limitations on spending is that the public is at best ambivalent about them. If public support for the idea is evidenced by the rate of taxpayer participation in the income tax checkoff, that support is diminishing. People are likely to be skeptical of reforms of campaign finance emanating from Congress. After all, it will be argued, the politicians are already the problem. Yet public financing and limits on spending are not likely to result from general demands for change. This is why the deep divisions at the elite level have resulted in stalemate. Because the public is not demanding change and politicians cannot agree, the status quo is the predictable result. There are, however, other approaches to reform that avoid the impasse over public financing and spending limitations. We will turn our discussion to some of those ideas in the next chapter.

10

Incentives and Subsidies

Provisions for public financing and changes in limitations on contributions and spending are not the only options for addressing problems with the current system of congressional campaign finance. Indeed, partisan differences about the merits of public financing and limitations on spending make an analysis of alternative reforms even more important. There are other reforms that, if enacted, would increase competition in congressional elections, improve disclosure of campaign activity, and simplify and speed administration of the campaign finance laws.

One alternative to direct cash transfers to candidates is for Congress to finance campaigns indirectly by subsidizing broadcast campaign advertising or requiring television and radio stations to provide time at discounted rates. Broadcast advertising is such an important part of the budgets for Senate candidates and many House candidates that reducing its costs would help those most strapped for money—challengers. Or Congress could buy time itself for the parties or candidates, or it could provide vouchers for candidates to use on the medium of their choice. Congress could also legislate further reductions in postage rates for the candidates and parties, another indirect subsidy that would benefit challengers more than incumbents. (In a sense, indirect public financing for campaigns already exists: Congress funds part of the election expenses for incumbents by paying for franking, frequent trips home, and office space in their districts.)

Competition could also be increased by providing incentives for individual donors to contribute to candidates. This could take several different forms, but is most frequently discussed as a full income tax credit for contributions up to $100. Other incremental reforms that would avoid the impasse on public financing and limits on spending include increased disclosure of soft money and changing the structure of the Federal Election Commission so that it could carry out its tasks more effectively. Should Congress seriously consider some of the reforms discussed earlier in this book, much more far-reaching changes in the procedures of the FEC would be needed.

Improving Competition

Some people think there is little competition in congressional races because constituents believe incumbents are doing a good job in Washington and are vigorously promoting the interests of their districts. No doubt many members meet this high standard, but it is not true for all of the 98 percent of House members reelected in the past few election cycles. Rather, it is more likely that congressional races, particularly for House seats, are not more competitive because of the high cost of running for office, the consequent difficulty in raising campaign money, and such advantages of incumbency as name recognition, an existing staff and offices, and the use of the frank.

One way to make campaigns more competitive is to reduce the costs, particularly for challengers and candidates for open seats. Because much of the increased cost of congressional campaigns can be attributed to the use of broadcast advertising, proposals have been advanced to provide free or discounted broadcast time and free or subsidized mailings.

Free or Reduced-Cost Broadcast Advertising

Free broadcast time would be most useful to Senate candidates and to candidates in competitive House districts. In 1986 the Center for Responsive Politics found that 89 percent of the Senate candidates surveyed and 87 percent of the candidates in competitive House races relied more on television than on any other medium to communicate with voters.[1] Robert Squier, a political consultant with considerable campaign experience, estimated in testimony before the Senate Telecommunications Subcommittee in September 1988 that 60 percent of the total spending in contested Senate races goes to broadcast advertising. Although the National Association of Broadcasters has produced figures suggesting that spending for radio and television spots is much less significant than that, Squier called the NAB's figures "absolutely absurd."[2]

---

1. Center for Responsive Politics, *Beyond the 30-Second Spot: Enhancing the Media's Role in Congressional Elections* (Washington, 1988), p. 5.
2. Robert Squier, testimony before the Senate Telecommunications Subcommittee, September 15, 1988.

Generally, proposals to reduce campaign advertising costs seek to provide free broadcast time, most often on television, to congressional candidates or to the two major political parties. In the 100th Congress, Representative Samuel Stratton introduced H.R. 521, which would have provided major-party Senate candidates with two hours of free time and major-party House candidates with one hour. Senator Claiborne Pell introduced S. 593, which would have given free time to the political party committees. Both bills would have required that the time be made available in segments longer than sixty seconds.[3]

The most obvious advantage of making free television or radio time available to candidates is that it would reduce campaign costs for most of them. In the 1986 survey by the Center for Responsive Politics, only House candidates in the six largest media markets did not spend more money for television or radio time than for anything else. The candidates in the large media markets reported spending more than half their communication budgets on direct mail.[4] Lower media costs would probably mean that candidates would need to raise less money, thus making it easier for nonincumbents to achieve parity with incumbents and reducing the time all candidates must spend raising money. But free air time is not without costs. First there is the question of who will provide it. Pell's and Stratton's proposals would require broadcasters to provide free time as a condition of their licensing agreement with the government.[5] H.R. 480, a bill introduced by Representative Andrew Jacobs in the 100th Congress, would have required the government to pay for the time.[6] Opposition to free air time provided by broadcasters comes, not surprisingly, from broadcasters but also from some candidates. In the survey by the Center for Responsive Politics, 45 percent of all

3. Most such reform proposals stipulate that the commercials be in segments of five minutes or longer to improve the level of information available to potential voters. The Center for Responsive Politics has argued that "free media proposals which grant time in segments longer than 30 or 60 seconds would certainly represent a new opportunity for the public to assess candidates, and to weigh their views on substantive issues." *Beyond the 30-Second Spot,* p. 20. However, thirty- and sixty-second campaign advertisements also have defenders. Larry Sabato concludes that "like it or not, Americans prefer their political advertisements to be short and sweet; the 'tune out' factor, i.e., channel switching, is devastating for political commercials that are lengthier than five minutes." *The Party's Just Begun* (Little, Brown, 1988), pp. 220–21. Candidates themselves prefer the shorter spots; in one survey only 10 percent bought air time for political advertising lasting longer than sixty seconds. Center for Responsive Politics, *Beyond the 30-Second Spot,* p. A-2.

4. Center for Responsive Politics, *Beyond the 30-Second Spot,* pp. 102–03.

5. Center for Responsive Politics, *Beyond the 30-Second Spot,* pp. 42–43.

6. Jacobs's bill would have provided government funds to candidates to purchase 90 minutes of television time in segments of 5 minutes or longer, 135 minutes of radio time, and 126 column inches or one page of newspaper advertising, whichever was longer.

candidates favored requiring broadcasters to provide free time, and 45 percent opposed it (58 percent of the incumbents were opposed). Challengers (61 percent) and candidates for open seats (52 percent) favored free time.[7]

Broadcasters oppose providing free time because their stations lose. Estimates are that granting House candidates 60 minutes of television commercial spots and 60 minutes of program time and Senate candidates 120 minutes of spot time and 90 minutes of program time would have cost the broadcast industry in 1986 as much as $200 million. However, $200 million represented less than 1 percent of the television industry's advertising revenues in 1986.[8] Broadcasters are also quick to respond that it is not fair to single them out to subsidize the cost of congressional campaigns while newspapers, campaign consultants, and direct mail companies go scot-free.

Of course, one way to avoid the loss of revenue to broadcasters would be to have the government pay for the free time for party committees or for candidates, as in Representative Jacobs's proposal. This would, however, be a form of public financing, with all its attendant problems, as discussed in chapter 9. Moreover, there is very little support for the idea among candidates. As one stated, "Because the license to broadcast is issued by the federal government, it should be the responsibility of broadcasters ... the government should not pay for the time."[9]

Broadcasters also oppose providing free time because, in large media markets with many congressional districts, to do so—even if it were restricted to major-party candidates—would strain, if not immobilize, television programming. As one network executive explained, "A requirement that broadcasters provide even one half-hour of free time to each of these federal candidates would have compelled WCBS-TV to present a total of 99 hours of free political programming prime time— almost 3 hours a night—during the 35 consecutive nights preceding the 1980 election. The resulting burden on the station would have been crippling, entailing an enormous revenue loss and the virtual total preemption of all other prime time programming." Another network executive predicted that free broadcast time "would mean an unending

7. Center for Responsive Politics, *Beyond the 30-Second Spot*, p. 45.

8. Center for Responsive Politics, *Beyond the 30-Second Spot*, p. 46. See also Andrew Buchsbaum, *Independent Expenditures in Congressional Campaigns: The Electronic Solution* (New York: Democracy Project, 1982).

9. Center for Responsive Politics, *Beyond the 30-Second Spot*, p. 24.

stream of political messages that would be calculated to turn off television sets as effectively as a power failure in the New York area."[10]

One way to reduce this inundation would be to require television and radio stations to provide free broadcast time only to the two major political parties, as in Senator Pell's proposal. Fewer hours would have to be set aside, because the parties could allocate the time available among their candidates. Although such a proposal would strengthen the role of the parties in congressional campaigns, candidates are wary, fearing that committees would not allocate the time fairly. Challengers and incumbents alike think that incumbents, because of their connections to the chairmen of the party committees, would most likely receive the time.[11] Whether such skepticism is warranted is unknown; deciding among candidates for free air time would be similar to deciding which candidates receive what contributions from the party committees.

Still another problem with providing free air time is what to do about third parties or candidates running as independents. The three proposals introduced in the 100th Congress all provided some free advertising time for third-party candidates, though in different ways. Jacobs's proposal would provide free time for all candidates; Stratton's and Pell's bills would allocate time to third-party and minor-party candidates based on the parties' percentage of the vote in past elections.

An alternative to free broadcast advertising would be reduced-cost, or discounted, broadcast rates. In theory, reduced-cost advertising already exists. As part of the Federal Election Campaign Act of 1971, Congress established a "lowest unit rate" for political advertising. In the forty-five days before a primary election and the sixty days before a general election, television stations can charge candidates no more than the "lowest unit rate" charged any advertiser for advertisements at the particular time of day the candidate wishes to air commercials.[12] In practice, however, the lowest unit rate is meaningless. Broadcast rates are in constant flux, depending on the nature of the market for air time. Stations charge different rates for various times of the day and seasons of the year. Moreover, the lowest unit rate applies only to preemptible time—spots that can be sold to another advertiser willing to pay a higher price. If candidates want to be sure their commercials air at the time

10. Both are quoted in Center for Responsive Politics, *Beyond the 30-Second Spot,* p. 48.
11. Center for Responsive Politics, *Beyond the 30-Second Spot,* p. 56.
12. 47 U.S.C. 315(b).

they want them to air, they must buy nonpreemptible, or fixed, time, which is the most expensive advertising time. One political consultant familiar with media buys in congressional campaigns has testified, "You would be malpracticing a political client if you went into October and purchased a pre-emptible spot."[13] Another commented, "I don't know of a campaign in [its] right mind that doesn't buy fixed time. You're crazy, in the pressure of a campaign, if you don't."[14]

Although candidates do not favor free media time for political advertisements, they do favor reduced rates. In one survey 46 percent believed that broadcasters should be required "to sell both nonpreemptible and preemptible time at a substantially discounted rate to candidates"; 39 percent opposed such a reform. Support for the proposal was highest among losers (65 percent), challengers (64 percent), and candidates for open seats (54 percent). Opposition came from winners (51 percent) and incumbents (49 percent).[15]

During the 100th Congress Senator Mitch McConnell introduced legislation to make the lowest unit rate nonpreemptible for political candidates. The proposal was incorporated into S. 7, the campaign finance reform bill Senator Dole introduced at the start of the 101st Congress. Such legislation would make the provision for lowest unit rates what it was originally intended to be and would reduce the costs of political advertisements substantially.[16]

One consequence of providing nonpreemptible time at the lowest unit rate would be to expand the number of commercials candidates can afford to buy, especially if nothing is done to constrain overall costs. Incumbents, who already are much more likely to be seen in television ads, would be even more visible. Challengers would also benefit, but only to the extent that they can raise the funds necessary to buy nonpreemptible time.

Free Mailings and Postal Subsidies

Although proposals for reducing the cost of communications have concentrated primarily on air time, communication costs could also be

---

13. Robert Squier, testimony before the Senate Telecommunications Subcommittee, quoted in Congressional Quarterly, *Campaign Practices Reports,* September 19, 1988, p. 3.

14. Center for Responsive Politics, *Beyond the 30-Second Spot,* p. 73.

15. Center for Responsive Politics, *Beyond the 30-Second Spot,* p. 81.

16. The National Association of Broadcasters testified that the loss in revenue to television stations under McConnell's proposal would be between 1 percent and 4 percent. Senator McConnell's own estimates put revenue losses at 0.75 percent. Author's notes from hearings before the Senate Telecommunications Subcommittee, September 15, 1988.

reduced by providing free mailings, which would help candidates other than incumbents overcome the advantage incumbents enjoy with the franking privilege.[17] (Currently, House and Senate rules prohibit mass mailings, defined as more than 500 pieces of essentially similar, unsolicited mail, in the sixty days before an election.) Free mailings would likely be most important for House candidates in the largest media markets, for whom broadcast time is least important. The mailings would probably provide minimal benefits for incumbents, who presumably have the entire election cycle to get their message to constituents.

Postal subsidies are another possible reform. Such subsidies now accrue only to the national, congressional, and state campaign committees of each party; candidates themselves are not eligible. The campaign finance reform bill introduced by Senator Boren at the beginning of the 101st Congress proposed that candidates who voluntarily accepted spending limits would be eligible for a first-class rate of 5.5 cents per piece or a rate 2 cents below current third-class rate.[18] However, postal subsidies are just as unpopular as free political advertising with at least some candidates. The 1986 survey by the Center for Responsive Politics found that 57 percent of all candidates opposed providing postal subsidies and only 30 percent favored them. Not surprisingly, 61 percent of incumbents opposed the subsidies, and just 17 percent favored them.[19]

Reducing the costs of broadcast advertising and postage would help reduce the overall costs of campaigns. The reductions would benefit nonincumbents most because they have the most difficulty raising money and are the least known to potential voters. If it became easier to establish a minimum level of recognition for these candidates, voters would be better able to evaluate the statements and records of both candidates in a congressional race, and competition would increase.[20]

17. For fiscal year 1989 Congress appropriated $54 million for franked mail, which was to be added to the $13.5 million assumed to be left over from previous years. Still, the $67.5 million available for franked mail in fiscal 1989 was less than the estimated cost, $75 million. Janet Hook, "Congress Avoids Pay Quarrel in Bill to Pay Its Own Expenses," *Congressional Quarterly Weekly Report,* October 1, 1988, p. 2695; and "Fiscal 1988 Legislative Appropriations," *Congressional Quarterly Weekly Report,* January 2, 1988, p. 16.

18. *Congressional Record,* daily ed., January 25, 1989, pt. 2, p. S466.

19. Center for Responsive Politics, *Beyond the 30-Second Spot,* p. 65.

20. Ed Blakely, a media consultant, calculated that a typical congressional challenger would have to purchase 750 gross rating points to establish the minimum name recognition necessary to be competitive. (A gross rating point is the percentage of a market viewing audience watching a particular program at a particular time. These points are used in setting advertising rates. Thus 750 gross rating points means that a market will have been exposed to a commercial 7.5 times.) The cost varies among media markets. In 1986 the

Tax Credits

Another way to increase competition in congressional elections is to make it easier for candidates—again, especially challengers—to raise campaign funds. Higher ceilings for individual contributions would be the best way to enable candidates to get more money from people who currently contribute the maximum allowed and are financially able to give more. However, a tax credit for contributions to congressional campaigns could also help because candidates would find it easier to raise small contributions from people who are not wealthy.

From 1972 until the Tax Reform Act of 1986 was passed, a tax credit for one-half of all political contributions up to $50 ($100 on a joint return) was allowed. Richard Conlon, the late director of the Democratic Study Group, had long advocated a 100 percent tax credit for congressional campaign contributions up to $100 because he believed it would encourage people to participate in the political process and would give candidates a greater incentive to try to raise money in small amounts. As we noted in chapter 4, the number of those who contribute less than $100 has fallen in the past decade.

There is some general opposition to reinstituting a tax credit because of the costs to the federal treasury. For the three most recent election cycles for which there are data (1979–84), the average cost per election cycle was $635 million in constant 1988 dollars.[21] There are also partisan disagreements over the size of the credit. Republicans favor a 50 percent credit, Democrats a 100 percent credit. The differences are based on assumptions that Democrats have less disposable income and therefore need a greater incentive to contribute, while the opposite is true for Republicans.

It is difficult to estimate how much a tax credit would encourage campaign contributions from people otherwise reluctant to make them. When the 50 percent credit was in place, about 7 percent of federal taxpayers used it.[22] But because a 100 percent credit has not been tried,

---

Center for Responsive Politics calculated that 750 gross rating points would cost $84,750 in Albany and $361,500 in Miami. Center for Responsive Politics, *Beyond the 30-Second Spot,* pp. 22–23.

21. Adapted from Joseph E. Cantor, *Campaign Financing in Federal Elections: A Guide to the Law and Its Operation,* Report 89-451 GOV, Congressional Research Service, July 31, 1989, pp. 28–29.

22. California Commission on Campaign Financing, *The New Gold Rush: Financing California's Legislative Campaigns* (Los Angeles: Center for Responsive Government, 1985), p. 15.

its effects on levels of contributions are uncertain. The National Republican Senatorial Committee monitored the effect of removing the tax credit on both the number of donors and the size of donations and found its absence had no effect on either.[23] In a 1984 survey conducted by the California Commission on Campaign Financing, however, 35 percent of Californians said that with a full tax credit they would either increase their political contributions or contribute for the first time.[24] Thus advocates may argue that a 100 percent tax credit would increase campaign contributions, but there are few facts to support the claim, and what information there is suggests a tax credit would have limited effects on increasing either the number of small contributors or the aggregate amounts given.

Another reason it is difficult to estimate how much a 100 percent tax credit would encourage contributions is that candidates have not had an incentive to use it as part of a fundraising strategy. Candidates could argue to potential contributors that under the 100 percent credit they are in essence loaning the money to a campaign.[25] Under the system of flexible spending limits proposed by the 1990 Senate campaign finance reform panel, candidates would have an additional incentive to use the credit: small individual contributions from within their states would not count against their spending limit.[26]

Tightening Disclosure Provisions

Although observers agree that the most successful part of the FECA has been the requirement that campaign contributions be publicly disclosed, the regulations could be improved. Undisclosed soft money has become an important source of funds for both the Democratic and Republican party committees. According to the press and the party committees' own reports, wealthy donors and, in some states, corporations and labor unions are making campaign contributions to both political parties well above the limits stipulated by the FECA. These contributions undermine the disclosure provisions of the act and allow

23. Ben Ginsberg, former general counsel, National Republican Senatorial Committee, remarks delivered at the Conference on Campaign Finance Reform and Representative Democracy, Marquette University, February 25, 1989.

24. California Commission on Campaign Financing, *New Gold Rush,* p. 15.

25. Richard P. Conlon, "The Declining Role of Individual Contributions in Financing Congressional Campaigns," *Journal of Law and Politics,* vol. 3 (Winter 1987), p. 470.

26. Campaign Finance Reform Panel, "Campaign Finance Reform: A Report to the Majority Leader and Minority Leader, United States Senate," March 6, 1990.

special interests to give substantial sums directly to federal, state, and local political parties and indirectly to candidates for federal office.

Although soft money received its greatest attention during the presidential campaign in 1988, its party-building objectives suggest that it also affects congressional campaigns. Disclosure of all contributions made to federal and state party committees would fulfill the original intent of the FECA and provide a truer picture of how much is spent in congressional campaigns. Nonprofit 501(c)(3) organizations, as well as others that engage in registration and get-out-the-vote activities, should also be required to disclose soft-money contributions. Once the extent of all such contributions is known, an informed discussion of what, if any, restrictions should be placed on soft money could occur.

Current disclosure requirements could also be strengthened by having the source of independent expenditures be fully identified in all campaign advertising. Giving the name of the person or committee sponsoring the independent expenditure and clearly stating that the advertisement was not sponsored by either candidate would alert voters to the possible motivations of the sponsor. Senator Boren's bill, S. 137, would require that all television spots paid for by independent expenditures display the name of the person, PAC, or organization responsible continually throughout the spot and state that it was not subject to campaign contribution limits.[27] Tightening the definition of independent expenditures, as Senator Dole has proposed, would also ensure that they are in fact independent.[28]

One group of experts has argued that when the independence of independent expenditures is in doubt, candidates should "be authorized to bypass the complaint procedures of the Federal Election Commission and seek relief from the federal courts."[29]

Simplifying Administration of Campaign Laws

Reforms that reduce difficulties in administration increase compliance with campaign laws and improve the effectiveness of the system. The ad-

27. *Congressional Record,* daily ed., January 25, 1989, pt. 2, p. S466.

28. Senator Dole's bill, S. 7, prohibits candidates and persons making independent expenditures from retaining the "professional services" of the same consultant "in connection with the candidate's pursuit of nomination for election, or election to Federal office . . . including any services relating to the candidate's decision to seek Federal office." *Congressional Record,* daily ed., January 25, 1989, pt. 2, p. S211.

29. Campaign Finance Reform Panel, "Campaign Finance Reform," p. 23.

ministration of the current system is weak because of flaws in the structure and procedures of the Federal Election Commission. The existing problems would only be magnified under some reform proposals, particularly those discussed in chapter 9, unless the structure and functioning of the FEC were also changed.

Given the general dissatisfaction with the present workings of the commission, reforming it is necessary even if no other changes in campaign finance law are made. One common criticism is the slowness of the commission's enforcement procedures, which is caused by the statutory procedures that must be followed. The procedures apply equally to all cases irrespective of their simplicity or complexity or the severity of the alleged violation of campaign law. Kenneth Gross, a former assistant general counsel at the commission, estimates that 50 to 75 percent of the matters under review at any one time are routine cases and could be handled fairly in an expedited manner.[30] Establishing a two-track system, one for routine cases and one for more difficult cases, would improve efficiency and enable the commission to spend most of its time on the more difficult matters. Gross proposes combining the "reason to believe" and conciliation phases into one procedure for routine cases, so that when the commission finds reason to believe, a conciliation agreement could be offered at the same time (see chapter 7). This would drastically reduce the time spent on most cases.

In 1981 the Administrative Law Section of the American Bar Association proposed a series of changes in the enforcement proceedings of the Federal Election Commission. The changes were recommended to both "increase the procedural safeguards for those who . . . may be investigated by the agency" and "to expedite the enforcement proceedings without increasing administrative burdens."[31]

In addition to its slowness, the commission is so partisan that a 3–3 deadlock regularly occurs in judging major cases. One way to change the situation would be to have an odd number of commissioners.[32] Another would be to appoint members for only one term: in the words of one former commissioner, "If an individual wishes to be reappointed for a second or third term, his or her votes will be closely scrutinized

30. Kenneth Gross, "Enhancing Enforcement of the Federal Campaign Finance Laws," paper prepared for the Conference on Campaign Finance Reform and Representative Democracy, Marquette University, February 25, 1989.

31. American Bar Association, Section on Administrative Law, Committee on Election Law, *Report on Reform of the FEC's Enforcement Procedures,* 1981, p. 2.

32. Brooks Jackson, *Honest Graft: Big Money and the American Political Process* (Knopf, 1988), p. 310.

by members of Congress and by the White House as the time for his or her reappointment approaches. There are those who would suggest that actual decisions have been affected by such considerations. . . . The mere perception that a commissioner might, consciously or subconsciously, tailor his or her views as reappointment time approaches is cause for concern."[33] Senator Boren's bill incorporates both proposals. It would establish a seven-member commission, with no more than four members affiliated with one political party, and each member would serve only one seven-year term.[34] Partisan control would rotate between parties from one year to the next as a commissioner from one party completed his or her term and a commissioner from the other was appointed to fill the vacancy.

It has also been proposed that an adjudicatory system be established outside the FEC to handle difficult cases. An administrative law judge would oversee an adjudicated proceeding, and the judge's decision would then go to the commission for a decision. If necessary, the decision could then be appealed directly to the court of appeals. Each of these proposals has the potential to reduce the partisanship that currently pervades the commission's actions.

In addition to slowness and partisan deadlocks, the FEC has been criticized for its lack of a strong chairman. Brooks Jackson has argued for a chairman with a four-year term and the power to hire and fire staff, authorize routine inquiries into alleged violations, and issue warning letters or citations for minor violations. Kenneth Gross, in contrast, fears that a strong chairmanship, without an effective chairman in the role, would create serious problems for the functioning of the commission. Few would disagree with Frank Reiche, a former chairman of the FEC, who believes that the current rotating chairmanship "damages the Commission by depriving it of stability and continuity. . . . A rotating chairmanship not only insures a weak chairmanship, but also contributes towards a weak Commission."[35]

Changes in both the commission's structure and procedures are clearly needed even if other provisions of campaign finance law remain

33. Frank P. Reiche, "The Future of the Federal Election Commission," remarks delivered at the Conference on Campaign Finance Reform and Representative Democracy, Marquette University, February 25, 1989.

34. *Congressional Record,* daily ed., January 25, 1989, pt. 2, p. S474.

35. Jackson, *Honest Graft,* p. 309; Gross, "Enhancing Enforcement"; and Reiche, "Future of the Federal Election Commission."

untouched. Campaign finance reform would likely necessitate still more changes. The function of the commission would very much depend on the kinds of reforms enacted. If spending limits and public financing were established for congressional campaigns, its work load would expand enormously. The opportunities for candidates to exceed the limits would increase, and the commission would have to resolve allegations that spending limits had been exceeded, which could come from external complaints or from internal recommendations of the FEC's Reports Analysis Division. Public funding would require audits of all congressional campaigns receiving public funds unless the law allowed random audits. The expansion of the work load would require more money and staff.[36]

In addition to a larger number of cases, the FEC's areas of responsibility would expand. Currently, certifying candidates to receive public funds occupies the commission only in the winter and spring before a presidential election and involves only a dozen or so candidates. Public funding in congressional elections could mean certifying more than 800 candidates. To meet such a demand, the commission would have to contract out work to independent auditors, borrow auditors from other agencies, or make random checks of candidates' submissions.

If new laws limiting campaign spending were passed, the commission's enforcement responsibilities would increase. Although it is already responsible for enforcing congressional candidates' compliance with the provisions of the FECA, most of the enforcement proceedings occur after an election. Under a system of spending limits for candidates, noncompliance could have determinative effects in close elections: a candidate could violate the campaign laws, win the election as a result, be seated, and then be assessed a penalty. The enforcement of both spending and contribution limits in the waning days of a campaign, coupled with expedited investigations of complaints, would force changes in FEC procedures. Unless the commission were able to act quickly, the consequence of spending limits for complying candidates could be disastrous.

---

36. The FEC estimated that implementation of S. 2, as it was introduced at the beginning of the 100th Congress, would have required $1.3 million and an additional thirty-three staff members for the 1988 election cycle. Internal FEC memorandum, March 5, 1987. In light of the responsibilities it would face with public funding or limits on spending or both in the House and the Senate, actual costs would probably be much more.

Other Reforms

The reform proposals already discussed could improve competition, expand disclosure provisions, and improve the functioning of the FEC. There are other proposals that would also change the current system of campaign finance but that do not fall neatly into easily described categories. The ones we have chosen are among the reforms most seriously discussed.

The first is to close what Senator McConnell has called the millionaire's loophole. The 1974 amendments to the FECA limited candidates' contributions to their own campaigns to $35,000 for Senate elections and $25,000 for House elections, but the Supreme Court ruled the limitations unconstitutional in *Buckley* v. *Valeo*. Given the costs of running for congressional office, there has been some concern that only wealthy candidates will be able to mount serious challenges to incumbents or run for open seats, thus turning the House and Senate into "millionaire's clubs."[37] Incumbents worry that challengers with independent wealth will spend more than the incumbents may be able to match. Because spending by wealthy candidates cannot be limited by law, proposals have been introduced to try to discourage it by compensating their opponents. For example, S. 7, introduced by Senators Dole and McConnell in January 1989, would require any candidates who intend to spend or loan more than $250,000 of their own money in a campaign to file an intent to do so at the same time they file for candidacy. The amount of money their opponents could raise from an individual donor would then be allowed to increase from $2,000 to $10,000.[38] The bill would also prohibit candidates from using campaign contributions to reimburse themselves for loans they made to their campaigns.

Compensating candidates to counter expenditures made by wealthy opponents may at first seem a fair way of increasing competition, but legislating such compensation could in fact result in a form of incumbent protection.[39] It is usually challengers and candidates for open seats who must rely on their own funds for seed money. In competitive Senate campaigns the average expenditure is $4 million. While expecting

---

37. *Congressional Record,* daily ed., January 25, 1989, pt. 2, p. S209.
38. *Congressional Record,* daily ed., January 25, 1989, pt. 2, p. S211.
39. Herbert E. Alexander, "Strategies for Election Reform," Report to the Project for Comprehensive Campaign Finance Reform, April 1989, pp. 79–83.

candidates to spend $250,000 out of their own pockets may not seem particularly excessive—it is, after all, only 6 percent of the total—$250,000 is still an amount of money beyond the reach of most Americans. And for House candidates to give or loan themselves $25,000, as campaign professionals recommend, when added to the time devoted to campaigning for the better part of two years, is a substantial commitment and one that rarely pays off. Similarly, prohibiting candidates from repaying loans to themselves out of campaign funds may discourage those who lack independent wealth from even considering congressional office.

Another proposal advocated by some proponents of reform is to end bundling, the practice of collecting contributions from individual donors and then presenting the contributions as a group, or bundle, to the candidate. Former Senators Lawton Chiles and Robert Stafford have described bundling as a practice that "is disingenuous in the extreme. It is a sleazy end-run around the FECA contribution limits and it distorts the role of PACs. Congress could strike a small but significant blow for cleaner elections if it would amend the FECA to end bundling."[40] S. 137, introduced by Senator Boren, would try to eliminate bundling by requiring that any contributions collected by a PAC, party committee, registered lobbyist, or "other intermediary" count toward both the intermediary's contribution limit and the original contributor's limit.[41] S. 7, introduced by Senator Dole, would prohibit bundling by all political committees except the national party committees.[42]

To the extent that bundling is used by PACs and individual donors to circumvent contribution limits, as Senators Chiles and Stafford argue, it undermines the FECA. However, to distinguish between bundling done to avoid contribution limits and simple aggregation of contributions by a fundraiser to ease candidates' own burdens of fundraising is often difficult. For example, if a person hosts a dinner to raise funds, collects the checks, and presents them to a candidate, is that bundling? As Herbert Alexander has argued, antibundling proposals "can be viewed as a first effort to regulate not just the giver but also those collecting the gifts, the aggregators. The enactment of such legislation thus might be only a first step aimed eventually at elite fund raisers, direct mail

40. Lawton Chiles and Robert Stafford, "The Reality of Money in the Senate," in Robert T. Braye, Ellen Miller, and Laura Weiss, eds., *The View from Capitol Hill: Lawmakers on Congressional Reform* (Washington: Center for Responsive Politics, 1989), p. 17.

41. *Congressional Record,* daily ed., January 25, 1989, pt. 2, p. S466.

42. *Congressional Record,* daily ed., January 25, 1989, pt. 2, p. S212.

specialists, and others who aggregate and pool smaller contributions into more significant larger contributions."[43] The goal of antibundling proposals may be to ensure compliance with contribution limits, but the consequence may be to make it harder for candidates to raise funds, which would invariably hurt challengers and further hinder campaign competition.

Conclusions

There are important alternatives to public financing and limitations on spending that would improve the system of congressional campaign finance. The visibility of candidates, especially challengers, could be increased by providing reduced-rate or subsidized broadcast advertising. For many House and most Senate candidates this alone would improve competitiveness a great deal. Competition would also be improved by providing reduced-rate or subsidized mass mailings.

People who make small donations need to become a more important part of financing congressional campaigns. One way to increase their participation might be to provide an income tax credit for their contributions. This reform could be instituted independently of other reform proposals or as part of a package. Candidates would especially find it in their interest to solicit small in-state individual contributions under flexible spending limits.

The administration of the current system of congressional campaign finance needs to be improved by requiring additional disclosure of sources of soft money. Further improvements in administering campaign laws will require changes in the Federal Election Commission.

43. Alexander, "Strategies for Election Reform," p. 26.

11

A Plan for Reform

Almost everyone favors changing some part of the current system of congressional campaign finance, but bipartisan agreement on which changes to make has thus far been beyond reach. There are two quite different approaches Congress could take. It could treat the problems comprehensively, recognizing the interconnectedness of trying to increase competition, control the influence of PACs, improve the participation of parties, limit contributions, and improve the functioning of the Federal Election Commission. With this approach Congress would devise a set of rules that takes current as well as anticipated behavior into account. But even holding aside partisan differences, which have stalled such comprehensive efforts in the past, there are problems of paying for a substantially altered system, administering it in a prompt and fair way, and addressing the constitutional challenges that are sure to arise.

Congress could, of course, decide instead to address only some of the problems. Such a limited or incremental approach could include adjustments in the contribution limits for parties and individual donors, subsidies for candidates in the form of reduced-rate or free postage, and reduced-rate or free broadcast advertising. The single reform most often discussed would be to further limit the amount special interest groups can give candidates, or perhaps to ban PACs altogether. The list of possible incremental reforms is extensive.

Incremental reforms pose their own problems. Experience shows that redirecting the flow of political money is not easy: damming it in one place often means that it simply finds a different channel to the candidates. Thus, taken alone, further limiting PACs or banning them will almost certainly mean that corporate, labor union, or trade association money will merely be diverted, and the problems of disproportionate resources going to incumbents, the growing costs of some campaigns, and the influence of special interests will not necessarily have been addressed. Isolated reforms also encounter political difficulties. One reform may

195

adversely affect Democrats, another Republicans, leading to opposition from one or both. Of course, both parties could be asked to accept a change they do not like as part of a package that includes reforms they want, but this leads to considering more comprehensive changes.

This chapter examines comprehensive reform and more limited reform, the reasons neither type has yet been enacted, and their prospects. But before turning to these issues, it is important to review the reasons for considering reform in the first place.

Current Problems

Perhaps the most important failing of the current system is the lack of competition in the vast majority of House elections. Electoral accountability presupposes elections that are free and open and provide viable alternatives. In many House races the challengers are not visible enough even to be considered by the voters.

Substantial campaign funds are a necessary, although not sufficient, condition of candidate visibility. But few challengers can raise enough money to reach this threshold. The current system is clearly stacked in favor of incumbents. They bring to their campaigns an impressive infrastructure of paid staff, franked mail, and media visibility. They can also raise far more money than challengers can, especially from PACs.

Prospective challengers are not unaware of these conditions. Typically, they can hope to raise about $40,000 from PACs and their parties. Even with something of a local base and a commitment of $25,000 of their own funds, they still cannot compete. With the difficulties of fundraising, the time required, and the long odds for unseating an incumbent, it is understandable why prospective candidates would choose not to run.

The marriage of incumbents and PAC money has other deleterious results. Although hard evidence of quid pro quo vote buying is rare, PAC contributions facilitate greater access to legislators, which the PACs then use to help draft or amend legislation, secure committee appointments for members who support their interests, suggest possible witnesses for hearings, and help define the legislative agenda. Interest groups can and should "petition their government," but incumbents' large and growing dependence on PAC money to finance their campaigns may lead to more than transmitting information and organizing support or opposition. It may lead to undue influence from special interests. This then is the second compelling reason to reform the campaign finance system—to balance special interests and the public interest by reducing the dependence of many incumbents on PACs.

A third reason the system of congressional campaign finance needs overhauling is the dramatic increase in costs in competitive races. The current psychology is to raise and spend as much as possible, and what is defined as possible has been expanding. Rising costs in turn affect the competitive calculations of parties, interested individual donors, and groups. For candidates it means a greater preoccupation with fundraising, a longer fundraising season, and a greater commitment to pursue financing in the most efficient way possible. For many Senate candidates this means getting most of their large individual contributions out of state; there is, after all, only so much money one can raise in many sparsely populated states. For House incumbents, who often lack the national stature of Senate candidates, it means reliance on PACs, from whom candidates can raise money in larger chunks. These practices may create dual constituencies. Are members more responsive to their electoral or their financial constituencies? Finally, how important should fundraising ability be as the threshold to service in the national legislature?

There are many other reasons to change the present system of campaign finance—the unintended growth in use of soft money, the use of independent expenditures, and the advantages that wealthy candidates enjoy, for instance. But the case for reform really rests on the three problems discussed above: lack of electoral competition, dependence on "interested" money, and unrestrained costs.

Anticipating Consequences of Reform

Past reforms of the congressional campaign finance system have shown that there are often unanticipated consequences of changing the laws. Some of the problems of the previous system were solved, but others arose as candidates, parties, and contributors learned how to function in the new system. Some observers therefore fear that further changes could make things worse and that it is best to leave well enough alone. But if the present system is left in place, lack of competition in most House elections, incumbents' dependence on PACs, and increasingly expensive contests will continue. The alternative to inaction is to try to anticipate the consequences of various reform proposals and compare them with those of the current system to be certain the reforms, on balance, justify themselves.

Unintended consequences are most likely to result from the failure to recognize the interconnectedness of reforms, and therefore piecemeal reforms are inherently more vulnerable than comprehensive ones. The Supreme Court's ruling in *Buckley* v. *Valeo* did not recognize the interdependent nature of the campaign finance problem when it struck key provisions of the FECA. The possibility that the courts can selectively overturn parts of a reform act concerns many reformers, because the consequent effects could vary substantially from what Congress intended in passing the legislation.

The most frequently cited unintended consequences of the Federal Election Campaign Act of 1971 and its amendments have been the growth in the number of political action committees and the dependence of candidates, especially House incumbents, on them. Other failings have been more the result of the Supreme Court's striking down key provisions limiting use of personal funds by candidates, curbing independent expenditures, and placing ceilings on expenditures. Congress had recognized that these matters needed attention and structured legislative responses to them.

The surest way to invite important unintended consequences of further reforms would be to ignore the reality that when limits are enacted some individual donors or groups will attempt to circumvent those limits. Money has a way of finding its way into campaigns, and the task of reformers is to think of new ways it may do so. If Congress were to institute an aggregate PAC contribution limit, for instance, the organizations that now spend beyond that limit could spend the excess for other purposes—on state-level campaigns, perhaps, or on issue advocacy—or they could attempt to exceed the limit by making larger independent expenditures. Thus aggregate PAC limits that do nothing about independent expenditures will have overlooked the most likely flow of newly regulated campaign money.

Some have suggested that limits would encourage sources to avoid disclosure. If Congress enacted an aggregate limit on the amount a candidate could accept from PACs and lowered the amount any PAC could give to a candidate, those who contribute to interest groups might be tempted to organize contributions from employees and spouses to give individually to candidates. Such bundling could be a problem. If, for instance, limits on PAC contributions were part of a system of public financing and limits on spending, with a threshold requirement of in-state contributions from individual donors, PACs would not be as likely to influence the outcome of elections. This, of course, assumes that spending limits would apply to both primary and general elections.

Campaign reform legislation that limits spending only in general election campaigns will result in front-loading; candidates will spend without limit during the unregulated primary campaigns, and some of those expenditures could have clear consequences for general election campaigns.

Any one change in the campaign finance system invites candidates, parties, and PACs to find alternative uses for political money. Limits on individual contributions to congressional candidates of $2,000 in each cycle have driven candidates to raise money from more and more people and placed a premium on the more efficient $10,000 PAC contributions allowed. An aggregate limit on what candidates could accept from PACs would almost certainly make individual contributions even more prized, because candidates would need more of them to make up for restricted PAC dollars. Changes in party contribution limits would differ in their partisan effects. Raising ceilings on party contributions or coordinated expenditures would help Republicans, at least in the short run. Indexing the limitations on PAC contributions to allow for inflation would probably help Democrats. In short, a comprehensive approach to reform will not eliminate unanticipated consequences, but the consequences are likely to be far less severe than those resulting from piecemeal solutions.

Comprehensive Reform

In the beginning of this book we outlined the goals for reform: increased competition among candidates for congressional seats, reduced dependence on special interests, a less frenetic pace of fundraising, stronger political parties, full disclosure of contributions and expenditures, and smoother, more effective administration of campaign finance laws. These goals would be achieved most effectively and with fewest unintended consequences by enacting a comprehensive package of reforms, difficult as that might be to accomplish. Figure 11-1 summarizes our specific proposals, which we now discuss in detail.

Public Financing and Spending Limits

To foster competition, decrease spending in the most expensive campaigns and increase it in underfunded ones, and reduce the emphasis on fundraising, we recommend public financing combined with limitations on spending. Public financing alone would increase competition by getting money to challengers, who need it most. It would also raise spending in underfunded campaigns. But it would not, by itself, lower

FIGURE 11-1. *Proposed Comprehensive Reforms*

Public financing and spending limits
Provide public grants to cover part of campaign spending
Require qualification for grants
Set campaign spending limits high enough to ensure competition
Set campaign spending limits for the election cycle
Index spending limits to inflation

Contribution limits
Raise individual contribution limit to $4,800 per candidate for each election cycle
Establish 100 percent tax credit for contributions to congressional candidates of $100 or
  less
Raise individual contribution limits to candidates to $10,000 for the calendar year before
  the election and impose an aggregate "early money" candidate limit of $200,000 for
  money raised in this way by House candidates and a limit two or three times this amount
  for Senate candidates.
Raise limit on individual contribution to national party committees to $48,000
Raise aggregate annual individual contribution limit to $60,000
Raise limits on party contributions to candidates
Index individual contribution limits to inflation
Limit aggregate amount candidates can receive from PACs to a percentage of the candidates'
  spending limit
Limit independent expenditures by including them in contribution limits
Permit candidates to seek judicial relief when the independence of independent expen-
  ditures is questioned

Bundling
Prohibit registered lobbyists and PACs from bundling
Allow individuals and party committees to do so only under specified conditions

Disclosure
Require any party, person, or foundation to disclose amounts spent on activities that could
  influence the outcome of federal elections
Require a mix of hard and soft federal dollars

Communication costs
Give all major party candidates two free or reduced-cost mailings during the 60 days
  before primary and general elections
Establish a nonvariable, nonpreemptible lowest unit rate for broadcast time during the 45
  days before primary elections and 60 days before general elections

Federal Election Commission
Establish a nonpartisan commission
Limit commissioners to one term
Establish a strong chairman
Enact reforms already proposed by commission

costs in those 10 or 20 percent of campaigns in which spending has increased most dramatically, nor would it necessarily reduce the emphasis on fundraising. Setting voluntary spending limits without provisions for public financing or other means to help challengers become visible would do nothing to improve competition. Nor would voluntary spending limits alone satisfactorily reduce the time candidates must spend raising money, which in turn would perpetuate difficulties in candidate recruitment and continue to draw incumbents away from legislative duties.

Public funding should be provided through grants. To qualify, major-party candidates would have to demonstrate support by raising a threshold amount of small individual contributions from within their states. Upon certification of their candidacies for the general election campaign, candidates would be eligible for the grants. Third-party and independent candidates would be eligible if either they or their party's candidate receives 25 percent or more of the vote in the previous election. If candidates receive 25 percent of the vote or more in the current election, they would be eligible for retroactive public funding. The grant must be high enough to ensure sufficient seed money for general election candidates to run competitive races. A system of partial grants rather than the full grants that some have proposed would allow individual donors or PACs to contribute to campaigns, but would avoid the difficulties of administration that matching grants would present.

Grants should be paid for from voluntary taxpayer contributions to the tax checkoff fund. If the checkoff does not provide enough money, the system should be allowed to draw from the public treasury. Candidates who accept spending limits and partial public financing must be able to count on the funds. Although the chances that checkoff funds will be insufficient are unlikely, the importance of competitive elections in a system of democratic government warrants using general treasury funds if necessary.

Public funding should be accompanied by, and contingent upon, candidates' acceptance of limitations on spending. For House candidates the limit needs to be at or above the average campaign expenditures, in constant 1988 dollars, of competitive challengers and competitive candidates for open seats since 1980. While such a limit would be lower than the amount spent in the most expensive House races, it would, if coupled with public financing, raise spending in many more House races, thus increasing competition. In the Senate the basic formula can be tied to the voting age population of each state. In heavily populated states, economies of scale would allow a declining schedule of expenditures per voter. Because the cost per voter of campaigning in sparsely populated states is higher, and the political reality is that these states have become competitive battlegrounds for parties and PACs, a floor must be set that is well above the average expenditure per voter.

Spending limits should apply to the entire election cycle, not just the general election campaign. In the absence of limits for primary or runoff campaigns, candidates would raise and spend very large sums in them to escape the constraints of the limits for the general election campaign, perhaps spending as much or more than they do now. Because such expenditures would probably have consequences for the general election, especially in states with late primaries, cycle limits are necessary.

Spending limits must be indexed for inflation. If the limits are not pegged to the consumer price index or a campaign cost index, candidates might increasingly choose not to accept them by not accepting public financing, and the money chase would continue.

Finally, although spending limits could be achieved either by a constitutional amendment or by statute, a legislative solution tying spending limits to public financing is far preferable. A constitutional amendment would open the door for Congress to address candidates' spending limits, but it would not necessarily resolve problems of how money should be raised, PAC spending limits, independent expenditures, limits on individual contributions, and other matters that are integrally connected. A constitutional amendment to give Congress the power to set spending limits could also run into challenges that it abridges some candidates' rights under the First Amendment.

Changes in Contribution Limits

One way to reduce the dependence on special interest money fostered by the current campaign finance system is to increase the amounts candidates can accept from individual donors and party committees. If limits on individual donors' contributions to candidates had been adjusted for inflation, they would now be more than $2,400 per election in 1988 dollars, or $4,800 for the cycle (excluding runoffs). The limits should be raised to take account of inflation and then indexed for future years. A 100 percent tax credit for contributions of up to $100 to congressional campaigns should also be allowed. Although there is no definitive evidence that a tax credit would increase the number or amounts of small contributions, it would have the potential to increase constituents' participation in campaigns and make it easier for candidates to raise contributions from individual donors who are not wealthy.

Our comprehensive reform proposal seeks to create a more competitive environment for challengers. Reasonably high spending limits combined with public financing are the most direct and probably most effective way to enhance competition. But if public financing remains a major stumbling block, as it has often been in the past, a means must be found to help challengers raise the funds necessary to mount a visible campaign. One way to help challengers over this initial hurdle would be to create a higher individual contribution limit—$10,000 or so—for persons giving to candidates' early campaign accounts. This early fundraising opportunity would stimulate competition by allowing challengers to mount a serious campaign. House candidates would be allowed to accept only $200,000 or $250,000 in this early seed money, and Senate candidates would be permitted to raise two or three times this amount. Adjusting the amount individuals can give to candidates in the first year of a two-year election cycle would also require increasing the individual contribution limit for that year. In nonelection years the aggregate individual contribution limit ought to be raised from $25,000 to $50,000. Raising the individual contribution limit for early contributions is an alternative to our proposal for public financing.

The limit on individual contributions to the national party committees and the aggregate annual limit on individual contributions should also be increased to adjust for inflation and then indexed for future years. In 1988 dollars the limit for contributions to the national party committees would be $48,000 and the aggregate annual limit $60,000. Raising the limits would strengthen the financial positions of the national party committees and enhance the importance of parties in the electoral process.

Ceilings on the contributions of party committees to candidates should also be raised. By deciding not to challenge contributions from the national senatorial committees to House candidates and from the national House committees to Senate candidates, in 1989 the FEC in effect raised these limits by $10,000 for each candidate. Allowing the parties to raise more money from individual donors and contribute more money to candidates would strengthen their role in congressional campaigns.

Reduced Role for Special Interests

Organized interests participate in various capacities in the legislative process, and they represent an additional way for people to contribute to congressional campaigns. Although some reform advocates have proposed decreasing the amount individual PACs can contribute to candidates, in practice a lower limit would affect only a small number of these organizations. In 1988, nine-tenths of all contributions to House members and three-quarters of those to Senate members were in amounts less than $3,000 (see chapter 5). And if PAC contributions to congressional candidates were to be banned, the money would probably reappear in the form of independent expenditures, or else corporations, trade associations, and labor unions would encourage individual members to contribute directly to candidates, thus creating a far less traceable influence of organized interests on elections than exists today.

In short, PACs are and will continue to be a part of the political landscape, but they should be less important to congressional campaigns. The best means to accomplish this would be an aggregate limit on how much candidates could accept from special interest groups. Ideally, contributions from PACs should be a given percentage of a candidate's total campaign funds, and the percentage should be substantially less than that contributed by individuals.

Any further restriction on PAC activity would probably lead at least some of them to increase their use of independent expenditures. Some reform proposals include provisions to counter them: for example, candidates who are hurt by independent expenditures would receive a public grant in the amount of the expenditure or be allowed to raise and spend additional funds. But these proposals are not very satisfactory solutions to the potential problem. The opportunity for a candidate to receive compensatory public funds to counter independent expenditures could lead PACs to engineer independent campaigns designed to trigger public funds for a favored candidate (see chapters 8 and 9). Permitting candidates who have been the target of independent expenditures to raise and spend additional funds may make sense in theory, but in practice they may have neither the time nor the ability to do so, particularly late in a campaign. In addition, deciding when candidates have been hurt would require the FEC to monitor the content of advertisements paid for by independent expenditures, something the commission is ill equipped to do.

The best solution would be for Congress to confront the *Buckley* v. *Valeo* decision head-on by restricting the amounts individuals and PACs can spend on independent expenditures. The limit should strike a balance between the rights of individuals and organizations to freedom of speech and the ability of candidates to compete fairly and effectively in elections. We propose that individual and PAC contribution limits cover both direct contributions to candidates and independent expenditures. That is, an individual could spend up to $4,800 per candidate in each election cycle in any combination of direct contributions or independent expenditures. Similarly, a PAC could give up to $10,000 in any combination. Limiting independent expenditures this way will lead to a court challenge, but asking the courts to reconsider the issue is preferable to any alternative solutions proposed so far.

Restrictions on Bundling

One consequence of the FECA was to elevate the importance of fundraising. Individual and PAC contribution limits mean not only that candidates constantly need to broaden their contributor base, but also that no individual or PAC contribution accounts for a very large share of total campaign receipts. To enhance their credit with members of Congress and get around this limit on the financial influence of contributors, some PACs and individuals, acting as intermediaries or conduits, engage in bundling. Bundling activity can range from a fundraising event in a volunteer's home to soliciting regular contributions from similarly interested contributors and then passing those contributions on to the candidate.

Bundling by PACs should be prohibited. These groups already have a significant effect on elections, and expanding their giving power through bundling only reinforces the suspicion that the objective of their contribution is influence. Similarly, registered lobbyists who currently enhance their influence with members of Congress by hosting fundraising events should be prohibited from doing so. These individuals are different from campaign volunteers in that they have an ongoing professional interest in legislation.

Party committees and individuals who are not registered lobbyists should be permitted to bundle so long as they meet the following conditions: contributions must be made payable to the candidate; be passed directly to the candidate and not deposited in the conduit's own account; and be fully reported by the candidate as contributions received. In addition, costs incurred by the conduit must be reported as in-kind contributions and count against the conduit's own contribution limit or against a party's coordinated expenditure limit. These new limitations on bundling will permit fully disclosed fundraising to continue except in cases where limits already apply or where there is compelling reason to restrict this activity.

Disclosure and Limitation of Soft Money

No one knows the extent to which undisclosed spending, or soft money, is used in congressional elections, or whether it has much effect. But to many observers, opening the door to such undisclosed activity has provided too great a temptation for parties and candidates to try to escape scrutiny. Such temptation would be even greater under a system of spending limits in congressional elections. It is therefore important that soft money be fully disclosed and limited as part of a system of comprehensive campaign finance reform.

Soft money is composed of both receipts and expenditures. Soft money receipts pose problems because they permit individuals and groups to contribute unlimited amounts of money. Such contributions have all the negative consequences of influence buying that prompted the enactment of the FECA. Soft money expenditures are clearly designed to influence the outcome of elections, and because they fall beyond any limits on expenditures they introduce instability into any system of spending limits—either the current system for presidential elections or the proposed system for congressional elections. Partisan efforts at voter registration, getting out the vote, generic advertising, and voter canvassing are certainly legitimate election activities. But permitting them to be financed by soft money undermines the integrity of any system of spending limits.

Another source of undisclosed campaign-related expenditures is nonprofit foundations that pursue voter registration and get-out-the-vote drives. Contributions to these foundations are generally tax deductible under section 501(c)(3) or 501(c)(4) of the Internal Revenue Code. Although they are in principle nonpartisan, in fact they often focus their election activities on demographic groups that have predictable partisan tendencies. Under a system of spending and contribution limits, the activities of such foundations would probably grow because those activities, unchecked by limits, could influence the outcome of elections.

The first step in dealing with soft money activity is to disclose it. We propose that any person, party, or foundation disclose the amount spent on any activity that could influence the outcome of a federal election, including nonpartisan registration and get-out-the-vote campaigns. Disclosure comes with varying levels of specificity. It is important to disclose in at least the detail of current candidate disclosure the sources of funds spent by parties and groups seeking to influence federal elections and how the money is spent. The soft money issue has been before the FEC and the courts for some time, and the FEC has been ordered to develop regulations to require a mix of disclosed and limited "hard" federal dollars and "soft" funds.

The use of soft money has caused concern most frequently when used for joint federal and state party activity involving federal and nonfederal candidates. The concern is that federal candidates benefit most from such activity and indeed have been its principal instigators. We propose that any activity that supports ticketwide or other federal-nonfederal activity be funded by at least one-third hard and limited federal dollars in nonpresidential years and one-half hard and limited federal dollars in presidential years. We have already recommended raising the limit on individual contributions to political parties; this should permit parties to provide at least one-third to one-half of such funds from "hard dollar" accounts. In states whose current laws require greater disclosure or impose limits on soft money, such disclosure and limits would be permitted.

Reduced Communication Costs

Communicating with potential voters is the largest expense in most congressional campaigns. Incumbents' communications are greatly aided by the frank and the use of district offices and congressional staff to help get their names and messages to potential voters. Indirectly, incumbents are helped by free media coverage. These situations cannot be eliminated, nor should they be, but reforms can give challengers and candidates for open seats some of the perquisites that now apply only to incumbents, thus cutting campaign costs and increasing competition.

First, we propose giving all major-party candidates two free, or at least reduced-cost, mailings during the sixty days before primary and general elections (that is, a total of four mailings). Candidates would thus have two opportunities before an election to communicate their campaign messages to potential voters at little or no cost to themselves. Such a reform would be most helpful to challengers and candidates for open seats. It would probably have minimal effects for incumbents, who, presumably, have the entire election cycle to communicate with constituents.

In addition, a nonvariable, nonpreemptible lowest unit rate for broadcast time should be established for forty-five days before primary elections and sixty days before general elections. Candidates would thus know in advance what broadcast time would cost and could purchase it without engaging in bidding wars with other advertisers. Again, all candidates would have access to such reduced-cost communication, but challengers and candidates for open seats would benefit most.

Improving Campaign Oversight and Administration

Both the structure and procedures of the Federal Election Commission must be changed to facilitate the handling of cases brought before it. The changes are necessary even without comprehensive reform of campaign laws. If spending limits and public financing were approved, changing the way the FEC functions would be imperative.

First, for the commission to be effective, it must be made nonpartisan, either by changing the number of commissioners to an odd number, as Senator Boren has proposed, or by removing the presumption of partisanship in selecting them. Limiting commissioners to just one term would perhaps also remove some of the partisan pressure to conform.

Second, establishing a strong chairman would give the commission the guidance and direction it now lacks. The chairman should serve for more than one year, be empowered to hire commission staff, and have the authority to speak for the commission before Congress.

In its annual reports to Congress, the commission itself has suggested reforms that would improve its functioning. Being allowed to seek injunctions in enforcement cases would increase its powers, and changing the language of the "reason to believe" finding would more accurately reflect its actions at the early stages of investigation (see chapter 7). The commission has also asked for authority to grant waivers or exemptions from reporting requirements in instances when they may not be appropriate and has asked that it be the sole point of entry for disclosure documents. To further facilitate bookkeeping and disclosure of campaign activity, it has recommended that limits on contributions for each election campaign be changed to cycle limits and that candidate committees file reports based on an election cycle rather than a calendar year cycle.

The FEC is presently just the kind of agency Congress wants to regulate campaign finance laws: it provides disclosure but rarely acts in a way that could influence an election outcome. Under many proposed reforms of election finance, however, including our own, it will need to be a much more aggressive agency—one that can respond quickly, make decisions, and administer the law impartially.

Consequences of Comprehensive Reform

Our proposal is very ambitious because it seeks to improve competition in congressional campaigns and permit a variety of individuals and groups to participate without allowing any one type of contributor to dominate. It would almost certainly attract more and better-qualified candidates. But it is likely to be opposed by some in both parties who might object on grounds of philosophy or self-interest.

Although we have set forth the outlines of reform, we are not wedded to a particular level of public funding or a particular spending limit in House races or formula for setting spending limits in Senate races. Appendix B presents several potential combinations of public funding, spending limits, and PAC limits for House and Senate campaigns.

In looking at spending limits, particularly, it is important to remember that they are meant to be part of a comprehensive reform that includes public funding, higher contribution limits for individual donors, and reduced communication costs. Both public funding and reduced communication costs will lessen the amount of private money that needs to be raised and the costs associated with raising that money. Higher individual contribution limits will make it easier for candidates to raise money in larger sums from individual donors. Thus it is important to evaluate spending limits within the context of a campaign finance system quite different from the system currently in place.

Many of these proposals could be enacted alone, but it would be difficult to control the consequences. Moreover, incremental reforms by their very nature address only some of the problems with the current system. Further restrictions on PAC contributions would reduce the importance of organized interests in congressional campaigns but would do nothing to stem rising costs. Enacting spending limits would reduce costs but would do nothing to curb spending by special interests. Public financing, in and of itself, would change the sources of funding for congressional campaigns but would not necessarily control costs. Disclosure of soft money would increase voters' understanding of where certain individuals and groups stand politically but would not address the other problems. Only through comprehensive reform can the collective problems of the current system of campaign finance be addressed and the consequences of reform adequately anticipated.

Although a comprehensive approach alleviates many of the unanticipated consequences of reform, it has its own risks and costs. For example, the goal of public financing is to encourage qualified candidates who presently are deterred from running because of the costs, but the prospect of public funds may also encourage candidates with little hope of election. Consequently, public financing may create artificial competition in some races, causing opponents to spend more money than they might otherwise. The risk of artificial competition in some races is, however, probably worth the more serious competition that would arise in most races. Another consequence is that, when coupled with spending limits, public funding will probably increase the overall amount of money spent in congressional campaigns, at least in the short term. Spending limits will control costs of the most expensive races, but public funding will provide an infusion of money into many more in which not enough money is now spent for the challenger to become competitive.

Another potential problem is how to set spending limits in campaigns for the House. The diversity among states can be accommodated reasonably well in Senate campaigns by tying spending limits to state voting age populations and building in floors for less populated states and ceilings for more populated ones. But House districts, which are similar to each other in numbers of people but show great diversity in geographic dispersion of the population and in the sizes of media markets, make it difficult to set spending limits that are reasonably fair to all candidates. Ideally, there would be a formula to adjust for these variations. However, the diversity makes devising any one formula probably impossible, and administering it would be a nightmare. The alternative is to set spending limits high enough to permit candidates to run competitive campaigns in all but the most expensive districts. In these districts, candidates already adjust their strategy to account for expensive television or other unusual costs (see chapter 9).

Comprehensive reform also requires a greater role for the federal government, particularly the Federal Election Commission. Given the failings of the commission in administering the current law, concern about any system that imposes more duties on it is warranted, although many of the commission's current shortcomings could be alleviated if its structure and procedures were changed, as they would be with comprehensive reform.

Finally, if incremental reform could encourage political money to pop up in unanticipated ways, even comprehensive reform will not be able to entirely control the sources and direction of campaign funds. Nevertheless, comprehensive reform still goes much farther toward solving the problems with the current system than does a more timid approach.

Prospects for Reform

Given the difficult choices of campaign finance reform and the disparate partisan and institutional perspectives that Republicans and Democrats, senators and representatives, bring to the issue, any reform at all might seem remote. But innovative policies do emerge that seem to run contrary to the interests of the participants, often because of a confluence of short-term and long-term interests. In the matter of campaign finance reform, Democrats and Republicans, particularly in the House, have very different short-term and long-term interests. Yet their recognition of these conflicting interests may itself lead to reform.

Differences in partisan and personal self-interest have been the most important stumbling blocks to accommodation. Republicans in both houses believe that any limitation on spending will hurt them as candidates and as a party. They believe they need to spend more than Democrats to be competitive because they have fewer partisan supporters. Their party infrastructure is less developed in many states and districts, and the Democrats have had the advantage of incumbency for most of the past fifty years. Democrats in the Senate see an advantage in putting a cap on spending; those in the House, given their success in attracting corporate PAC money to add to their support from organized labor, are increasingly confident that the present system works well for them.

Whether it is financed by voluntary tax checkoffs or other sources, reform also brings with it a potentially larger role for government, and perhaps greater costs, to which Republicans are philosophically opposed. Democrats are not generally opposed to reform on these grounds. Republicans are not, however, opposed to campaign subsidies or to tax incentives for individual contributors. These indirect forms of public financing may actually cost more than a grant system. Republican opposition to public financing appears to have more to do with how money is spent than with total cost.

Because Democrats are in the majority in both the House and Senate, it would seem to be in their short-term interest to continue the current system of campaign finance with few if any changes. Similarly, because Republicans are in the minority, short-term self-interest would suggest that they should support reform.

The differences in partisan short-term and long-term interests are more clearly defined in the House than in the Senate. House Democrats are comfortably in the majority and have no reason to fear a change in their status in the foreseeable future. They are successful in raising campaign funds, including funds from corporate and trade association PACs whose perspectives on policy and ideological interests do not always square with those of the Democrats. However, were Democrats to lose control of the House, PAC money would presumably flow to the majority Republicans, who also have a greater policy and ideological affiliation with corporate and business PACs. Thus, if it is not necessarily in the short-term interest of House Democrats to change the current system, it is in their long-term interest to create one that is less dominated by incumbents and gives more opportunities to challengers.

House Republicans are not faring very well under the current system because it so favors incumbents. If Republicans were to become the majority party, however, they would likely do very well under the current system. House Republican incumbents would benefit from contributions by business PACs. The Republican party committees, which even now have more money than their Democratic counterparts, would be able to support Republican incumbents and provide more resources to challengers than they presently can. But Republicans are not in the majority in the House and are not likely to become the majority unless there are changes in the current system. Thus it is in their short-term interest to support campaign finance reform.

In the Senate, neither party has any particular advantage under the current system. Each controlled the Senate at some point during the 1980s, and candidates in both face competitive races in almost any election. Both Republicans and Democrats must raise substantial sums to run against a serious competitor and must endure the costs of fundraising. Consequently, it is in the interest of both to change the current system. Senators must move beyond their differences over spending limits and agree on a package of reforms. If spending limits were the last issue discussed rather than the first, the possibilities for agreement would be improved.

The lessening of sharp partisan feelings and the new spirit of cooperation that seemed to be building in the House and the Senate at the close of the 1980s offer renewed opportunities for campaign finance reform in the 1990s. Neither Republicans nor Democrats are immune to the demands of the money chase or the influences of special interest money. The Senate will remain competitive in the 1990s, and campaign costs will increase. House races will continue to suffer from lack of competition unless the system is changed to allow greater opportunities for challengers to run serious campaigns. And although there may be particular candidates who benefit from the current system, in the long run those in both parties and both houses are hurt by it. Perhaps the widespread recognition that the current system needs changing will lead to serious efforts to enact bipartisan reform.

Appendix A:
Data Sources

Any assessment of reform proposals must be based on an understanding of how the present system is working. Fortunately, for more than a decade the Federal Election Commission has been gathering data on congressional campaigns. These data include candidates' reports of receipts and expenditures, as well as the financial activities of political parties, PACs, and individuals acting independently. The FEC data we used for 1980–88 were primarily on computer tape and were provided by the Inter-university Consortium for Political and Social Research or directly by the FEC. The data for 1978, which are not on computer tape, were taken largely from *FEC Reports on Financial Activity, 1977–78, Interim Report No. 5, U.S. Senate and House Campaigns.* Some data tables were provided directly by the commission or were found in one of the frequent FEC press releases. In some instances where we wanted to compare financial activity over a longer period of time (as far back as 1972), we relied on data compiled by Common Cause.

We also gathered information through interviews with key participants in congressional elections. We interviewed past and present staff of the party campaign and national committees of both parties, media consultants, fundraising consultants, pollsters, campaign managers, PAC managers and directors, past and present officials of the FEC, and attorneys who have frequent dealings with the commission, as well as key participants in legislative battles on campaign finance during the past fifteen years. In addition to these interviews we hosted two dinners at Brookings that brought together some of these people in an effort to see whether there were shared perceptions about problems and possible solutions that cut across partisan and institutional boundaries. The dinners did not result in a set of agreed-upon reforms, but they did inform and add insight to the book. In addition to the FEC campaign finance data and interviews, we employed several public opinion surveys conducted over the past two decades, as well as surveys of relevant elites conducted by the Center for Responsive Politics.

U.S. Federal Election Commission Data Tapes

For 1976: Inter-university Consortium for Political and Social Research, Study 7570, *Survey of United States Congressional Candidates, 1976* (from FEC data).

For 1978 and 1980: Inter-university Consortium for Political and Social Research, Study 8158, *Campaign Expenditures by Party and Non-Party Political Committees [United States]: 1977–1978 and 1979–1980* (from FEC data).

For 1982: Inter-university Consortium for Political and Social Research, Study 8238, *Campaign Expenditures in the United States, 1981–1982* (from FEC data).

For 1984: Inter-university Consortium for Political and Social Research, Study 8511, *Campaign Expenditures in the United States, 1983–1984* (from FEC data).

For 1986: Federal Election Commission, *FEC Reports on Financial Activity, 1985–1986: House/Senate; FEC Reports on Financial Activity, 1985–1986: Non-Party;* and *FEC Reports on Financial Activity, 1985–1986: Party.*

For 1988: Federal Election Commission, *FEC Reports on Financial Activity, 1987–1988: House/Senate;* and *FEC Reports on Financial Activity, 1987–1988: Party.*

Campaign Expenditures

For 1972: Common Cause, Campaign Finance Monitoring Project, *1972 Federal Campaign Finances: Interest Groups and Political Parties,* vol. 3, p. iv.

For 1974: Common Cause, "Common Cause Study Reveals $74 Million Spent by Congressional Candidates Who Ran in 1974 General Elections," press release, April 11, 1975; and Norman J. Ornstein, Thomas E. Mann, and Michael J. Malbin, *Vital Statistics on Congress 1985–1986* (Washington: American Enterprise Institute for Public Policy Research, 1984), pp. 65–66, 69–70.

For 1976: Federal Election Commission, Disclosure Series No. 6, *1976 Senatorial Campaigns, Receipts and Expenditures,* 1977, pp. 3, 6;

Disclosure Series No. 9, *1976 House of Representatives Campaigns, Receipts and Expenditures,* 1977, pp. 4, 11; and Ornstein, Mann, and Malbin, *Vital Statistics on Congress 1985–86,* pp. 65–66, 69–70.

For 1978: Federal Election Commission, *Reports on Financial Activity, 1977–1978, Interim Report No. 5, U.S. Senate and House Campaigns,* 1979, pp. 31, 38; and FEC, press release, June 29, 1979.

For 1980–88: FEC data tapes (see above).

For 1988: Federal Election Commission, "$458 Million Spent by 1988 Congressional Campaigns," press release, February 24, 1989.

Campaign Receipts

For 1978: Federal Election Commission, *Reports on Financial Activity, 1977–1978, Interim Report No. 5, U.S. Senate and House Compaigns;* and FEC, "FEC Releases Year-End 1978 Report on 1977–78 Financial Activity of Non-Party and Party Political Committees," press release, May 10, 1979.

For 1980–88: FEC data tapes (see above).

For 1980: Federal Election Commission, "FEC Releases Final PAC Report for 1979–80 Election Cycle," press release, February 21, 1982.

For 1982: Federal Election Commission, "FEC Publishes Final 1981–82 PAC Study," press release, November 29, 1983.

For 1984: Federal Election Commission, "FEC Final Report for '84 Elections Confirms Majority of PAC Money Went to Incumbents," press release, December 1, 1985.

For 1986: Federal Election Commission, "FEC Releases Final Report on 1986 Congressional Candidates," press release, May 5, 1988.

For 1988: Federal Election Commission, "FEC Finds Slower Growth of PAC Activity in 1988 Election Cycle," press release, April 9, 1989.

PACs

For 1978: Federal Election Commission, *FEC Reports on Financial Activity 1977–78: House/Senate;* and FEC, "FEC Releases Year-End 1978 Report on 1977–78 Financial Activity of Non-Party Political Committees," press release, May 10, 1979.

For 1980: Federal Election Commission, "FEC Releases Final PAC Report 1980: for 1979–80 Election Cycle," press release, February 21, 1982.

For 1982: Federal Election Commission, "FEC Publishes Final 1981–82 PAC Study," press release, November 29, 1983.

For 1984: Federal Election Commission, "FEC Final Report for '84 Elections Confirms Majority of PAC Money Went to Incumbents," press release, December 1, 1985.

For 1986: Federal Election Commission, "FEC Releases Final Report on 1986 Congressional Candidates," press release, May 5, 1988.

For 1988: Federal Election Commission, "FEC Finds Slower Growth of PAC Activity in 1988 Election Cycle," press release, April 9, 1989; additional 1988 data provided by the FEC.

Additional multiyear data: FEC data tapes (see above); Federal Election Commission, *Final Reports on Financial Activity, Party and Non-Party Political Committees,* vol. 1, *Summary Tables* (1978, 1980, 1982, 1984, 1986); and FEC, "PAC Growth—From 1974," press release, July 18, 1988.

Appendix B: Hypothetical Funding Proposals

As we discussed in chapter 9, a major danger in setting spending limits is setting them too low. In the hypothetical examples for House and Senate spending limits presented in table B-1, we have set the limits sufficiently high to permit competition in both houses. These limits are in 1988 dollars and would need to be adjusted upward for inflation or for changes in technology that might significantly increase costs. A spending limit of $500,000 for the House is well above the actual average of roughly $450,000 (in constant 1988 dollars) for competitive nonincumbents between 1980 and 1988. Had such a limit been in place between 1980 and 1988, 349 incumbents would have spent beyond the limit, compared with 111 challengers and 111 candidates for open seats. Of all major general election House candidates since 1980, about 88 percent spent less than $500,000 (in constant 1988 dollars).

Setting spending limits high enough to foster visible and competitive elections is our primary objective. At the same time, however, we recognize that there will be some cases of extraordinary spending. For instance, in one 1988 California House race the two candidates spent nearly $1.5 million each. It would be a mistake to set all spending limits by reference to such cases. Since the limits we propose are voluntary, candidates may choose to go beyond them if they are willing to forgo public funds and other benefits that accrue from participating in the partial public financing system.

Discussing the effect of spending limits in the Senate is made more complex by the fact that there would be a different limit for each state in all but the least populous states. This results from the necessity of

TABLE B-1. *Funding for House Candidates under Two Hypothetical Election Cycle Limits*

1988 dollars

	Cycle limits			
	500,000		750,000	
Source of funds	50 percent grant	67 percent grant	50 percent grant	67 percent grant
Public grant	250,000	337,000	375,000	502,000
Qualification threshold (10 percent)[a]	50,000	50,000	75,000	75,000
Subtotal	300,000	387,000	450,000	577,000
Remainder[b]	200,000	113,000	300,000	173,000
Maximum individual contributions beyond threshold[c]	200,000	113,000	300,000	173,000
Maximum direct and coordinated party contributions (for all party committees)	86,100	86,100	86,100	86,100
Maximum PAC contributions (20 percent)	100,000	100,000	150,000	150,000

a. Small individual contributions.
b. Can come from any of the three sources listed.
c. For every dollar raised from PACs or parties, a dollar must be deducted from these permitted limits for individual contributions.

pegging Senate spending limits to population. Despite this variability in spending limits, we can summarize the effect of our proposal on states that in 1990 had populations near the three thresholds we have chosen. In the thirteen states with populations under 1 million, there were fifty Senate elections (one hundred general election candidates) between 1978 and 1988. In these less populated states we would expect the greatest pressure on spending limits because of the greater efficiency of spending there. Had our $2.5 million spending limit been in effect, only twelve of the one hundred candidates would have spent beyond the limit, and of these twelve, six were incumbents, five challengers, and one a candidate for an open seat. The years in which spending tended to exceed the limit were, not surprisingly, 1980 and 1986. For the medium and large states, there are two with 1990 populations very near each hypothetical population: Missouri and Indiana have populations near 4 million, and Texas and New York have populations near 12 million. Of the thirty-three major-party general election candidates who

TABLE B-2. *Funding for Senate Candidates under Three Hypothetical Election Cycle Limits, by Voting Age Population of State*
1988 dollars

| | Cycle limits | | | | | |
| | 2,500,000 (small state)[a] | | 4,000,000 (medium state)[b] | | 6,000,000 (large state)[c] | |
Source of funds	50 percent grant	67 percent grant	50 percent grant	67 percent grant	50 percent grant	67 percent grant
Public grant	1,250,000	1,675,000	2,000,000	2,680,000	3,000,000	4,020,000
Qualification threshold (10 percent)[d]	250,000	250,000	400,000	400,000	600,000	600,000
Subtotal	1,500,000	1,925,000	2,400,000	3,080,000	3,600,000	4,620,000
Remainder[e]	1,000,000	575,000	1,600,000	920,000	2,400,000	1,380,000
Maximum individual contributions beyond threshold[f]	1,000,000	575,000	1,600,000	920,000	2,400,000	1,380,000
Maximum direct and coordinated party contributions (for all party committees)	129,700	129,700	421,520	421,520	1,189,564	1,189,564
Maximum PAC contributions (20 percent)	500,000	500,000	800,000	800,000	1,200,000	1,200,000

a. Under 1 million voting age population.
b. Four million voting age population.
c. Twelve million voting age population.
d. Small individual contributions.
e. Can come from any of the three sources listed.
f. For every dollar raised from PACs or parties, a dollar must be deducted from these permitted limits for individual contributions.

have run in these four states since 1978, nine would have exceeded our hypothetical limits. Five were incumbents and four were candidates for open seats. No challengers in these four states spent as much as permitted under our limits.

In several of the Senate elections summarized in table B-2, the spending beyond the hypothetical limit was by two candidates in the same race—for example, the Missouri open-seat election in 1986 and the Texas open-seat election in 1984. In these instances, as in others in the small-state category, spending limits would affect both candidates equally, and both would be permitted to spend sufficient funds to mount visible and competitive campaigns. A limit in cases like these would discipline spending and focus the competition between the candidates on issues and candidate qualities.

Index